Study Guide
David Eaton

Microeconomics
Principles, Applications, and Tools
6th Edition

Arthur O'Sullivan
Steven M. Sheffrin
Stephen J. Perez

Prentice Hall

Boston   Columbus   Indianapolis   New York   San Francisco   Upper Saddle River

Amsterdam   Cape Town   Dubai   London   Madrid   Milan   Munich   Paris   Montreal   Toronto

Delhi   Mexico City   Sao Paulo   Sydney   Hong Kong   Seoul   Singapore   Taipei   Tokyo

Editor-in-Chief: Natalie E. Anderson
Executive Editor: David Alexander
Editorial Project Manager: Virginia Guargilia
Production Project Manager: Lynne Breitfeller
Operations Specialist: Diane Peirano

Prentice Hall
is an imprint of

www.pearsonhighered.com

10 9 8 7 6 5 4 3 2

ISBN-13: 978-0-13-609408-1
ISBN-10: 0-13-609408-2

Contents

The numbers in brackets indicate the Economics volume chapter.

Preface

This Study Guide was written to be used with *Microeconomics: Principles, Applications, and Tools, 6th Edition*, and also with *Economics: Principles, Applications, and Tools, 6th Edition*, by O'Sullivan, Sheffrin, and Perez. The chapter numbers and figure numbers in brackets refer to the economics volume of the book. If used consistently, the Study Guide will aid your understanding of the main book's content and give you additional problems and exercises to help you apply economic concepts to various situations and interpret graphs.

Study Guide Features

Each chapter of the Study Guide contains the following features:

Chapter Summary
Summarizes the main points of the chapter and corresponds to the summary that appears at the end of each chapter of the main book.

Applying the Concepts
Lists the key questions that are answered by the Applications in the main book.

Section-by-Section Overview
Highlights important concepts, principles, definitions, and figures in each numbered section of the main book.

Extra Examples
Provides short, additional examples not found in the main book. These extra examples are identified with the following icon: ☞

Study Tips, Cautions, Key Equations, and Remember Boxes
Highlight important items to remember. The Caution boxes warn you against common mistakes that students make. The Remember boxes highlight material that is particularly important.

Application Summary
Provides an overview of the Applications used to answer the key questions that open the chapter.

Activity and Answer
Helps you complete an activity to further build your understanding of economic concepts.

Key Terms
Provides all the terms and definitions that appear in the margin of the chapter.

Practice Quiz
Helps you prepare for exams. There are multiple-choice questions and short-answer questions. Several questions ask you to interpret a graph. Several questions also support the Applications you learned about in the chapter. Answers are provided so you can confirm your understanding.

Use the Study Guide to Do Better on Tests

1. Figure out what you don't know. Often students spend time studying everything, when there are some things they actually know very well and some things that they need to work on. Use the exercises in the Study Guide and on **www.myeconlab.com** to help you figure out what you know well and what you need to spend extra time on. See the section entitled "Other Learning Resources" for more about MyEconLab.

2. Practice in a test environment. Often when working problems you may have the text or notes and use those resources to help get the right answer. That's a good thing, that's how you learn. At test time, however, you don't realize how much you depended on those resources. Also, you sometimes know how to solve a problem, but don't solve problems quickly and feel rushed in a test environment. Here's a suggestion. Use the Study Guide as a source of questions to mimic a test environment. Set a timer for 15 minutes and answer 15 multiple-choice questions without using any study aid. This will let you know what things you really know and will also help you feel comfortable with a time constraint.

Study Tips

1. The Study Guide doesn't replace the text! The Study Guide is intended to be used *along with* the text. It has been written to provide an overview of the key topics, but you should always read the text chapter first. In addition, the Study Guide references figures and graphs that are found in the text. To get the most out of the Study Guide, you really need to use it alongside the text.

2. Attend class and read chapters before you go to class. Reading the chapter first will give you an idea of what your instructor will discuss in class. Often you will find that you are able to understand many basic ideas simply from your reading of the text. You can then use class time to learn how to apply those basic ideas, to understand more difficult concepts, and to ask questions.

3. See economics in the world around you. Almost every decision you make has an economic component to it. Suppose that you watched the Golf Channel every day or read all you could about playing the piano, but you never went to the golf course or sat down at a piano. All the knowledge in the world doesn't benefit you much if you never put it into practice. It is the same with economics. Don't just learn the material; put it into practice as you go about your daily routine.

4. Do extra exercises. Economics is a problem-solving discipline. The more problems you do, the better you will understand the material and the more comfortable you will be working with the material. The activities and exercises in the Study Guide are a great practice ground. Also visit **www.myeconlab.com** to complete more exercises and get tutorial help.

Other Learning Resources

Here is another resource you can use in addition to this Study Guide to help you understand economic concepts and build your skills solving problems and exercises:

Get Ahead of the Curve

MyEconLab puts you in control of your learning through a collection of tests, practice, and study tools tied to the online, interactive version of the textbook, and other media resources. At the core of MyEconLab are the following features:

1. Sample Tests, two per chapter
2. Personal Study Plan
3. Tutorial Instruction
4. Graphing Tool

Sample Tests
Two Sample Tests for each chapter are preloaded in MyEconLab, enabling you to practice what you have learned, test your understanding, and identify areas in which you need further work. You can study on your own, or you can complete assignments created by your instructor.

Personal Study Plan
Based on your performance on tests, MyEconLab generates a personal Study Plan that shows where you need further study. The Study Plan consists of a series of additional practice exercises with detailed feedback and guided solutions and keyed to other tutorial resources.

Tutorial Instruction
Launched from many of the exercises in the Study Plan, MyEconLab provides tutorial instruction in the form of step-by-step solutions and other media-based explanations.

Graphing Tool
A graphing tool is integrated into the Tests and Study Plan exercises to enable you to make and manipulate graphs. This feature helps you understand how concepts, numbers, and graphs connect.

Additional MyEconLab Tools
MyEconLab includes the following additional features:

1. Economics in the News—This feature provides weekly updates during the school year of news items with links to sources for further reading and discussion questions.

2. eText—While you are working in the Study Plan or completing homework assignments, part of the tutorial resources available is a direct link to the relevant page of the text so that you can review the appropriate material and complete the exercise.

3. Glossary—This searchable version of the textbook glossary provides additional examples and links to related terms.

4. Glossary Flashcards—Every key term is available as a flashcard, allowing you to quiz yourself on vocabulary from one or more chapters at a time.

5. Ask the Author—You can e-mail economics-related questions to the author.

6. Research Navigator (CourseCompass™ version only)—This feature offers extensive help on the research process and provides four exclusive databases of credible and reliable source material, including *The New York Times*, the *Financial Times*, and peer-reviewed journals.

Learning economics can be interesting and rewarding. The skills you develop in your economics class will be with you throughout your life. Enjoy the class, the book, and this Study Guide.

David Eaton
Murray State University

Study Guide

Microeconomics
Principles, Applications, and Tools

1
Introduction:
What Is Economics?

Chapter Summary

This chapter explains what economics is and why it is useful. Here are the main points of the chapter:
- Most of modern economics is based on positive analysis, which answers the question "what is?" or "what will be?" Economists contribute to policy debates by conducting positive analyses about the consequences of alternative actions.
- Normative analysis answers the question "what ought to be?"
- The choices made by individuals, firms, and governments answer three questions: What products do we produce? How do we produce the products? Who consumes the products?
- To think like economists, we (a) use assumptions to simplify, (b) use the notion of *ceteris paribus* to focus on the relationship between two variables, (c) think in marginal terms, and (d) assume that rational people respond to incentives.
- We use macroeconomics to understand why economies grow, to understand economic fluctuations, and to make informed business decisions.
- We use microeconomics to understand how markets work, to make personal and managerial decisions, and to evaluate the merits of public policies.

Applying the Concepts

After reading this chapter, you should be able to answer these two key questions:
1. Do people respond to incentives?
2. What is the role of prices in allocating resources?

1.1 What Is Economics?

Economics is the study of how people, businesses, governments, and other organizations make choices when there is scarcity. **Scarcity** means that the resources we use to produce goods and services are limited. Human wants, however, are unlimited. For instance, you may earn enough money each month to make a lease payment on a Lexus, but if you do that you won't have money to pay for rent and buy food. Because your resources are limited, you have to choose between a nice car, and food and a place to sleep.

We call the resources used to produce goods and services **factors of production** and typically think of five types of factors:

- **Natural resources**, which are provided by nature and include land, mineral deposits, oil and gas deposits, and water.
- **Labor**, the physical and mental effort people use to produce goods and services.
- **Physical capital**, the stock of equipment, machines, structures, and infrastructure that is used to produce goods and services.
- **Human capital**, the knowledge and skills acquired by a worker through education and experience.
- **Entrepreneurship**, the effort to co-ordinate the factors of production to produce and sell products.

☞ Think about the factors of production needed to open a coffee shop near your campus. You would need some physical capital such as a building, an espresso machine, tables, and chairs. You would need labor, workers who would make the coffee drinks and who, hopefully, could suggest and help develop new recipes as they learn what your customers like. You would provide the entrepreneurial ability as you find a location and make decisions on the best way to use the resources at your disposal.

Economic analysis takes on two primary forms: **positive analysis,** which answers the question "What is?" or "What will be?" and **normative analysis,** which answers the question "What ought to be?"

An example of a positive question is "Why do athletes make more money than schoolteachers?" A related normative question would ask "Should athletes make more money than schoolteachers?" Another positive question is "How does a monopoly affect market outcomes?" A related normative question is "Should society regulate monopolies?"

📄 Remember

Most of what is covered in this book will take the form of positive analysis, trying to understand the world the way it is, not the way we might like it to be.

Economics seeks to answer three primary questions:
- What products do we produce? Should a coffee shop sell breakfast food and lunch food along with coffee?
- How do we produce the products? Should the coffee shop hire bakers to make breakfast pastries or should they buy pastries from someone else?
- Who consumes the products? Should prices determine who buys coffee or should the coffee shop use some other mechanism?

Most of the time markets will provide the answers to these three questions. There are times when legal or regulatory restrictions are imposed on the market. We will explore how those impact economic outcomes. We will also see that there are times when legal or regulatory action improves market outcomes.

To simplify analysis, we use **economic models.** A model is a simplified representation of an economic environment. At this level, our models will often employ a graph. A model focuses on the main issues in an economic situation. Most of our models ignore certain aspects of real markets, but the models do contain the essential features that let us understand how markets work. For example, we might assume in a model that firms sell identical goods. In most cases we know that the goods offered by different companies are not technically identical. However, if most consumers don't care what color facial tissues they buy, we can simplify analysis by assuming that all facial tissues are the same. By making this assumption we remove a factor that would add a great deal of complexity to the analysis, but little understanding.

1.2 Economic Analysis and Modern Problems

Policy makers, economists, company executives, and you can use the tools of economic analysis to understand and solve a variety of problems in the world. For instance, we might ask "What is the best way to reduce pollution?" and even "What is the right amount of pollution?" Economic analysis is often used to provide answers to these questions.

We can also use the tools of economics to measure the level of economic activity and to examine how changes in policy or education affect the level of economic activity and the amount of economic growth in a country.

Your book provides three examples of real-world problems that can be addressed by economics:
- Traffic congestion: How do you help people realize the true cost of driving on a road, and will this reduce congestion?
- Poverty in Africa: As economies grow, the poorest households share in the prosperity. A key source of economic growth missing from this is a well-functioning legal and regulatory system.
- Japan's economic problems: How can changing the financial system revitalize a once rapidly growing economy?

These will be used as examples in more detail in later sections of the book.

1.3 The Economic Way of Thinking

In many cases multiple things are happening at once. Most economic analysis attempts to understand how changing one **variable**, a measure of something that can take on different values, changes the economic outcome. To do this we often assume that all other variables are held constant in the analysis. *Ceteris paribus* is the Latin expression that means "to hold other variables fixed."

Perhaps the most important thing to remember about the economic way of thinking is that economics focuses on the **marginal change**, that is, a small, one-unit change. Even though we may not consciously make decisions in this manner, it provides a very nice framework to understand decision making. Decisions made by individuals and institutions are usually very close to the decisions predicted by marginal analysis.

☞ As an example of a marginal change, suppose that a store is selling sweaters for $40 each, two for $70 and three for $85. To find the marginal cost, the additional cost we must pay, of each sweater, we ask, "How much more do we have to spend to buy an additional sweater?" For the first sweater, we must spend $40. The marginal cost of the second sweater is only $30. Why? We have already spent $40 to purchase one sweater. Since we can buy two sweaters for $70 we need to spend only an additional $30 to acquire the second sweater. The third sweater will only cost us only $15 because we have paid $70 for two sweaters and to purchase the third we must increase our payments to $85.

ᏠᏏ **Study Tip**

Throughout your study of economics, you will use the concept of a marginal change. Be sure that you understand that a marginal change considers how a small change in economic activity affects some other economic variable. For instance, marginal cost tells us how the production of one more unit of output changes our total costs. The marginal benefit of a slice of pizza is the change in satisfaction that comes from eating one more slice of pizza.

There are four main elements to the economic way of thinking:

1. **Use assumptions to simplify**: In any problem there are certain key elements we need to understand along with other elements that don't affect the current decision. We use assumptions to eliminate the other elements so we can focus on the key elements for the decision.

☞ For example, when you decide which road to take to travel from Seattle to San Francisco, you don't take into account the curvature of the earth or all the smaller side roads along the path. You examine a flat highway map that shows only main roads. You have assumed away factors that don't affect the decision at hand.

2. **Isolate variables**: Examine how a change in one factor (say, the price of apples) affects another (say, the quantity of apples a person purchases) while assuming all other factors, such as income, remain unchanged. We can then ask how a change in income affects the quantity of apples purchased, assuming the price of apples remains constant.

3. **Think at the margin**: Analyze a problem by asking, "What happens if we make a small change from our current point?"

☞ For instance, a firm might ask, "If we hire one more worker, how will our output change, holding everything else constant?" Or consider that no one tries to decide whether they should drop out of high school or become a doctor. In part because those aren't the two options available. A marginal decision would be "do I drop out of high school or do I graduate?" The next decision would be "do I go to college or not?" Only after you graduate from college can you decide to go to medical school to be a doctor.

4. **Rational people respond to incentives**: People will change their behavior as the benefits and costs of their actions change.

☞ Imagine how your behavior would change if police could confiscate your car if they catch you speeding. Since the price of speeding would increase, you would be more careful to drive the speed limit. Some states will confiscate your car if you are caught driving under the influence.

Your book uses traffic congesting in London as an example. To solve the problem of traffic congestion, we first assume that all drivers and all cars have the same effect on congestion. This is an important simplifying assumption. We then examine how a government policy of charging a toll to drive on the road will affect the number of cars, holding constant things such as income and the price of gasoline. This assumption lets us focus on just the policy variable. To determine how well the toll works, we examine the effects of adding only one more car to the highway, that is, we think at the margin. In the book example, an additional car added two seconds to the travel time for each of the 900 other cars on the road. This amounted to 30 minutes of additional travel time. London decided to charge a tax of $8 per day to drive in the city between 7AM and 6:30PM. This higher price led some people to avoid driving in the city during the day, thus easing congestion.

Let's review two Applications that answer the key questions we posed at the start of the chapter:

1. Do people respond to incentives?

    APPLICATION 1: PEDALING FOR TELEVISION TIME
    In this Application, researchers increased the cost of watching TV by making children ride a bike to power the TV. Children that didn't have to pedal to watch TV watched 21 hours per week. For the children who had to pedal the bike to watch TV, this higher cost reduced their TV viewing time to only 2 hours per week. This is a nice example of people responding to incentives—as the cost of watching TV increased (because now the person had to work to power the TV), the amount of TV viewing decreased.

2. What is the role of prices in allocating resources?

    APPLICATION 2: THE ECONOMIC SOLUTION TO SPAM
    In this Application we examine the problem of spam, unwanted e-mail and text messages. The application suggests that changing the price of sending spam e-mail, will get firms sending spam e-mail to allocate promotional resources to other activities.

1.4 Preview of Coming Attractions: Macroeconomics

Macroeconomics is the study of the nation's economy as a whole. Macroeconomists study questions of inflation, unemployment, and economic growth. These are the economic issues you frequently hear about on the news or read about in the paper and on the web. Macroeconomics answers questions such as "What makes economies grow?" "How can we smooth out business cycles?" "How does the Federal Reserve affect economic performance?"

Three important reasons for studying macroeconomics are:
*   To understand why economies grow.
*   To understand economic fluctuations.
*   To make informed business decisions.

1.5 Preview of Coming Attractions: Microeconomics

Microeconomics studies the choices of individual economic agents such as households, firms, and governments. Microeconomics also studies how the choices made by these agents affect the market for goods and services. Questions of output and pricing would be microeconomic questions. Some questions addressed by microeconomics might be "How will a hurricane in Florida affect the price of citrus fruits?" "Who pays when a tax is imposed in a market?" "When will a new business enter a market?" "Why does the price of bottled water rise after a hurricane?"

Three important reasons for studying microeconomics are:
- To understand markets and predict changes.
- To make personal and managerial decisions.
- To evaluate public policies.

𝒶𝓇 Study Tip

Economics is a way of looking at the world and understanding how the world works. To be successful in this class you must become comfortable thinking like an economist. While this may seem difficult at first, as with many things, practice will help this become second nature. That is one of the reasons it is important to work a lot of problems as you try to learn economics. Working the problems helps you to begin to see the world as an economist.

Activity

An important concept introduced in this chapter is that people respond to incentives. You can see this around you every day. As an example, think about all of the lectures and other campus events students attend because they are given extra credit. The incentive (extra credit) has changed their behavior. How incentives affect behavior is an important part of understanding economic decisions.

List a few ways that you and your fellow students respond to incentives. A good place to start is to ask yourself if you have ever attended a campus function that you normally wouldn't attend to earn extra credit points. If you have, you have changed your behavior in response to the incentives offered.

Key Terms

Ceteris paribus: The Latin expression meaning other variables being held fixed.

Economics: The study of choices when there is scarcity.

Economic model: A simplified representation of an economic environment, often employing a graph.

Entrepreneurship: The effort used to coordinate the factors of production—natural resources, labor, physical capital, and human capital—to produce and sell products.

Factors of production: The resources used to produce goods and services; also known as production inputs.

Human capital: The knowledge and skills acquired by a worker through education and experience.

Labor: The physical and mental effort people use to produce goods and services.

Macroeconomics: The study of the nation's economy as a whole; focuses on the issues of inflation, unemployment, and economic growth.

Marginal change: A small, one-unit change in value.

Microeconomics: The study of the choices made by households, firms, and government and how these choices affect the markets for goods and services.

Natural resources: Resources provided by nature and used to produce goods and services.

Normative analysis: Answers the question "What ought to be?"

Physical capital: The stock of equipment, machines, structures, and infrastructure that is used to produce goods and services.

Positive analysis: Answers the question "What is?" or "What will be?"

Scarcity: The resources we use to produce goods and services are limited.

Variable: A measure of something that can take on different values.

Appendix: Using Graphs and Percentages

Graphs are a visual way of representing a relationship between variables. The relationship is usually either a **positive relationship**, meaning that the two variables move in the same direction, or a **negative relationship**, meaning that the two variables move in opposite directions. Figure 1A.4 shows a graph of a positive relationship. Figure 1A.6 shows a graph of a negative relationship. Graphs, particularly graphs of two variables, are used extensively in economics and a good understanding of the material in the appendix is needed for success.

ᨆ Study Tip

We will use graphs throughout the text. Now is the time to make sure you understand how to understand information presented in a graph. In particular, understand the difference between those factors that cause us to move between two points on a fixed curve and those factors that cause the position of the curve to shift. Being able to work with graphs will be particularly important in Chapter 4 when you study supply and demand.

The **slope of a curve** tells us by how much a change in one variable affects the value of another variable. You can find the slope by dividing the vertical difference between two points (the rise) by the horizontal difference between the two points (the run). A graph of two variables with a positive relationship will have a positive slope. A graph of two variables with a negative relationship will have a negative slope. The slope answers questions in economics such as, "By how much does quantity demanded fall when the price of a good increases by $1?"

We move along a curve when we move from one point on a graph to another point on the same graph. This would be a movement from point *f* to point *g* in Figure 1A.5. You can see that both hours and income have changed along the line representing income with a $90 allowance. We shift the curve when one of the variables changes while the other variable stays the same. This would be a shift from point *f* to point *b*. Our income per week now takes on a different value at the same number of hours worked per week.

☑ Key Equations: Finding the slope of a line

$$\text{slope} = \frac{\text{vertical distance between two points}}{\text{horizontal distance between two points}}$$

$$\text{slope} = \frac{\text{rise}}{\text{run}}$$

$$\text{slope} = \frac{\Delta y}{\Delta x}$$

The equations above all represent the same concept.

☑ Key Equations: Calculating percentage changes

$$\text{Percentage change} = \frac{(\text{new value} - \text{initial value})}{\text{initial value}} \times 100$$

In some cases, we will use the midpoint formula:

$$\text{Percentage change} = \frac{(\text{new value} - \text{initial value})}{\text{average value}} \times 100$$

where the average value is:

$$\frac{(\text{new value} + \text{initial value})}{2}$$

Key Terms for Appendix

Negative relationship: A relationship in which two variables move in opposite directions.

Positive relationship: A relationship in which two variables move in the same direction.

Slope of a curve: The vertical difference between two points (the rise) divided by the horizontal difference (the run).

Practice Quiz

(Answers are provided at the end of the Practice Quiz.)

1. Economics is the study of choice under conditions of:
    a. supply.
    b. scarcity.
    c. opportunity.
    d. abundance of resources.

2. Which of the following terms would best describe the consequence of scarcity?
    a. Limited resources
    b. Tradeoffs
    c. Unlimited wants
    d. Poverty and possibly starvation

3. The resources provided by nature and used to produce goods and services are also known as:
    a. factors of production.
    b. natural resources.
    c. physical capital.
    d. productive inputs.

4. Select the best answer. Which questions usually lie at the heart of policy debates?
    a. Positive questions
    b. Normative questions
    c. All economic questions, both positive and normative
    d. Questions about the choices made by individuals

5. If the president of Colombia commented that "we should do something to reduce inflation in Colombia," this would be an example of:
    a. a normative statement.
    b. a positive statement.
    c. a statement that has both positive and normative components.
    d. neither positive analysis nor normative analysis.

6. Economic decisions are made at every level in society. When we try to decide which production method to use among several alternatives, which of the key economic questions are we trying to answer?
    a. What products do we produce?
    b. How do we produce the products?
    c. Who consumes the products?
    d. Which government agency should supervise the production of goods?

7. Economic models are:
    a. precise representations of reality that include as many details as possible in order to accurately predict behavior.
    b. simplifications of reality that focus only on key relationships and ignore less relevant details.
    c. presentations of all the possible outcomes under all real world circumstances.
    d. analytical interpretations of economic behavior involving a good deal of the surrounding social and political structure of society.

8. Economists develop analytical tools to deal with specific problems. Which of the problems below is an economist prepared to discuss?
   a. The economic view of Japan's economic problems
   b. The economic view of poverty in Africa
   c. The economic view of traffic congestion
   d. All of the above

9. A roadmap is a good example of one of the four elements of economic thinking. Which one?
   a. Using assumptions to simplify
   b. Isolating variables—*ceteris paribus*
   c. Thinking at the margin
   d. Acting rationally and responding to incentives

10. This question tests your understanding of Application 1 in this chapter, *Pedaling for Television Time*. Do people respond to incentives? To illustrate the notion that people are rational and respond to incentives, an experiment was conducted by researchers at St. Luke's Roosevelt Hospital in New York City. Which of the following best illustrates the findings of that experiment?
    a. Children are rational and respond to incentives in the manner we would expect any rational person to respond.
    b. Children don't seem to respond to incentives in the same manner as adults do.
    c. Sometimes children act in a manner consistent with the incentives provided to them, but other times they don't seem to pay attention to incentives.
    d. Adult behavior is closely linked to childhood development.

11. Macroeconomics can be used to understand all of the topics below, EXCEPT:
    a. how the national economy works.
    b. how consumers decide which car to buy based on their preferences vs. prices.
    c. what causes economic booms and downturns.
    d. how to make informed business decisions.

12. In which of the following situations can we use economic analysis?
    a. To determine how well the government performs its roles in the market economy and to examine the tradeoffs associated with various public policies
    b. To answer many practical questions about markets and how they operate
    c. To explain why some resources increase over time and how an increase in resources translates into a higher standard of living
    d. All of the above

13. If Y = 800 - 4X, what is the slope of this line?
    a. -1/4
    b. 1/4
    c. 4
    d. -4
    e. 800

14. Refer to the graph below. The solid line can be expressed algebraically as Y = a + bX. What causes the line to shift, from the solid line to the dashed line?

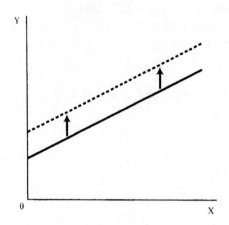

   a. A change in the value of a
   b. A change in the value of b
   c. A change in the value of X
   d. A change in the value of bX

15. Refer to the graph below. Which move describes the impact of an increase income on consumption?

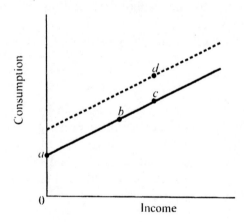

   a. The move from *b* to *c*
   b. The move from *c* to *d*
   c. The move from *d* to *c*
   d. A simultaneous move from *b* to *c*, and from *c* to *d*

16. Refer to the graph below. The relationship between output produced and cost of production can be described as follows:

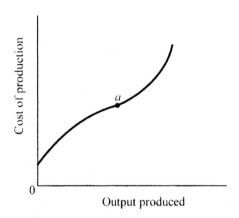

  a. The cost of production decreases up until point *a*, then it increases.
  b. The cost of production increases rapidly up until point *a*, then it increases slowly.
  c. The cost of production increases at a decreasing rate up until point *a*, then it increases at an increasing rate.
  d. The cost of production equals zero if there is no output produced.

17. Refer to the graph below. Which of the following statements is true about the value of the slope of this line?

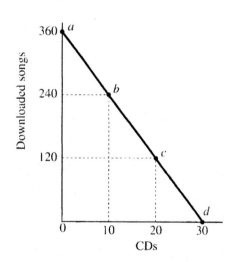

  a. The value of the slope is greater between points *a* and *b* than between points *c* and *d*.
  b. The value of the slope is smaller between points *a* and *b* than between points *c* and *d*.
  c. The value of the slope is the same between points *a* and *b* and points *c* and *d*.
  d. The value of the slope increases as the value of the variable along the horizontal axis increases.

18. Refer to the graphs below. Which graph shows a negative and increasing relationship between X and Y?

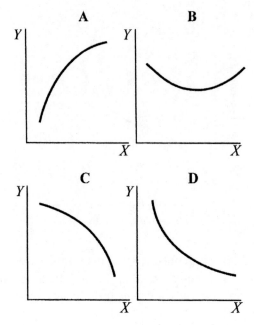

   a. A
   b. B
   c. C
   d. D

19. Refer to the figure below. The expression for the slope of this line between points a and b equals:

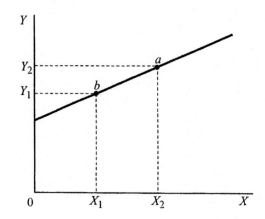

  a) $\dfrac{Y_2 - Y_1}{X_2 - X_1}$

  b) $\dfrac{Y_2 - X_2}{Y_1 - X_1}$

  c) $\dfrac{X_2 - X_1}{Y_2 - Y_1}$

  d) $\dfrac{X_2 - Y_1}{Y_2 - Y_1}$

20. The sale price of a shirt is $8. There is a sign on the clothing rack that states "price marked is 20% off original price." What was the original price of the shirt?
    a. $49.60
    b. $50
    c. $65
    d. $60

21. Define "economics" and explain the most fundamental economic problem.

Answers to the Practice Quiz

1. b. Scarcity is a situation in which resources are limited in quantity and can be used in different ways. Economics is the study of choice under conditions of scarcity.

2. b. Economists are always reminding us that there is scarcity—that there are tradeoffs in everything we do.

3. b. Natural resources are provided by nature. Some examples are fertile land, mineral deposits, oil and gas deposits, and water. Some economists refer to all types of natural resources as *land*. Factors of production refers to all of the resources, not only natural resources but also labor, physical capital, human capital, and entrepreneurship, used to produce goods and services; also known as production inputs. Physical capital is the stock of equipment, machines, structures, and infrastructure that is used to produce goods and services. Some examples are forklifts, lathes, computers, factories, airports, roads, and fiber-optic cables. Productive inputs are all of the resources, not only natural resources but also labor, physical capital, human capital, and entrepreneurship, used to produce goods and services; also known as factors of production.

4. b. Correct. Normative economics answers the question: What ought to be? Normative questions lie at the heart of policy debates. Positive economics only lays out the possibilities and their likely consequences; it does not suggest decisions among these alternatives which are based on values and priorities. Policies often do influence how individuals make choices but policy debates are centered around the choices made by policy makers based on their judgments on which policy will be best for society.

5. a. The word "should" implies a value judgment. Only normative statements involve value judgments.

6. b. When we try to decide which production method to use among several alternatives, we ask questions such as: Should power companies use coal, natural gas, or wind power to produce electricity? Should professors teach in large lecture halls or small classrooms?

7. b. Abstraction and simplification, as opposed to concrete and complex information, are the preferred characteristics of economic models. Models ignore all non-essential elements of real world complexity. They also ignore a good deal of the social and political reality in order to study the underlying economic concepts.

8. d. Economic analysis provides important insights into real-world problems. Economists attempt to diagnose and provide solutions to problems such as traffic congestion, pollution, taxation, or the problems of an entire economy.

9. a. Economists use assumptions to make things simpler and focus attention on what really matters. If you use a road map to plan a car trip from Seattle to San Francisco, you make two unrealistic assumptions to simplify your planning: The earth is flat: The flat road map doesn't show the curvature of the earth. The roads are flat: The standard road map doesn't show hills and valleys. Instead of a map, you could use a globe that shows all the topographical features between Seattle and San Francisco, but you don't need those details to plan your trip. A map, with its unrealistic assumptions, will suffice, because the curvature of the earth and the topography of the highways are irrelevant to your trip.

10. a. In the experiment, kids responded to incentives as expected, watching less TV when the cost of watching is higher. The experiment does not differentiate between children and adults, nor does it establish a relationship between child behavior and subsequent adult behavior.

11. b. The decision between two types of cars is an individual choice. This is a topic of microeconomics.

12. d. Economic analysis includes all of the above.

13. d. The slope of this line is -4. You can calculate this by finding any two points on the line and remembering that the slope is the change in Y divided by the change in X. Alternatively, for any linear function of the form $Y = a + bX$, b is the slope.

14. a. The value of a represents the Y-intercept. An increase in the value of the intercept causes the upward, parallel shift of the line. The value of b represents the value of the slope of the line. A change in the value of the slope makes the solid line steeper or flatter, but it does not shift the line. A change in the value of X causes a move along the solid line, not a shift to the dashed line. Only a change in a would result in a parallel shift of the line.

15. a. As income increases we move to the right along a fixed income/consumption line.

16. c. The relationship is first positive and decreasing, then positive and increasing.

17. c. The value of the slope is the same between any two points along a line.

18. c. As the value of X increases, the value of Y decreases at an increasing rate.

19. a. The difference between Y2 and Y1 is the vertical distance, or the change in Y. The difference between X2 and X1 is the horizontal distance, or the change in X. The ratio of the changes is commonly called "rise over run."

20. d. A reduction of 20% means that the new price is 80% of the old price. If $40 equals 80%, then how many dollars are equivalent to 100%? The answer is (48 x 100)/80 = 60.

21. Economics studies the choices that can be made when there is scarcity. Scarcity is a situation in which resources are limited in quantity and can be used in different ways. Because our resources are limited, we must sacrifice one thing for another. Economists are always reminding us that there is scarcity—that there are tradeoffs in everything we do.

2

The Key Principles of Economics

Chapter Summary

This chapter introduces five key principles of economics. You'll see these principles again in each chapter of the book. The five key principles are:

- **Principle of Opportunity Cost:** The opportunity cost of something is what you sacrifice to get it.
- **The Marginal Principle:** Increase the level of an activity as long as its marginal benefit exceeds its marginal cost. Choose the level at which the marginal benefit equals the marginal cost.
- **Principle of Voluntary Exchange:** A voluntary exchange between two people makes both people better off.
- **Principle of Diminishing Returns:** Suppose that output is produced with two or more inputs, and we increase one input while holding the other inputs fixed. Beyond some point—called the point of diminishing marginal returns—output will increase at a decreasing rate.
- **The Real–Nominal Principle:** What matters to people is the real value of money or income—its purchasing power—not the face value of money or income.

Applying the Concepts

After reading this chapter, you should be able to answer these seven key questions:
1. What is the opportunity cost of running a business?
2. What are society's tradeoffs between different goods?
3. How do firms think at the margin?
4. What is the rationale for specialization and exchange?
5. Do farmers experience diminishing returns?
6. How does inflation affect the real minimum wage?
7. How does inflation affect lenders and borrowers?

⤳ Study Tip

While the concepts introduced in this chapter may seem very elementary, they are quite important. In fact, the rest of the book is an application of the principles in this chapter. As you go through the text, you may wish to look back and see how different topics are examples of these five principles.

2.1 The Principle of Opportunity Cost

To make a good decision we must compare the benefits of the decision with the costs. The important cost concept for decision making is that of the **opportunity cost**, what you sacrifice to get something. It is important to recognize that opportunity costs often don't involve spending money. Waiting in line is a cost: You sacrifice time you can't get back. Would you wait in line for 15 minutes at a gas station to save $1 on a tank full of gas instead of paying $1 more at a gas station with no line? In this case you need to recognize that sacrificing your time is part of the cost of the gasoline. Only if you value 15 minutes of time at less than $1 would you want to wait in line.

An opportunity cost can involve both time and money. When evaluating the costs of college, some costs, such as tuition and books, are obvious because they involve spending money. Some costs are not obvious, because they don't involve spending money. The income you give up by going to college instead of taking a full-time job is a cost. You sacrificed the income you could have earned to go to college. Some things we think of as costs are not relevant to the decision. For instance, whether you go to college or find a full-time job, you must have a place to live and food to eat. As a result, room and board aren't relevant costs to the decision to go to college—you would have to pay these costs regardless of your choice.

Like you and other people, economies (countries) face opportunity costs. Economists use the **production possibilities curve** to represent these costs. The production possibilities curve shows the possible combinations of products that an economy can produce, given that its productive resources are fully employed and efficiently used. The production possibilities curve shows us the cost of one good in terms of the amount of the other good we must sacrifice. The bowed-out shape of the production possibilities curve reflects the fact that the opportunity cost of a good increases as we produce more of it. Look at Figure 2.1 in your text. The first few tons of wheat, moving from point *a* to point *b*, require little sacrifice of steel. This makes sense as there are some resources (fertile land) that are very suited for wheat production, but not very well suited for steel production. As we produce more and more wheat, however, we must begin to use resources that are better suited for steel production and, thus, we give an increasing amount of steel for each additional unit of wheat. You can see this as we move from point *c* to point *d* in Figure 2.1.

✍ Study Tip

The concept of opportunity cost is one of the most important concepts in microeconomics. Make sure that you can recognize all the costs of a particular decision, both the monetary costs and the opportunity costs. For an individual, the other uses of your time are an important source of opportunity cost. You also need to recognize when particular costs are not relevant to a decision.

Let's review two Applications that answer key questions we posed at the start of the chapter:

1. What is the opportunity cost of running a business?

APPLICATION 1:
DON'T FORGET THE COSTS OF TIME AND INVESTED FUNDS
When you use your own time and money in a business, you sacrifice the opportunity to use those resources in other ways. You sacrifice the opportunity to trade your time for the money you could earn working for someone else as well as the interest you could have earned investing the money you invest in your business. Even though you don't write a check for these costs, they are important costs for decision making. As a result Betty's revenues must not only cover the explicit costs of doing business, they must also replace the implicit costs of her time and invested funds in order for her business to be profitable. If she is not able to cover these implicit costs, she will likely not start her own business.

2. What are society's tradeoffs between different goods?

APPLICATION 2: THE OPPORTUNITY COST OF MILITARY SPENDING
If society has a fixed amount of money to spend on goods and services, buying one type of good or service means we sacrifice the opportunity to buy others. In this example, $100 billion can pay for the war in Iraq or 13 million children enrolled in Head Start programs. To see this idea in another way, suppose that your state legislature, in an attempt to make college more affordable, gives each full-time college student $500 to offset the cost of textbooks. The state now has less money to spend on the other goods and services the state provides, such as police patrols and highway maintenance. So, the true cost of the $500 per student may be that fewer potholes are repaired on state highways.

2.2 The Marginal Principle

Economics is concerned with making choices. We will assume that the relevant choice is whether to change a current activity level by a little bit. That is, do we hire one more worker? Produce one more unit of output? Purchase one more slice of pizza? This is what is known as a marginal change. To make a good decision, we compare the **marginal benefit**, the additional benefit resulting from a small increase in some activity, with the **marginal cost**, the additional cost resulting from a small increase in some activity. If the marginal benefit is greater than the marginal cost, we want to increase the level of the activity. Doing so will increase our total well-being by the difference between the marginal benefit and the marginal cost. If the marginal benefit is less than the marginal cost, we want to reduce the level of the activity. If they are equal, we are at the optimal amount of the activity.

☞ A marginal change refers to a small change in some activity. You can think of a marginal change as taking the next step in a logical sequence. You would never, for instance, compare the salary of someone with a Ph.D. against someone who didn't finish high school. Why not? These aren't two logical options. A person doesn't decide to either earn a Ph.D. or drop out of high school. She decides whether to drop out of high school or get a high school diploma. She next decides whether to go to college or not. Upon graduating college she decides whether to take a job or go to graduate school. These are each sequential steps, and thus we can make relevant comparisons between them. A person will continue to go to school as long as the marginal benefit of the next level of schooling exceeds the marginal cost.

Let's review an Application that answers one of the key questions we posed at the start of the chapter:

3. How do firms think at the margin?

APPLICATION 3:
THE MARGINAL BENEFIT AND MARGINAL COST OF SPEED
This Application considers whether a driver should drive faster than their current speed. The marginal benefit of driving 1 mile per hour faster is that you will arrive at your destination more quickly. The marginal cost is the increased likelihood of injuries and accidents, not to mention speeding tickets. If the marginal benefit exceeds the marginal cost, a driver should speed up.

The Application also highlights unintended outcomes of auto safety equipment. If the marginal cost of driving faster is reduced by increased safety equipment, rational drivers will increase their speed, which may lead to an undesirable result for bicyclists on the road

☞ A restaurant might use the marginal principle when deciding whether to open for breakfast in addition to lunch. Since many of the costs of the restaurant (rent, payments for equipment) are fixed, the only additional cost of opening for breakfast would be the food, labor, and utilities needed to open earlier. If the revenue from selling breakfast exceeds these costs, the restaurant should open for breakfast.

ᰔ Study Tip

Decision making based on the marginal principle is the basis for all decisions in this book. Be sure you understand the concepts of marginal benefit and marginal cost. Recognize that people should continue to take an action as long as the marginal benefit is greater than the marginal cost.

2.3 The Principle of Voluntary Exchange

The principle of voluntary exchange states that a voluntary exchange between two people makes both people better off. Think about the last time you purchased a movie ticket. Since you were willing to pay the price of a ticket, you must have valued seeing the movie more than the ticket cost. The theater manager knows that the ticket price was higher than the theater's cost of letting you see a movie. Neither of you felt cheated in the transaction because you were both better off.

☞ Most of us recognize this principle in practice. All of us realize that we are better off trading our time for money and then spending that money on other goods and services. Many people choose to eat dinner in a restaurant, even though they could make the same food at home. This principle works for trades between individuals and, as we will see later in the book, for trades between countries as well.

Let's review an Application that answers a key question we posed at the start of the chapter:

4. What is the rationale for specialization and exchange?

APPLICATION 4: TIGER WOODS AND WEEDS

Tiger Woods can earn $1,000 in the time it takes him to weed his garden. Should Tiger pay someone to weed his garden, even if that person takes longer to weed the garden than Tiger Woods? Yes, if Tiger pays that person less than $1,000. If Tiger pays someone $200 to weed his garden, Tiger has a weed-free garden, and $800 (the $1,000 he earned minus the $200 he paid). If Tiger weeds his garden himself, he has only a weed-free garden. In this case, Tiger Woods is better off paying someone to weed his garden.

📄 Remember

A voluntary trade between two people will always leave both people better off.

2.4 The Principle of Diminishing Returns

The principle of diminishing returns says that if we produce output using two or more inputs and change the amount of only one input, beyond some point output will increase at a decreasing rate.

☞ Think of a local fast-food restaurant and imagine that they currently have only two workers on a shift. If the restaurant hired an additional person for that shift, would they be able to serve more food? Yes. That person could staff another register or cook more burgers, or take care of the drive-thru business. What if the restaurant kept hiring people? With a fixed number of registers, preparation areas or grill space, it would be harder for additional workers to add much to output because of the fixed amount of capital. In fact, at some point the workers would start to get into each other's way and output might actually fall as we hire more workers.

Let's review an Application that answers a key question we posed at the start of the chapter:

5.   Do farmers experience diminishing returns?

APPLICATION 5: FERTILIZER AND CROP YIELDS

Adding fertilizer increases crop yields, but after adding the first bag, each additional bag adds less to our output than the previous bag. So, as you can see in Table 2.1, adding the first bag of fertilizer increases output by 35 bushels per acre. The second bag increases output by only 15 bushels, and each additional bag of fertilizer adds a smaller amount to output. This is the principle of diminishing returns. More fertilizer increases output, but each additional bag adds a smaller and smaller amount to total output.

📄 Remember

Diminishing returns refers to the rate of change in output: Output grows at a smaller rate as we add additional units of a variable input. Diminishing returns does *not* refer to the level of output.

2.5 The Real–Nominal Principle

This principle states that what matters to people is the purchasing power of money, not its face value. Suppose that you earn $500 per month, and you spend $250 on rent, $150 on food, and $100 on entertainment. If your money income increases to $1,000, are you better off? If prices stay the same you are because you'll be able to buy more things. If, however, your rent increases to $500, food to $300, and the cost of entertainment to $200, you are no better off earning $1,000 than you were earning $500. Why? What you can purchase with your money income is the same in both cases.

📄 Remember

The important concern in economics is not how many dollars you have, but what you can purchase with those dollars. This is why we distinguish between real and nominal amounts.

Let's review two Applications that answer key questions we posed at the start of the chapter:

6. How does inflation affect the real minimum wage?

APPLICATION 6: THE DECLINING REAL MINIMUM WAGE
Would you rather earn $2 per hour or $5.85 per hour? The answer depends on what you can buy with that money. Even though at $5.85 per hour the dollar amount of the minimum wage is higher in 2007 than it was in 1974, the purchasing power of the 1974 minimum wage of $2 per hour was much greater. That is, even though you earned a smaller number of dollars (the **nominal value**, or the face value of an amount of money) those fewer dollars were able to purchase more stuff (the **real value**, or the value of money in terms of the quantity of goods it can buy).

7. How does inflation affect lenders and borrowers?

APPLICATION 7: REPAYING STUDENT LOANS
Inflation reduces the purchasing power of a given sum of money. Borrowers may like inflation (as they give up fewer goods in repaying their loans) while lenders do not like inflation (the nominal dollars they receive in repayment can't buy as much as the dollars they loaned). When the nominal amount of the loan is fixed, inflation allows the loan to be repaid in less time. Deflation increases the amount of time that it takes to repay the loan.

Activity

Suppose that you earn $12 per hour. (That's the same as 20 cents per minute.) Think about the following situations and consider the opportunity cost involved.

a. At the grocery store you have the choice to spend $1.50 for a package of unsliced mushrooms or to spend $1.90 for a package of pre-sliced mushrooms. How long would you have to spend slicing mushrooms to be better off buying the presliced mushrooms?

b. There are two gas stations on opposite corners of the street. One sells gasoline for $2.35 per gallon, the other for $2.32 per gallon. Your gas tank holds 10 gallons of gas. There is a line at the gas station with the lower price, and you anticipate that you will spend five minutes waiting in that line. You could buy gas now at the gas station with the higher prices. What should you do?

Answers

a. Since you can earn 20 cents per minute, if you would spend more than 2 minutes slicing mushrooms you should buy the pre-sliced mushrooms.

b. You will save 30 cents buying gasoline at the lower priced station since you save 3 cents per gallon on each of the 10 gallons that you purchase. In terms of time, 30 cents is only one and a half minutes. You are better off buying the higher priced gasoline.

Key Terms

Marginal benefit: The extra benefit resulting from a small increase in some activity.

Marginal cost: The additional cost resulting from a small increase in some activity.

Nominal value: The face value of an amount of money.

Opportunity cost: What you sacrifice to get something.

Production possibilities curve: A curve that shows the possible combinations of products that an economy can produce, given that its productive resources are fully employed and efficiently used.

Real value: The value of an amount of money in terms of what it can buy.

Practice Quiz

(Answers are provided at the end of the Practice Quiz.)

1. The principle of opportunity cost evolves from the concept of:
    a.   consumer spending.
    b.   wealth.
    c.   poverty.
    d.   scarcity.

2. A friend offers you a Coke, a Pepsi, or a Diet Coke. You don't like Diet Coke, so after some thought, you take the Pepsi. What is the opportunity cost of your choice?
    a.   The Pepsi
    b.   The Coke
    c.   The Coke plus the Diet Coke
    d.   The Coke plus the Diet Coke plus the Pepsi

3. Which of the following is NOT an opportunity cost of attending college?
   a. The wages that you could have earned while going to class
   b. Tuition
   c. The cost of books
   d. The cost of housing

4. This question tests your understanding of Application 1 in this chapter. From the choices A, B, and C below, choose the ones that you would include in your estimate of the opportunity cost of doing business:

   A: The expenses for fuel and other supplies
   B: The interest that the funds invested in the business could have earned at the bank or elsewhere
   C: The value of your time when used in the best alternative activity

   a. A and B
   b. B and C
   c. A and C
   d. A, B, and C

5. The table below shows the production possibilities for an economy that produces two goods: lobsters and boats. What is the opportunity cost of moving from point C to point D?

	Lobsters	Boats
A	0	10
B	100	9
C	200	7
D	300	4
E	400	0

   a. 3 boats
   b. 100 lobsters
   c. 100 lobsters and 3 boats
   d. 4 boats

6. Refer to the graph below. Which move best describes an increase in efficiency in the use of existing resources?

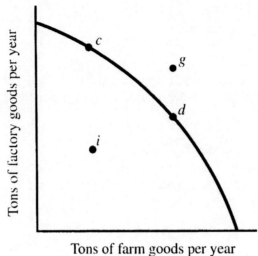

a. A move from *i* to *d*
b. A move from *c* to *d*
c. A move from *d* to *g*
d. None of the above. Higher efficiency in the use of resources is not represented by a move but by a shift of the production possibilities curve.

7. Refer to the graph below. At which point, or points, are resources fully and efficiently employed?

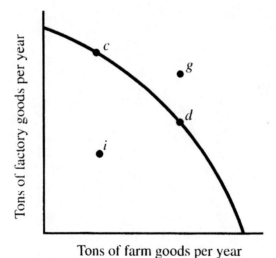

a. At points *c* and *d* only
b. At point *g* only
c. At points *c*, *d*, and *g*
d. At point *i* only

8. Refer to the graph below. Which of the following factors can cause a move from point *d* to points *g* or *h*?

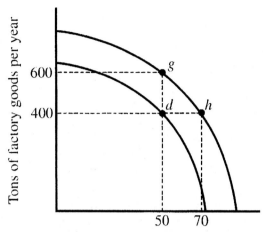

Tons of farm goods per year

(a.) The economy's resources increase.
b. The opportunity cost of producing farm goods or factory goods changes.
c. The economy utilizes its resources fully.
d. Resources that used to be more suitable for producing farm goods are now perfectly adaptable to the production of either farm goods or factory goods.

9. Refer to the graph below. According to this graph, the opportunity cost of producing an additional 20 tons of wheat, from 140 to 160 tons, is:

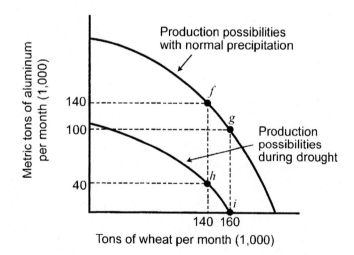

Tons of wheat per month (1,000)

a. higher with normal precipitation than during a drought.
b. higher during a drought than with normal precipitation.
(c.) the same with normal precipitation or during a drought.
d. zero during a drought.

10. Refer to the graph below. What can we conclude about opportunity cost based on the shape of this production possibilities curve?

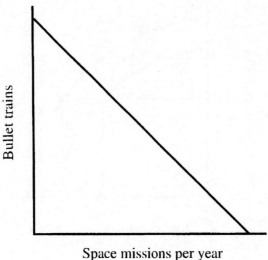

Space missions per year

a. The curve shows that as more of a good is produced, the higher the opportunity cost of producing that good.
b. Resources appear to be perfectly substitutable, or equally adaptable to the production of either bullet trains or space missions.
c. We can conclude that as you move downward along the curve, the opportunity cost of producing bullet trains decreases.
d. The economy's resources are abundant.

11. Refer to the table below. What is the marginal benefit of the fourth slice of pizza?

Slices of Pizza	Total Cost	Total Benefit
1	$1.50	$4.00
2	$3.00	$7.00
3	$4.50	$9.00
4	$6.00	$10.50
5	$7.50	$10.75

a. $6.00
b. $1.50
c. $10.50
d. $4.50

12. The table below shows the marginal benefit that Ted earns from keeping his store open one more hour. Ted has a marginal cost of $90 per hour. How many hours should Ted stay open?

Hours	Marginal Benefit Per Hour
20	200
21	140
22	110
23	70
24	40
25	10
26	0

   a. 21
   b. 22
   c. 23
   d. 24

13. The optimal amount of an activity is determined at the point where the activity yields:
   a. maximum marginal benefit.
   b. minimum marginal cost.
   c. equal value of marginal benefit and marginal cost.
   d. zero marginal cost.

14. Refer to the graph below. The price line indicates the additional revenue (or additional benefit) obtained from selling an additional unit of output. The marginal cost curve shows the cost of producing an additional unit. What is the optimal level of output?

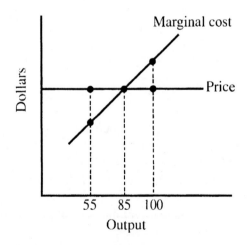

   a. 55 units, where price is greater than marginal cost
   b. 85 units, where price equals marginal cost
   c. 100 units, where price is below marginal cost
   d. Either 55 units or 100 units, or as long as price differs from marginal cost

15. This question tests your understanding of Application 5 in this chapter: Fertilizer and crop yields. Do farmers experience diminishing returns? The table below shows the relationship between the amount of fertilizer and the corn output, all else the same.

Table 2.1 | FERTILIZER AND CORN YIELD

Bags of Fertilizer	Bushels of Corn Per Acre
0	85
1	120
2	135
3	144
4	147

What causes a farmer to experience diminishing returns?
a. The fact that he doubles up all of his inputs at once in order to increase his crop yield.
b. The fact that he changes just one of the inputs, fertilizer, in order to increase crop yield.
c. The ability of the farmer to increase his crop yield faster than the rate of increase in fertilizer.
d. The farmer experiences diminishing returns anytime this year's crop is less than last year's crop.

16. Which of the following key principles of economics is the principle of voluntary exchange?
a. If participation in a market is voluntary, both the buyer and the seller must be better off as a result of a transaction.
b. What matters to people is the real value of money or income—its purchasing power—not the face value of money or income.
c. What matters in decision making is what happens at the margin.
d. The opportunity cost of something is what you sacrifice to get it.

17. From the principle of voluntary exchange, we conclude that:
a. often buyers are made better off and sellers are worse off when an exchange is made.
b. often sellers are made better off and buyers are worse off when an exchange is made.
c. both the buyer and the seller must be better off as a result of a transaction.
d. both the buyer and the seller might be worse off as a result of a transaction.

18. According to the real-nominal principle, what matters to workers is the real wage rate (or purchasing power of wages). The real wage rate:
a. always increases when the nominal wage rate increases.
b. always increases when the nominal wage rate decreases.
c. may increase or decrease when nominal wages change.
d. will not change with a change in the nominal wage rate.

19. Which of the following is NOT an example of nominal value?
a. A price shown on a clothing tag in a retail store
b. The value you could sell your house for at an auction today
c. Tuition costs that are adjusted for inflation
d. The amount of money you receive from the bank as interest on a deposit

20. James has enough money to buy a car at the market price from fifteen years ago, but that amount of money is only half of what he would need to buy it today. Which principle does this problem represent?
    a. The principle of opportunity cost
    b. The principle of voluntary exchange
    c. The principle of diminishing returns
    d. The real-nominal principle

21. During your next job interview, you will use the marginal principle to explain why you should be hired. What will you say?

22. Think about opportunity cost. What is the opportunity cost of you attending college? Write a short essay describing what it *really* costs you to attend.

23. Which economic principles are involved in the analysis of scarcity using a production possibilities curve?

24. Among the reasons for the use of marginal analysis in economics is that there are natural and technical constraints that prevent us from achieving unlimited results. Provide five examples of situations in which additional effort yields diminishing returns.

25. This question tests your understanding of Application 3 in this chapter: The marginal benefit and marginal cost of speed: How do firms think at the margin? Drivers have to decide whether or not to speed as they drive down the interstate. Explain how each of the following factors affects the decision to speed:
    i. a smaller likelihood of getting caught speeding.
    ii. better safety equipment in cars.
    iii. increased fines for speeding.

Answers to the Practice Quiz

1. d. The concept of opportunity cost is based on the principle of scarcity. Because resources are scarce, there exists a tradeoff for every choice you make.

2. b. Opportunity cost is the value of your next best choice, which in this case, is the Coke.

3. d. Housing is not an opportunity cost because you have to live somewhere anyway. However, you are implicitly giving up the wages that you could have earned.

4. b. Opportunity costs are costs stated in terms of the alternative use, such as how the funds could have been used, or the value of your time when used in the best alternative activity.

5. a. Three boats must be sacrificed (7 - 4) in order to increase the production of lobsters by 100.

6. a. When the economy moves from a point inside to a point on the production possibilities curve, resources become fully and efficiently employed.

7. a. As long as a point lies on the curve, resources are fully and efficiently employed at that point.

8. a. An increase in the amount of resources available to the economy shifts the production possibilities curve outward.

9. c. In both instances, the economy must give up to 40 metric tons of aluminum in order to increase wheat production from 140 to 160 tons.

10. b. Since the production possibilities curve is a straight line, the opportunity cost remains constant as you move downward along the line. A linear production possibilities curve reflects perfect substitutability of resources in production.

11. b. The marginal benefit is the extra benefit provided by the 4th slice of pizza: $10.50 - $9.00 = $1.50.

12. b. The marginal benefit of the 23rd hour is only $70, and so Ted would not want to pay costs of $90 to stay open for an hour if the benefit is only $70.

13 c. According to the marginal principle, we should increase the level of an activity if its marginal benefit exceeds its marginal cost; reduce the level of an activity if its marginal cost exceeds its marginal benefit. If possible, pick the level at which the activity's marginal benefit equals its marginal cost. Maximum, minimum, or zero are not the measures of optimality.

14. b. Stop the level of an activity where marginal benefit (or price in this case) equals marginal cost.

15. b. The notion of diminishing returns applies to all inputs to the production process. Because the farmer is changing just one of the inputs, fertilizer, the output will increase, but at a decreasing rate. Eventually, additional fertilizer will actually decrease output as the other nutrients in the soil are overwhelmed by the fertilizer.

16. a. According to the principle of voluntary exchange, a voluntary exchange between two people makes both people better off.

17. c. According to the principle of voluntary exchange, if participation in a market is voluntary, both the buyer and the seller must be better off as a result of a transaction.

18. c. Changes in the real wage rate depend not only on the nominal wage rate but also on the price level.

19. c. When costs are adjusted for inflation, they represent real values. An increase in prices due to inflation does not represent an actual increase in the amount of the good or service provided.

20. d. The real value of a good is a sum of money in terms of the quantity of good it can buy. The real value of this car has not changed—only its nominal value, the face value of a sum of money, has changed.

21. In accordance with the marginal principle, you should be hired because the additional cost to the company (your salary and benefits) will outweigh the contributions you will make to the firm, or the additional revenue the firm will obtain from your productive activity.

22. What is the opportunity cost of a college degree? Consider a student who spends a total of $40,000 for tuition and books. Instead of going to college, the student could have spent this money on a wide variety of goods, including housing, stereo equipment, and world travel. Part of the opportunity cost of college is the $40,000 worth of other goods the student sacrifices to pay for tuition and books.

of college is the $40,000 worth of other goods the student sacrifices to pay for tuition and books. Also, instead of going to college, the student could have worked as a bank clerk for $20,000 per year and earned $80,000 over four years. That makes the total opportunity cost of this student's college degree $120,000.

23. The production possibilities curve involves two of the fundamental principles: the principle of opportunity cost, and the principle of diminishing returns. The principle of opportunity cost is described by a move from one point to another along the curve. The curve shows combinations of two goods, or sets of goods, that can be produced when resources are fully and efficiently employed.

    As we increase the production of one good, we must sacrifice some of the other good. The principle of diminishing returns explains the shape of the curve. The curve is bowed out because resources are not perfectly substitutable in production. For this reason, it takes an ever greater amount of resources to produce additional units of a good, particularly when the production of that good is already high.

24. a.   Additional water into a flowerpot does not cause a flower to grow proportionally to the amount of water added.
    b.   As speed rises, it becomes harder and harder to gain an extra mile of speed.
    c.   As consumption rises, an extra bite does not yield as much satisfaction as the previous one.
    d.   The knowledge gained from an extra hour of study is less than the knowledge gained from the previous hour, particularly when you have been studying for a long time already.
    e.   In an eight-hour workday, the productivity of the last hour is smaller than the productivity of the first hour.

25. A lower likelihood of getting caught speeding would lower the marginal cost of speeding. For instance, if there is a 10% chance of getting a ticket, and a ticket costs $100, the expected cost of getting caught is .1(100) = $10. If there is only a 5% chance of getting caught, the marginal cost of speeding drops to $5 and more people will speed. As cars become safer the risk of injury in an accident decrease, as does the expected injury if one occurs. This also lowers the marginal cost of speeding and should lead to more speeding. Increased fines make speeding more expensive, raising the marginal cost and discouraging people from speeding.

3

Exchange and Markets

Chapter Summary

This chapter explores specialization and exchange as well as the virtues and shortcomings of markets. Here are the main points of the chapter:

- It is sensible for a person to produce the product for which he or she has a comparative advantage, that is, a lower opportunity cost than another person.
- Specialization increases productivity through the division of labor, a result of the benefits of repetition, continuity, and innovation.
- A system of international specialization and trade is sensible because nations have different opportunity costs of producing goods, giving rise to comparative advantages.
- Under a market system, self-interested people, guided by prices, make the decisions about what products to produce, how to produce them, and who gets them.
- Government roles in a market economy include establishing the rules for exchange, reducing economic uncertainty, and responding to market failures.

Applying the Concepts

After reading this chapter, you should be able to answer these three key questions:
1. Does the protection of one domestic industry harm another?
2. What is the role of opportunity cost in the development of markets?
3. Why do markets develop wherever people go?

3.1 Comparative Advantage and Exchange

The concept of comparative advantage is an application of the principle of opportunity cost from Chapter 2.

 Principle of Opportunity Cost
The opportunity cost of an item is what you must sacrifice to get the item.

To get more of one item you must sacrifice some other item. For Fred and Kate in the survivor example, the opportunity cost of a coconut is the number of fish that could have been produced in the time it takes to produce one coconut.

Trade is based on **comparative advantage**, the ability of one person or nation to produce a good at a lower opportunity cost than another person or nation. If Fred wishes to consume both fish and coconuts he can either produce both goods, or he can buy one of the goods from Kate. Since Kate can produce

34

coconuts at a lower opportunity cost than Fred, he would prefer to buy coconuts from her. Trade encourages individuals to specialize, and in so doing, increase the total output produced by all parties.

Trade benefits both parties, even if one person can produce more of both goods. We define **absolute advantage** as the ability of one person or nation to produce a product at a lower resource cost than another person or nation. While Fred spends less time producing each coconut than does Kate, he still wants to buy coconuts from her because she gives up fewer fish to produce a coconut than does Fred. Fred gives up fewer fish buying coconuts from Kate than he would give up producing coconuts on his own. This is an example of the principle of voluntary exchange from Chapter 2. As long as Fred and Kate both agree to the trade, both will be better off as a result of the trade. This is an example of the principle of voluntary exchange:

Principle of Voluntary Exchange
A voluntary exchange between two people makes both people better off.

🖹 Remember

It is important to recognize that we are concerned with opportunity cost, the amount of one good which must be foregone to produce some other good. Comparative advantage refers to who has the lowest opportunity cost of producing a certain good. Be sure that you are comfortable not only understanding the concept of opportunity cost, but calculating opportunity costs as well.

Trade is based not on who can produce the most of a good, but who can produce a good at the lowest cost. Thus, trade is based on comparative, not absolute, advantage.

3.2 Comparative Advantage and International Trade

Countries also engage in trade. An **import** is defined as a product produced in a foreign country and purchased by residents of the home country. An example of an import would be a Hyundai car, which is produced in Korea and sold in the United States. An **export** is a product produced in the home country and sold in another country. An example of an export would be agricultural products produced in the United States and sold in other countries.

<u>Why do firms move jobs to other countries?</u>

Firms take advantage of the principle of comparative advantage to shift production to facilities around the world. This practice is known as outsourcing or offshoring. This Application suggests that the employment effects of outsourcing are smaller than we may think. Estimates suggest that only 2 percent of layoffs in the first three months of 2004 were due to job movement overseas. In addition, lower labor costs reduce the prices that consumers have to pay and allow firms to produce more output.

☞ It is also worth remembering that while some U.S. companies are shifting production overseas, some non-U.S. companies are shifting jobs into the United States. Toyota, BMW, and Mercedes all have production plants in the United States. From Japan's perspective, Toyota jobs in Georgetown, Kentucky would be viewed as "outsourced."

☞ To see how "outsourcing" can increase the number of jobs, think about the Tiger Woods example in Chapter 2. If Tiger Woods earns $1,000 while paying his gardener $200 to weed his garden, Tiger Woods now has an additional $800 he can spend on goods and services. In fact, he might decide to spend some of the extra money hiring a personal chef. The same holds true for companies that move some jobs overseas. By lowering labor costs in one area, this provides additional resources for the firm to hire other types of labor.

🖹 Remember

Principles of trade are the same whether we are examining individuals, firms, or countries. Total output increases when individuals or countries specialize in those goods for which they have a comparative advantage. Voluntary trade between individuals or countries makes both parties to the trade better off.

4. Let's review an Application that answers a key question we posed at the beginning of the chapter.

   1. Does the protection of one domestic industry harm another?

APPLICATION 1:
CANDY CANE MAKERS MOVE TO MEXICO FOR CHEAP SUGAR

To keep the price of sugar high, the U.S. government restricts the amount of sugar which can be imported into the United States. This restriction leads to price disparities for sugar in the U.S. relative to other countries. This Application states that sugar costs six cents per pound in Mexico, but twenty-one cents per pound in the United States. Because of this cost disparity, candy makers have relocated to Mexico to take advantage of lower sugar costs. Since 1998 about 3,000 candy making jobs have left the Chicago area in part because of the difference in sugar prices between the United States and other countries. While the trade restrictions benefit U.S. sugar producers, they harm U.S. workers involved in candy production.

3.3 Markets

A **market economy** is one in which people specialize and exchange goods and services in a market. Most of us specialize in a few things and exchange our time doing those things for money. We then trade money for the other goods and services we wish to consume. In this situation money is a medium of exchange. At the most basic level we trade our time for money, and use the money to facilitate trades for other goods.

There are a number of inventions that help markets work better:
- Contracts: Specify terms of exchange and rights and obligations of the parties to the exchange.
- Insurance: Reduces the risk from low probability, random events such as severe storms.
- Patents: Encourage innovation in new products.
- Accounting rules: Provide a common set of information on the financial status of firms.

In contrast to a market economy, a **centrally planned economy** is one in which a planning authority decides how much of each good to produce, how to produce the goods, and who gets them. In a market system these same decisions are made in a very decentralized manner with prices providing the information about relative scarcity and the incentive to provide goods by means of higher prices for goods that are relatively scarce.

To see the challenges of a centrally planned economy, suppose you were in charge of securing all the food and clothing needed in your city. Could you imagine the amount of information you would need to identify all the food products that stores should carry or trying to arrange for the production of all those products? How much should you pay the workers who produce those goods? Where will those goods be produced? What about the transportation to bring them to the stores? The market system answers these questions using prices to convey information to decentralized decision makers. The market provides incentive for farmers to grow food that people wish to eat, for truckers to transport the food from the farm to the stores and for grocery managers to stock the shelves with the food that people want to buy. As you will see later in the text, profits and losses provide incentives for firms to enter and exit markets.

🖹 Remember

Prices serve an important function in markets. Prices provide information and incentives to participants in markets to provide the goods and services demanded by the market.

Let's review two Applications that answer key questions we posed at the start of the chapter:

2. What is the role of opportunity cost in the development of markets?

APPLICATION 2: GOLD FARMING FROM WORLD OF WARCRAFT

Why would you ever pay real money for online game items that you earn "free" in the game? This application points out that for some gamers, it is less expensive to buy gold coins in the World of Warcraft game than it is to earn them. The value of the gamer's time is what provides the opportunity cost. Suppose a gamer earns $10 per hour at their job. Suppose also that in an hour of playing, they earn 12 gold coins. Would you rather spend an hour earning 12 gold coins or work for that hour, earn $10 and then spend $2.40 for the gold coins. If you play the game for an hour at the end you have 12 gold coins. If you work at the end of an hour you have 12 gold coins, and $7.60.

3. Why do markets develop wherever people go?

APPLICATION 3: MARKETS IN A PRISONER OF WAR CAMP

Markets exist as a way to allocate goods and services to those who desire them. This Application illustrates that principle in POW camps during World War II. Prisoners all received the same goods, regardless of their desire for the goods. Prisoners would then trade for the goods they desired, using cigarettes as "money." You can see in this example how these trades improved the allocation of goods as tea-drinking British prisoners were able to trade unwanted coffee for other, more desirable goods.

3.4 Market Failure and the Role of Government

In general, markets work well and allocate resources to those who most value the resources. There are some circumstances in which markets don't do a very good job of allocating resources. These situations are known as market failure. In these cases government can intervene in the market and improve outcomes. Some examples of market failures you will study later in the book are:

- Pollution. What happens when one person's action negatively impacts someone else? Government can force polluters to consider the costs they impose on others in the economy. An example would be a tax requiring polluters to bear the cost that their actions impose on others. The tax provides a financial incentive for polluters to reduce the amount of pollution they produce.

- Public goods. What if we can't keep non-payers from consuming a good, such as a fireworks display? What if more people could use a good at no additional cost of providing the good? How do markets respond in these cases? In most cases, markets will not provide an appropriate amount of public goods, which requires the government to step in and encourage production or in many cases produce the goods itself. Police protection would be an example of a public good.

- Imperfect information. What happens in a market if the buyers of a product know less about the product's condition than the sellers? Government can take steps to provide complete information so that both sides of the market can make an informed decision. For example, the government requires that food manufacturers provide nutritional information on labels so consumers can know what is contained in the food they are eating.

- Imperfect competition. What happens when only a few firms exist in a market? Think about a utility that is the only provider of electricity in a particular area. Government will regulate the prices that the utility can charge so that it can't exploit its monopoly power.

The government plays other roles in the market economy as well, including:

- enforcing property rights.
- establishing and enforcing rules for market exchange.
- reducing economic uncertainty and providing social insurance.

Activity

Darrin Hobbes is a very skilled carpenter, though his regular career is practicing law. At the moment, Darrin is trying to put an addition on his house. He estimates that it would take him 3 weekends of work, working eight hours a day on Saturday and Sunday to complete the addition. This means it would take Darrin 48 hours of time to complete the addition.

WeBuildIt Contractors has provided Darrin an estimate to complete the addition to his house. They estimate that they would have two people spend 4 days at Darrin's house to complete the addition. This is a total of 64 hours to complete the addition. WeBuildIt charges $35 per labor hour.

a. Who has the absolute advantage in completing the addition? Why?
b. What would it cost Darrin to pay WeBuildIt to complete the addition? _____
c. Suppose Darrin earns $60 per hour in his legal practice and can work as many hours as he chooses. What would it cost Darrin to build the addition himself? _____
d. Who has the comparative advantage in completing the addition? Why?

Answers

a. Darrin, because it will take him 48 hours as opposed to 64 hours to do the same work.
b. It would cost $35(64) = $2,240 to have WeBuildIt complete the addition.
c. It would cost Darrin $60(48) = $2,880 to complete the addition himself.
d. WeBuildIt Contractors has the comparative advantage because the company can do the work at a lower cost than Darrin.

Key Terms

Absolute advantage: The ability of one person or nation to produce a product at a lower resource cost than another person or nation.

Centrally planned economy: An economy in which a government bureaucracy decides how much of each good to produce, how to produce the goods, and who gets them.

Comparative advantage: The ability of one person or nation to produce a good at a lower opportunity cost than another person or nation.

Export: A product produced in the home country and sold in another country.

Import: A product produced in a foreign country and purchased by a resident of the home country.

Market economy: An economy in which people specialize and exchange goods and services in markets.

Practice Quiz

(Answers are provided at the end of the Practice Quiz.)

1. Which of the following is NOT among the fundamental questions that every economy must solve?
    a. What goods and services will be produced?
    b. How will the goods and services be produced?
    c. At what prices will goods and services be exchanged?
    d. Who will receive the goods and services produced?

2. When people participate in markets, they are encouraged to practice:
    a. self-sufficiency.
    b. specialization.
    c. restraint in consumption.
    d. care in selecting the government officials that run the markets.

3. Which of the following key principles of economics do we use to explore the details of specialization?
    a. The nominal-real principle
    b. The principle of diminishing returns
    c. The principle of opportunity cost
    d. The marginal principle

4. Absolute advantage is the ability of an individual, firm, or country to:
    a. produce more of a good or service than competitors using the same amount of resources.
    b. produce a good or service at a lower opportunity cost than other producers.
    c. consume more goods or services than others at lower costs.
    d. reach a higher production possibilities frontier by raising opportunity costs.

5. We say that a person has a comparative advantage in producing a particular product if he or she:
    a. is self-sufficient.
    b. also has an absolute advantage.
    c. has a lower opportunity cost than another person.
    d. All of the above

6. According to the theory of comparative advantage, specialization and free trade will benefit:
    a. only the owner of a monopoly.
    b. all trading parties who specialize in the production of the good in which they have a comparative advantage.
    c. only that trading party that has an absolute advantage in the production of all goods.
    d. only the party which specializes the most.

7. The table below shows the maximum output of widgets and gadgets for two countries: Utopia and Nirvana. Which of the following is correct?

	Widgets	Gadgets
Utopia	500	500
Nirvana	250	125

    a. Nirvana has a comparative advantage in both goods.
    b. Utopia has a comparative advantage in both goods.
    c. Nirvana has a comparative advantage in widgets.
    d. Nirvana has a comparative advantage in gadgets.

8. Refer to the table below. Which of the following statements is correct?

	Cakes	Pies
Jorge	3	6
Rocky	6	9

    a. Rocky has the comparative advantage in pies.
    b. Jorge has the absolute and comparative advantage in pies.
    c. Jorge has a comparative advantage but not an absolute advantage in pies.
    d. Rocky has an absolute advantage but not a comparative advantage in pies.

9. The fact that specialization and exchange make people better off is an illustration of one of these principles. Which one?
    a. The principle of voluntary exchange
    b. The principle of diminishing returns
    c. The principle of opportunity cost
    d. The marginal principle

10. In his 1776 book *An Inquiry into the Nature and Causes of the Wealth of Nations*, Adam Smith noted that specialization increases productivity. Which of the following was the cause of this phenomenon?
    a. Increased slavery
    b. Combining various steps into a single job raised productivity
    c. Turning small factories into large factories
    d. The division of labor

11. A product produced in a foreign country and purchased by residents of the home country is called:
    a. an import.
    b. an export.
    c. self-sufficiency.
    d. outsourcing.

12. Which of the following is NOT a reason for the increase in productivity that comes with specialization?
    a. Repetition
    b. Continuity
    c. Innovation
    d. Absolute advantage

13. Contracts, insurance, patents, and accounting rules are:
    a. things that came naturally with the creation of markets.
    b. ideas that are unnecessary in a free-market place.
    c. inventions that make a market work better.
    d. enforced primarily in non-market economies, such as centrally planned economies.

14. In what type of economy does the government decide how economic resources will be allocated?
    a. In a market economy
    b. In a centrally planned economy
    c. In both of the above
    d. In none of the above. The government does not allocate resources in any type of economy.

15. In a market system, which of the following provides the information that individuals need to make decisions?
    a. Primarily, the government
    b. Public libraries
    c. Prices
    d. Production costs

16. Whenever markets do not produce the most efficient outcomes on their own, we call this phenomenon:
    a. the invisible hand.
    b. market failure.
    c. absolute disaster.
    d. diminishing returns.

17. Refer to the figure below. Each graph represents one country. Which country in this graph has a comparative advantage in the production of shirts?

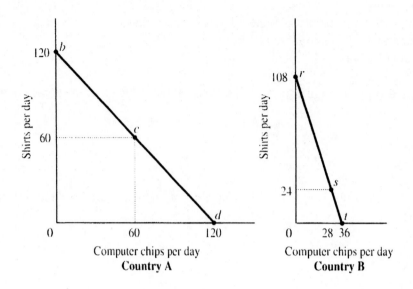

Country A   Country B

    a. Country A
    b. Country B
    c. Neither country
    d. Both countries

18. Refer to the figure below. Each graph represents one country. Which country in this graph should specialize in the production of chips?

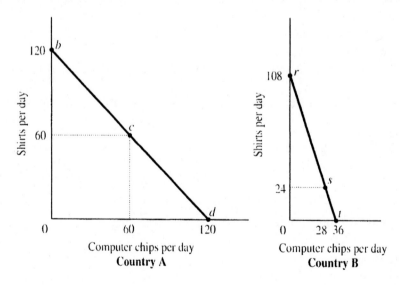

Country A   Country B

    a. Country A
    b. Country B
    c. Neither country. They both should produce some chips.
    d. Both countries should specialize in the production of chips.

19.   The impact of outsourcing on the domestic economy can be summarized as follows:
    a.   Outsourcing has resulted in a substantial loss of jobs, insignificant cost savings for outsourcing companies, higher prices for consumers, and less output for firms.
    b.   Outsourcing has resulted in a minimal loss of jobs, as well as significant cost savings for domestic companies, lower prices for consumers, and more output for firms.
    c.   The results of outsourcing have been mixed. Lower prices for consumers have been overshadowed by a substantial loss of domestic jobs.
    d.   The benefits of outsourcing have not outlasted the increases in communication costs and the costs of the standardization of software necessary to allow firms to outsource business services.

20.   This question tests your understanding of Application 3 in this chapter: Markets in a prisoner of war camp. Why do markets develop wherever people go?

To illustrate the pervasiveness of exchange, this application illustrates the emergence of markets in prisoner of war (POW) camps in World War II, as documented by economist R. A. Radford. The exchange of goods that took place among prisoners of war (POWs) during World War II is an example of how:

    a.   markets cannot work properly when severe restrictions are imposed on people.
    b.   markets in restricted places, such as prisoner camps, work poorly because product prices do not reflect the actual scarcity of goods.
    c.   even in prisoner camps, the market system can work because people, motivated by self-interest, rely on exchange to make themselves better off.
    d.   exchange that takes place through barter does not allow for the emergence of markets. Only monetary economies can support market exchange.

Answers to the Practice Quiz

1.   c. The three questions are: What goods and services will be produced? How will the goods and services be produced? Who will receive the goods and services produced?

2.   b. A market is an institution or arrangement that enables people to buy and sell things. The alternative to buying and selling in markets is to be self-sufficient, with each of us producing everything we need for ourselves. Rather than going it alone, most of us specialize: We produce one or two products for others and then exchange the money we earn for the products we want to consume.

3.   c. A person specializes in the good for which he or she has a lower opportunity cost. We say that a person has a comparative advantage in producing a particular product if he or she has a lower opportunity cost than another person's marginal cost.

4.   a.. Absolute advantage is the ability of an individual, firm, or country to produce more of a good or service than competitors using the same amount of resources.

5.   c. The lesson is that those who are self-sufficient have an incentive to specialize and trade. Having an absolute advantage does not guarantee that a person also has a comparative advantage. We say that a person has a comparative advantage in producing a particular product if he or she has a lower opportunity cost than another person.

6. b. According to the theory of comparative advantage, if both nations specialize and trade in the production of goods/services in which they have a comparative advantage, both nations will be better off.

7. c. Utopia's opportunity cost is 1 for either good. Nirvana's opportunity cost of widgets is 125/250= 1/2. Since 1/2 < 1, Nirvana has a comparative advantage in widgets.

8. c. Jorge produces fewer pies per hour than Rocky, thus Rocky has an absolute advantage in pies. Jorge gives up less cake for each pie than Rocky. Thus, Jorge has a comparative advantage.

9. a. The fact that specialization and exchange make both people better off illustrates the key principle of voluntary exchange.

10. d. Adam Smith explains how the making of a pin is divided into many operations, and then he points to the very high output that can be produced in that factory through such division of labor.

11. a. An import is a product produced in a foreign country and purchased by residents of the home country.

12. d. Repetition, continuity, and innovation are the three reasons that cause an increase in productivity that comes with specialization.

13. c. Although it appears that markets arose naturally, a number of social and government inventions have made them work better: Contracts, insurance, patents, and accounting rules are part of those inventions.

14. b. A centrally planned economy is one where the government decides how economic resources will be allocated.

15. c. Under a market system, decisions are made by the thousands of people who already have information about consumers' desires, production technology, and resources. These decisions are guided by prices of inputs and outputs. In a market system, prices provide individuals the information they need to make decisions. Prices provide signals about the relative scarcity of a product and help an economy respond to scarcity.

16. b. "Market failure" is what happens when markets fail to produce the most efficient outcomes on their own. The role of government is to correct this problem.

17. b. The opportunity costs are as follows: The opportunity cost of shirts is: 1 chip for country A, and 1/3 chip for country B. The opportunity cost of chips is: 1 shirt for country A and 3 shirts for country B. Country B has a comparative advantage in the production of shirts because it sacrifices fewer chips to produce one shirt. Country B should therefore produce shirts.

18. a. The opportunity costs are as follows: The opportunity cost of shirts is: 1 chip for country A, and 1/3 chip for country B. The opportunity cost of chips is: 1 shirt for country A and 3 shirts for country B. Therefore, country A has a comparative advantage (or lower opportunity cost) in the production of chips because it sacrifices fewer shirts to produce one chip. Country A should therefore produce chips.

19. b. According to recent studies, the benefits of outsourcing have significantly outweighed the costs. Outsourcing has resulted in a minimal loss of jobs, substantial cost savings for domestic companies, lower prices for consumers, and more output for firms.

20. c. The prisoners used barter to exchange one good for another, and cigarettes emerged as the medium of exchange. Prisoners wandered through the camp calling out their offers of goods. In addition to food, the prisoners bought and sold clothing (80 cigarettes per shirt), laundry services (two cigarettes per garment), and hot cups of coffee (two cigarettes per cup). The prices of products reflected their scarcity.

4

Demand, Supply, and Market Equilibrium

Chapter Summary

This chapter shows how demand and supply determine prices. In addition, this chapter illustrates how to predict the effects of changes in demand or supply on market prices and quantities. Here are the main points of the chapter:

- A market demand curve shows the relationship between the quantity demanded and price, *ceteris paribus*.
- A market supply curve shows the relationship between the quantity supplied and price, *ceteris paribus*.
- Equilibrium in a market is shown by the intersection of the demand curve and the supply curve. When a market reaches equilibrium, there is no pressure to change the price.
- A change in demand changes price and quantity in the same direction: An increase in demand increases the equilibrium price and quantity; a decrease in demand decreases the equilibrium price and quantity.
- A change in supply changes price and quantity in opposite directions: An increase in supply decreases price and increases quantity; a decrease in supply increases price and decreases quantity.

ᎅ Study Tip

In this chapter, pay careful attention to factors that shift the position of the demand and supply curves.

Applying the Concepts

After reading this chapter, you should be able to answer these five key questions:
1. How do changes in demand affect prices?
2. How do changes in supply in one market affect other markets?
3. How does the adoption of new technology affect prices?
4. How do changes in supply affect prices?
5. How do producers respond to higher prices?

4.1 The Demand Curve

The **quantity demanded** of a particular good is the amount of a product that consumers are willing and able to buy. A number of factors affect how much of a good a consumer wants to purchase:

- the price of the product.
- the consumer's income.
- the price of substitute and complement goods.
- the consumer's preferences or tastes.
- the consumer's expectations of future prices.

To begin we examine a **demand schedule**, a table that shows the relationship between the price of a product and the quantity demanded of that product.   When we talk about a demand schedule, we assume that all of the other factors listed above (tastes, income, etc.) are held constant and only the price of the good changes.   Figure 4.1 of the text shows both the demand schedule and the demand curve. The **demand curve** is a graphical representation of the demand schedule. The curve shows the relationship between the price of a good and the quantity demanded of that good.

An **individual demand curve** shows the relationship between the price of a good and the quantity demanded by an individual consumer. A **market demand curve** shows the relationship between price and quantity demanded by all consumers.

☞ Think of the students in your microeconomics class. Each of you has some desired number of music downloads that you would purchase each month at a variety of prices. The relationship between price and how many downloads you purchase in a month is your individual demand curve. If your class represented the entire market for music downloads, the market demand curve would be the total number of music downloads that people in the class would buy at a particular price. This exercise gives us the market quantity demanded at that price. When we do this for a number of different prices we can find the market demand schedule or the market demand curve.

As the price of a good rises, the quantity demanded decreases. This is known as the law of demand. Formally, the **law of demand** states that there is a negative relationship between price and quantity demanded, *ceteris paribus*. The movement along a demand curve is known as a **change in quantity demanded**. This refers to how the quantity purchased changes in response to a change in the price of a good.

4.2 The Supply Curve

Much of the logic for demand also applies to the supply side of the market. The **quantity supplied** is the amount of a product that firms are willing and able to sell. A number of factors affect the decision of the sellers:

- the price of the product.
- the wage paid to workers
- the price of materials
- the cost of capital
- the state of production technology.
- expectations about future prices.
- government taxes and subsidies.

As Figure 4.3 in the text illustrates, we define a **supply schedule** as a table that shows the relationship between the price of a product and quantity supplied (holding all the other supply factors constant), and a

supply curve as a curve showing the relationship between price and quantity supplied. Notice that these definitions are similar to the ones you learned for the demand schedule and the demand curve.

The **law of supply** states that there is a positive relationship between price and quantity supplied. This is true of both the **individual supply curve**, which shows the relationship between price and quantity supplied by an individual firm, and the **market supply curve**, which shows the relationship between price and quantity supplied by all firms. As output increases, the cost of producing each additional unit increases. This leads to an upward sloping supply curve. This is an application of the marginal principle:

Marginal Principle

Increase the level of an activity as long as its marginal benefit exceeds its marginal cost. Choose the level at which the marginal benefit equals the marginal cost.

☞ As a way of thinking about supply, consider the market in which you are a supplier, the labor market. An employer offers you a wage (the price of labor) and you determine how many hours you are willing to work in exchange for that wage. If an employer offers you too little money (say $3 per hour) you will choose not to work at all. The price is below your **minimum supply price**, the lowest price at which a product will be supplied. As the wage offers increase you will become willing to work and at higher prices you will be willing to offer more hours of labor. You may be willing to work five hours per week for $6 per hour but if the wage is $10 per hour, you may be willing to work 15 hours per week. The market supply curve would illustrate the number of hours that all workers in the market would be willing to supply at each wage rate.

4.3 Market Equilibrium: Bringing Demand and Supply Together

We have seen that at each price, the quantity demanded tells us how many units buyers are willing to buy and the quantity supplied tells us how many units sellers are willing to sell. **Market equilibrium** occurs at the price where the quantity demanded is equal to the quantity supplied. The price at which this occurs is called the equilibrium price because it is the price that balances the quantity demanded and the quantity supplied. At this price buyers are buying all the goods they desire, sellers are selling all the goods they desire, and there is no pressure for the market price to change.

At prices other than the equilibrium there in an imbalance between the quantity supplied and the quantity demanded. You can see this in Figure 4.6 in the text. At prices below $8, buyers want to buy more pizzas per month than sellers want to sell. This situation is known as **excess demand**, or a **shortage**, a situation where the quantity demanded exceeds the quantity supplied at the prevailing price. In a situation of excess demand the price for a good will increase causing the quantity demanded to fall and the quantity supplied to rise until they are in equilibrium. A *price ceiling* (prices capped by law below equilibrium) will create excess demand in the affected market. Rent control would be an example of a price ceiling.

At prices above $8, suppliers are willing to sell more pizzas per month than demanders wish to purchase at those prices. This is known as an **excess supply** or **surplus**, a situation in which the quantity supplied exceeds the quantity demanded at the prevailing price. A *price floor* (prices held above equilibrium by law will create excess supply in the affected market. A minimum wage is an example of a price floor.

☞ To get a picture of this situation, imagine a concert coming to your campus. Now imagine people standing in line for concert tickets, with those in the front of the line having the highest willingness to pay, and those at the back of the line the lowest willingness to pay. The face value for the tickets is $25 and we will assume, for simplicity (see chapter 2), that each person in line wants to buy one ticket. If the number of people in line exceeds the number of tickets available then the ticket window will close while people are still waiting in line to buy tickets. This is a situation of excess demand and indicates that the face value for the tickets is too low relative to equilibrium. Some buyers will be unhappy because they will not be able to buy a ticket.

If the last person in line buys a ticket and the ticket office still has tickets available to sell, we have a surplus and we can infer that the price of the tickets is too high: There are more tickets available at that price than there are buyers for the tickets. The seller will be unhappy because they will not be able to sell all their tickets.

At the equilibrium price, the last person in line will buy the last ticket available. All buyers and sellers will be happy as they are all able to make a trade at this price.

4.4 Market Effects of Changes in Demand

A **change in demand** occurs when a variable other than the price of the product changes. When demand changes, people want to buy more or less of a product at the same price. Since the price of the good has not changed, the demand curve must have shifted.

An *increase in demand* occurs when consumers want to buy more of a good holding the price constant. An increase in demand causes the equilibrium price and quantity to increase. Here are factors that increase demand:
- Increase in income. If a good is a **normal good**, an increase in income increases demand for the good. Restaurant meals would be an example of normal goods.
- Decrease in income. If a good is an **inferior good**, a decrease in income will increase demand. Store-brand cola would be an example of an inferior good.
- Increase in the price of a substitute. A **substitute** is a good for which an increase in the price of one good increases the demand for another good. As the price of coffee increases, we expect the demand for tea to increase, holding the price of tea constant.
- Decrease in the price of a complement. A **complement** is a good for which a decrease in the price of one good increases the demand for the other good. As the price of French fries falls, people will demand more ketchup, holding the price of ketchup constant.
- Increase in population. As more people enter the market, the amount of a good demanded at any price will increase. If 1,000 new students enroll at your university, the demand for spiral bound notebooks at the campus bookstore will increase, holding the price of the notebooks constant.
- Shift in consumer preferences. When a celebrity advertises a product, more people may want that product, holding the price of the product constant.
- Expectations of higher future prices. If we anticipate that the price of a good is going to increase in the future, we will demand more of the good, at its current price.

A *decrease in demand* occurs when consumers want to buy less of a good holding the price constant. A decrease in demand lowers the equilibrium quantity and price in the market. Here are the factors that decrease demand:
- Decrease in income. Consumers will buy fewer normal goods when their incomes decrease.
- Decrease in the price of a substitute good. If the price of going to the movies falls, there will be an increase in the quantity demanded of movies. Consumers will rent fewer movies, holding the price of movie rentals constant.
- Increase in the price of a complementary good. If the price of coffee increases, leading people to decrease their quantity demanded of coffee, the demand for cream will fall. People will buy less cream, holding the price of cream constant.
- Decrease in population. If the number of people in a market decreases, there will be fewer units of a good demanded, holding the price of the good constant.

- Shift in consumer tastes. A health scare such as E. coli in fresh spinach and mad cow disease in beef will cause people to want to buy fewer units of these goods, holding the price of the good constant.
- Expectation of lower future prices. If people anticipate that the price of a good will fall in future periods, they will want to buy fewer units of that good at any price in the current period. This often happens with consumer electronics as people hold off purchasing new technology in anticipation of lower future prices.

📄 Remember

When demand changes, equilibrium price and quantity move in the same direction as demand. An increase in demand increases price and quantity. A decrease in demand decreases price and quantity.

When something changes in a market, be careful to ask yourself whether the change will cause people to want to buy a different amount of the good holding the price constant. If the answer is yes, then the demand curve will shift. If the answer is no, the demand curve remains constant.

💣 Caution!

Be very careful to understand the difference between a movement along a demand or curve and a change in demand. A movement along a demand curve is caused only by a change in the price of that good. A change in demand is caused by a change in some factor other than the price of the good changing. One way to keep the difference straight is to understand that when we move along a curve, both the price of the good and the quantity of the good are changing. When a curve shifts, people want to buy a different amount of the good, *holding the price constant.*

4.5 Market Effects of Changes in Supply

A **change in supply** is caused by a change in a variable other than the price of the product. A change in supply means that holding the price constant, suppliers now want to sell more or less of their product. Since the price has not changed, the supply curve must have shifted.

An *increase in supply* means that firms are willing to sell more units at any given price. When supply increases, the equilibrium price of the good falls, and the equilibrium quantity of the good increases. Here are the factors that increase supply:
- Decreases in input prices. When the firm can pay lower prices for its workers or materials, it is willing to sell more of a good, holding the price of the good constant.
- Technological advance. Better technology allows a firm to produce (and sell) more units of a good, holding the price constant.
- Government subsidy. If the government gives money to a firm for each unit it produces, the firm can sell its goods at a lower price in the market (the downward idea of the supply shift).
- Expected future price. If the firm anticipates that the price of its product is going to fall in the future, it will be willing to sell more units of the good now, holding the price constant.

- An increase in the number of producers. As more firms enter the market, there will be more units of the good available for sale, holding the price of the good constant.
- A *decrease in supply* means that firms want to sell fewer units of a good, holding the price of the good constant. A decrease in supply lowers the equilibrium quantity of the good and raises the equilibrium price. Here are the factors that decrease supply:
- Increases in wages and prices of materials. When the costs of producing output increase, firms require a higher price to sell any given number of units.
- Tax. If the government requires the firm to pay a tax each time it sells a unit of a good, the price required to sell any number of units of the good will increase.
- Higher future prices. If the firm expects the price of the good to increase in the future, it will be willing to sell fewer units of the good in the current period, holding the price of the good constant.
- A decrease in the number of producers. As firms stop producing a good and leave the market, there will be fewer units of a good available, holding the price of the good constant.

📄 Remember

It is sometimes helpful to think of supply changes in this way: Supply increases when a firm is willing to sell the same output for a lower price. If the wages paid to a worker fall, a firm is able to sell its output for a lower price. Graphically this shifts the supply curve down—indicating that the price required to sell any quantity will decrease—and to the right—indicating that the firm will sell more holding the price constant. See Table 4.3 of the text.

In the same way, if the wages paid to a worker increase, the firm now needs to sell its product at a higher price to be willing to sell the same quantity. Graphically, the supply curve shifts up—indicating that the price required to sell any quantity has increased—and to the left—indicating that at a constant price the firm is willing to sell fewer units of the good. See Table 4.4 of the text.

When supply changes, equilibrium quantity moves in the same direction as supply and equilibrium price moves in the opposite direction. An increase in supply increases quantity and decreases price.

〰 Study Tip

When something changes in a market, ask yourself whether the change will make suppliers want to sell a different amount of the goods holding the price constant. If the answer is yes, then the supply curve will shift. If the answer is no, the supply curve remains constant.

4.6 Predicting and Explaining Market Changes

We use our knowledge of demand and supply changes to both predict future price and quantity movements and to explain past price and quantity movements.

Examples:
- An increase in price occurs when demand increases or supply decreases.
- A decrease in price occurs when demand decreases or supply increases.
- An increase in quantity occurs when demand increases or supply increases.
- A decrease in quantity occurs when demand decreases or supply decreases.

💣* Caution!

If both curves are shifting at the same time, you will be able to predict only the movement of quantity *or* price—not both. For instance, an increase in demand combined with an increase in supply will increase the market quantity. However, the two shifts have offsetting price effects and you won't be able to forecast the price movement. After the two shifts have occurred, you will be able to determine which effect was stronger. If the price in the market increases, you know that the increase in demand was stronger than the increase in supply.

An increase in demand will cause a movement along the supply curve. Suppliers will offer more goods in the market but this is a result of a higher price being offered. A demand change can't cause the supply curve to shift. Similarly a change in supply will cause a movement along the demand curve, but won't cause the demand curve to shift.

4.7 Applications of Demand and Supply

Let's review five Applications that answer the key questions we posed at the start of the chapter:

1. How do changes in demand affect prices?

APPLICATION 1:
HURRICANE KATRINA AND BATON ROUGE HOUSING PRICES
In the aftermath of Hurricane Katrina, about 250,000 residents of New Orleans relocated to Baton Rouge, LA. With the arrival of the new residents, the demand for housing in Baton Rouge increased. Note that nothing happened that would cause suppliers to want to change the amount of housing offered in the market, holding the price constant. This shift in demand led to both higher prices for housing, and a higher quantity of homes sold. Note in Figure 4 we have a change in demand, but a movement along a fixed supply curve.

2. How do changes in supply in one market affect other markets?

APPLICATION 2: HONEYBEES AND THE PRICE OF ICE CREAM
While honeybees and ice cream may not seem to have anything to do with one another, growers of fruits, vegetables and nuts depend on honeybees to pollinate their plants. As the number of honeybees has decreased, the supply of strawberries, raspberries and almonds has decreased. With the decrease in supply comes a higher price for these products. Strawberries, raspberries and almonds are inputs into the production of ice cream. As the price of the inputs has increased, the supply curve of ice cream has shifted to the left leading to a higher price and lower quantity of ice cream using these ingredients. Figure 4.15 illustrates this.

3.   How does the adoption of new technology affect prices?

APPLICATION 3: ELECTRICITY FROM THE WIND
Between 2000 and 2006 new windmill technology has shifted the supply curve of wind-generated electricity to the right. As a result, the price of wind-generated electricity has fallen from 50 cents per kilowatt-hour to 4 cents per kilowatt-hour, as we would expect with an increase in supply, and the quantity produced has increased from 600 megawatt hours to 9,200 megawatt hours, again as we would expect from an increase in supply.

4.   How do changes in supply affect prices?

APPLICATION 4: THE BOUNCING PRICE OF VANILLA BEANS
What has caused the price of vanilla to change from $50 per kilo in 2000 to $500 in 2003 only to fall to $25 in 2006? In 2000, a cyclone hit Madagascar, a leading vanilla producer, and destroyed a large number of vanilla vines. The destruction reduced the amount of vanilla that suppliers could offer for sale, and as a result of the decrease in supply the price of vanilla increased. Over time, workers planted vines to replace the destroyed vines and a new variety of vanilla plants allowed other countries to grow vanilla beans for the first time. These two events increased the supply of vanilla so much that the price fell below its 2000 level.

5. How do producers respond to higher prices?

APPLICATION 5: DROUGHT IN AUSTRALIA AND THE PRICE OF RICE
Water is an important input in the production of rice. As drought continued in Australia for a sixth year, farmers responded to higher water prices by reducing the amount of land used to grow rice. As a result, the supply of rice decreased leading to a near doubling of the price of rice. The higher price of rice has inspired some farmers to try to innovate and develop new growing techniques and new varieties of rice that use less water. While these new growing techniques are more costly, the current high price of rice would allow farmers to still profit even with higher costs. If the price of rice were to fall, the new growing techniques would no longer be profitable, and would no longer be used.

Activity

Fill in the following table for music downloads. List the number of music downloads you would be willing to purchase per month at each price:

Price	Quantity	Quantity (2)
$2.00	_____	_____
$1.75	_____	_____
$1.50	_____	_____
$1.25	_____	_____
$1.00	_____	_____
$0.75	_____	_____
$0.50	_____	_____
$0.25	_____	_____
$0.00	_____	_____

a. Fill in the quantity of downloads you would want to purchase each month in the column marked Quantity.
b. Suppose that your income increased by $100 per week from its current level. In the column marked Quantity (2), indicate how many downloads you would be willing to purchase per month at each price.
c. On a graph, draw the demand curves corresponding to the Quantity and Quantity (2) columns.
d. Indicate in the table and graph a change in quantity demanded.
e. Indicate in the table and graph a change in demand.

Answers

d. This would be a move along a demand curve or within a quantity column.
e. This would be a move from one demand curve to the other, or from one quantity column to the other, holding price constant.

Key Terms

Change in demand: A shift of the demand curve caused by a change in a variable other than the price of the product.

Change in quantity demanded: A change in the quantity consumers are willing and able to buy when the price changes; represented graphically by movement along the demand curve.

Change in quantity supplied: A change in the quantity firms are willing and able to sell when the price changes; represented graphically by movement along the supply curve.

Change in supply: A shift of the supply curve caused by a change in a variable other than the price of the product.

Complements: Two goods for which a decrease in the price of one good increases the demand for the other good.

Demand schedule: A table that shows the relationship between the price of a product and the quantity demanded, *ceteris paribus*.

Excess demand (shortage): A situation in which, at the prevailing price, the quantity demanded exceeds the quantity supplied.

Excess supply (surplus): A situation in which at the prevailing price, the quantity supplied exceeds the quantity demanded.

Individual demand curve: A curve that shows the relationship between the price of a good and quantity demanded by an individual, *ceteris paribus*.

Individual supply curve: A curve showing the relationship between price and quantity supplied by a single firm, *ceteris paribus*.

Inferior good: A good for which an increase in income decreases demand.

Law of demand: There is a negative relationship between price and quantity demanded, *ceteris paribus*.

Law of supply: There is a positive relationship between price and quantity supplied, *ceteris paribus*.

Market demand curve: A curve showing the relationship between price and quantity demanded by all consumers, *ceteris paribus*.

Market equilibrium: A situation in which the quantity demanded equals the quantity supplied at the prevailing market price.

Market supply curve: A curve showing the relationship between the market price and the quantity supplied by all firms, *ceteris paribus*.

Minimum supply price: The lowest price at which a product will be supplied.

Normal good: A good for which an increase in income increases demand.

Perfectly competitive market: A market with so many buyers and sellers that no single buyer or seller can affect the market price.

Quantity demanded: The amount of a product that consumers are willing and able to buy.

Quantity supplied: The amount of a product that firms are willing and able to sell.

Substitutes: Two goods for which an increase in the price of one good increases the demand for the other good.

Supply schedule: A table that shows the relationship between the price of a product and quantity supplied, *ceteris paribus*.

Practice Quiz

(Answers are provided at the end of the Practice Quiz.)

1. The model of supply and demand explains how a perfectly competitive market operates. Which of the following is a characteristic of a perfectly competitive market?
    a. The market has a very large number of firms.
    b. The market has very few buyers so firms have to compete for them.
    c. In this market, large business firms produce large amounts of output and have a strong influence over price.
    d. All of the above

2. The *demand schedule* is:
    a. a curve that shows the relationship between price and quantity demanded, ceteris paribus.
    b. a table that shows the relationship between price and quantity demanded, ceteris paribus.
    c. a list of time periods during which the quantity of a good is demanded.
    d. the order in which individual consumers arrive to demand a good or service.

3. Refer to the figure below. Which move best illustrates a *change in quantity demanded*?

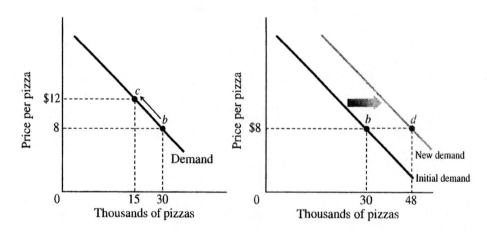

    a. The move from *b* to *c* on the graph in the left side
    b. The move from *b* to *d* on the graph in the right side
    c. A combination of the two moves above
    d. None of the above

4. Which of the following will NOT cause a shift in the demand curve for houses?
   a. A decrease in income
   b. An increase in the price of condominiums
   c. A decrease in the price of houses
   d. A change in lifestyles so that people prefer living in apartments.

5.

   Which of the following variables has an effect on the decisions of sellers, using the market for pizza as an example?
   a. Producer expectations about the future price of pizza
   b. The cost of the inputs used to produce the product, for example, wages paid to workers and the cost of the pizza oven
   c. The state of production technology, such as the knowledge used in making pizza
   d. All of the above

6. Refer to the figure below. Which of the following moves best describes a change in supply?

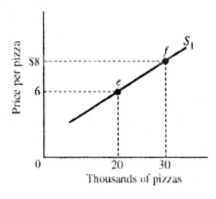 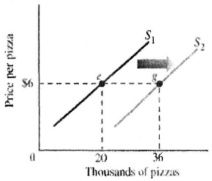

   a. The move from *e* to *f* on the graph on the left side
   b. The move from *e* to *g* on the graph on the right side
   c. Either move. Both moves above illustrate a change in supply.
   d. A change in supply is actually a combination of the moves described in each graph.

7. Refer to the figure below. If there are 100 identical pizzerias, how much is the quantity supplied when the market price equals $10?

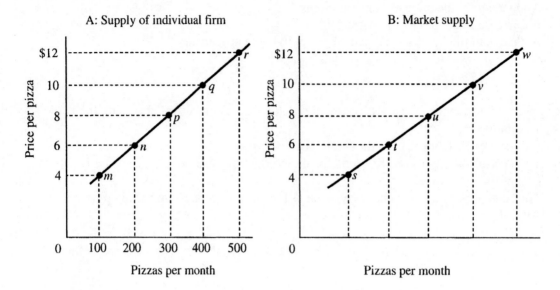

A: Supply of individual firm

B: Market supply

a. 400 pizzas
b. 4 pizzas
c. 40,000 pizzas
d. 400,000 pizzas

8. Refer to the figure below. When market price equals $12, we have a situation called:

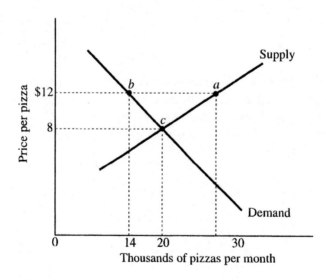

a. consumer protection.
b. market equilibrium.
c. excess demand.
d. excess supply.

9. Refer to the figure below. After the increase in demand, at the initial price of $8, there is now:

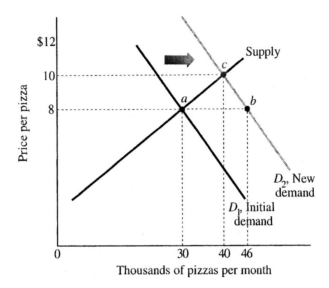

a. equilibrium.
b. excess quantity supplied.
c. excess quantity demanded.
d. a tendency for price to decrease.

10. Refer to the figure below. Which of the graphs best describes the impact of a decrease in the wages and input prices that firms must pay in order to produce output?

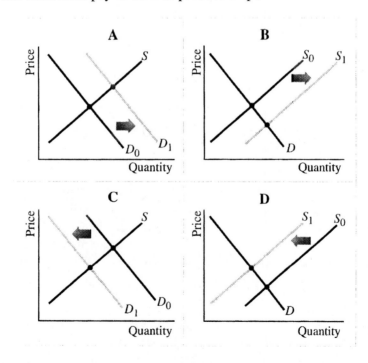

a. A
b. B
c. C
d. D

11. Refer to the figure below. Which graph shows an increase in *quantity demanded*?

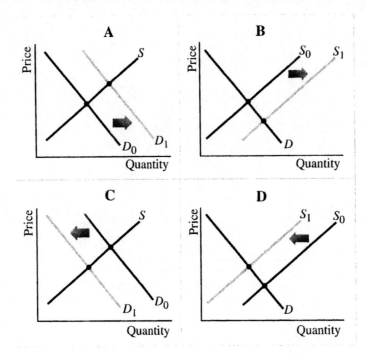

a. A
b. B
c. C
d. D

12. Refer to the figure below. This graph shows that:

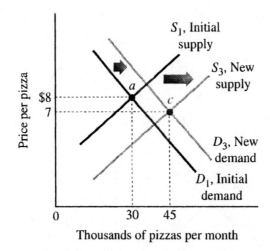

a. when the magnitude of a decrease in supply is greater than the magnitude of an increase in demand, equilibrium price will rise, and quantity will fall.
b. when the magnitude of an increase in supply is greater than the magnitude of an increase in demand, equilibrium price will fall, and quantity will rise.
c. when supply and demand both increase, price always decreases.
d. in equilibrium, quantity demanded is not always equal to quantity supplied.

13. This question tests your understanding of Application 2 in this chapter: Honeybees and the price of ice cream. How do changes in supply in one market affect other markets?

This Application notes that the supply of honey bees is decreasing. Honeybees are important for their role in pollinating plants. Fewer honeybees leads to smaller harvests of such items as strawberries, raspberries and almonds. As such the price of these items, which are inputs into certain types of ice cream, increases. How would this affect the market for ice cream?

a. The demand for ice cream will decrease.
b. The supply of ice cream will increase.
c. The demand for ice cream will increase.
d. The supply of ice cream will decrease.

14. This question tests your understanding of Application 4 in this chapter: The bouncing price of vanilla beans. How do changes in supply affect prices?

The price of vanilla beans has been bouncing around a lot. Using the information below, we can explain the bouncing price of vanilla in the context of the supply and demand model.

"The 2000 cyclone that hit Madagascar, the world's leading producer, destroyed that year's crop and a large share of the vines that produce vanilla beans. But then, in the following years, the vines in Madagascar were replanted, and other countries, including India, Papua New Guinea, Uganda, and Costa Rica, entered the vanilla market. This entry was facilitated by the development of a sun-tolerant variety of the vanilla plant that allows it to be grown as a plantation crop."

Refer to the figure below. The return of Madagascar to the industry, technological advances, and the entry of other countries in the vanilla market is best represented by:

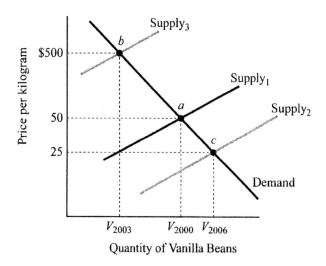

Quantity of Vanilla Beans

a. The upward shift of the supply curve, from $Supply_1$ to $Supply_3$, and higher prices
b. The rightward shift of the supply curve, from $Supply_3$ to $Supply_2$, and lower prices
c. The move along the demand curve, from point a to point b
d. The move of the supply curve, from $Supply_1$ to $Supply_2$, then over to $Supply_3$

15. Markets have a natural tendency to arrive at equilibrium. Expand.

16. Use the model of supply and demand to explain why ticket scalpers exist.

17. If supply and demand both increase, equilibrium price may increase or decrease. Explain.

18. Describe the role of expectations in the model of supply and demand

Answers to the Practice Quiz

1. a. The model of supply and demand explains how a perfectly competitive market operates. A perfectly competitive market is a market that has a very large number of firms, each of which produces the same standardized product in amounts so small that no individual firm can affect the market price.

2. b. The demand schedule is a table that shows the relationship between price and quantity demanded by an individual consumer, *ceteris paribus* (everything else held fixed).

3. a. A *change in quantity demanded* is a change in the amount of a good demanded resulting from a change in the price of the good. Such a move is illustrated by a move along the demand curve, from one point to another.

4. c. A decrease in the price of houses will result in movement along the demand curve, NOT a shift in the demand curve.

5. d. All of the above are known as the main determinants of supply.

6. b. A change in supply (movement of the supply curve) is different from a change in quantity supplied (movement along a supply curve). A change in quantity supplied is a change in the amount of a good supplied resulting from a change in the price of the good; represented graphically by a movement along the supply curve in the graph on the left side. A change in supply is caused by changes in determinants of supply other than price; represented by a shift of the entire supply curve on the right-side graph.

7. c. Market supply equals 100 times the quantity supplied by a single firm at each price level.

8. d. Excess supply is a situation in which, at the prevailing price, producers are willing to sell more than consumers are willing to buy.

9. c. At the initial price of $8, there is now excess quantity demanded. Equilibrium is restored at point *c*, with a higher equilibrium price and a larger equilibrium quantity.

10. b. Lower input prices will increase supply, that is, will shift the supply curve to the right, resulting in a higher equilibrium quantity and lowerequilibrium price for the good produced by the firms.

11. b. In this graph, there is an increase in supply and an increase in quantity demanded.

12. b. The price decreases because the increase in supply is greater than the increase in demand.

13. d. Almonds, strawberries and raspberries are inputs into the production of certain types of ice cream. As the price of an input increases, the supply of the product decreases. As a result we should see the supply of ice cream fall, the price rise and the quantity traded fall.

14. b. The price was $50 per kilo (2.2 pounds) in 2000, then rose to $500 in 2003, then dropped to $25 in 2006. The changes in the supply of vanilla between 2003 and 2006 are shown by a shift of the supply curve downward and to the right. The entry of additional producers in the vanilla market causes the supply curve to shift to the right.

15. Only in equilibrium, quantity supplied equals quantity demanded, and the wishes of buyers coincide with the wishes of sellers; buyers and sellers agree on a single price at which the good is exchanged. When a market is not in equilibrium, price is either too high or too low. When price is too high, quantity supplied is greater than quantity demanded, resulting in a surplus of output. This surplus, or excess supply, will put downward pressure on price. When the price is too low, quantity demanded will exceed quantity supplied. Excess demand will put upward pressure on price. In either case, the market has a natural tendency to move toward equilibrium.

16. When a stadium sells tickets for a popular event, it issues a number of tickets equal to the number of seats available. The stadium assumes that quantity supplied will equal quantity demanded once the tickets are sold out. Ticket scalpers, however, have a hunch that the quantity demanded greatly exceeds the quantity supplied at the price determined by the stadium. In other words, they assume that equilibrium price is higher than the price determined by the stadium. The excess of quantity demanded over quantity supplied means that someone must be willing to pay a higher price than the official price. Scalpers are first in line to buy the tickets at the official price, then, they go out in the streets to look for those who are willing to pay a price closer to the equilibrium market price.

17. In order to establish the impact on price from a change in supply and demand, we must examine the magnitudes of the change in each. By itself an increase in supply pushes price down while an increase in demand by itself pushes price up. If supply increases more than demand does, equilibrium price will fall. If demand increases more than supply does, equilibrium price will rise. And, if the magnitudes of change are the same, price will remain the same; only equilibrium quantity will change.

18. Expectations are an important component of both supply and demand. On the demand side, expectations determine whether buyers will buy more of a good today, or wait until tomorrow. Expectations are built into all rational household decisions. Decisions about how much to buy, how much to save, and how much labor to supply take into account both the present and the future. If households feel optimistic about the future, they may increase their present consumption. Pessimism, on the other hand, will cause households to hold back on their consumption expenditures. On the supply side, expectations also play a major role in decision making. Business firms decide what and how much output to produce based on a plan. This plan includes a forecast of future expected input and output prices. If producers are optimistic about the future, they will plan to expand capacity and increase production in future periods. If they feel pessimistic, they may plan to reduce capacity and output in the future. It is important to understand that the expectations of producers and consumers are independent. This means that producers do not have complete control of production and investment decisions.

5 [20]
Elasticity: A Measure of Responsiveness

Chapter Summary

This chapter explores the numbers behind the laws of supply and demand and develops the concept of elasticity. Here are the main points of the chapter:
- The price elasticity of demand—defined as the percentage change in quantity demanded divided by the percentage change in price—measures the responsiveness of consumers to changes in price.
- Demand is relatively elastic if there are good substitutes.
- If demand is elastic, the relationship between price and total revenue is negative. If demand is inelastic, the relationship between price and total revenue is positive.
- The price elasticity of supply—defined as the percentage change in quantity supplied divided by the percentage change in price—measures the responsiveness of producers to changes in price.
- If we know the elasticities of demand and supply, we can predict the percentage change in price resulting from a change in demand or supply.

Applying the Concepts

After reading this chapter, you should be able to answer these seven key questions:
1. How does the elasticity of demand very over time?
2. How can we use the price elasticity of demand to predict the effects of public policies?
3. If demand is inelastic, how does an increase in price affect total expenditures?
4. If demand is inelastic, how does a decrease in supply affect total expenditures?
5. How does a change in demand affect the equilibrium price?
6. How does a change in supply affect the equilibrium price?

5.1 [20.1] The Price Elasticity of Demand

The **price elasticity of demand** measures the responsiveness of the quantity demanded to changes in price. Since demand curves always slope downward, the natural sign of the price elasticity is negative. It's more convenient to work with positive numbers, so we take the absolute value and eliminate the negative sign. While we use the absolute value so we can deal with positive numbers, it is important to remember that price and quantity move in opposite directions along the demand curve.

☑ Key Equation

$$E_d = \left| \frac{\text{percentage change in quantity demanded}}{\text{percentage change in price}} \right|$$

💣 Caution!

Remember that along a demand curve, price and quantity always move in the opposite direction, so an increase in price will cause a decrease in quantity, even though our elasticity number is positive.

We define products in five ways depending upon the price elasticity:
- **Elastic demand.** The price elasticity of demand is greater than 1. For this to happen, the quantity change (in percentage terms) must be larger than the price change (in percentage terms).
- **Inelastic demand.** The price elasticity of demand is less than 1. For this to happen, the quantity change (in percentage terms) must be smaller than the price change (in percentage terms).
- **Unit elastic demand.** The price elasticity of demand is equal to 1. For this to happen, the quantity change and the price change must be equal (in percentage terms).
- **Perfectly inelastic demand.** The price elasticity of demand is 0 and the demand curve is vertical. The quantity demanded stays the same regardless of a price change.
- **Perfectly elastic demand.** The price elasticity of demand is infinite and the demand curve is horizontal. Any price increase will eliminate all quantity demanded. Price decreases won't occur since the firm can sell all the output it wants at the going rate. You will see this later in the book as a key assumption about the demand facing a perfectly competitive firm.

The number of available substitutes is a key factor in determining the price elasticity for a product. It is important to recognize that while the demand for eggs is relatively inelastic—because there are no natural substitutes—the demand for eggs purchased from a particular supermarket will be more elastic than the demand for eggs in general since eggs from one store are an almost perfect substitute for eggs from another store. Also, the demand for a particular brand of coffee will be more elastic than the demand for coffee since Folger's coffee is a good substitute for Maxwell House. The demand for corn will be more elastic than the demand for food since there are no substitutes for food, but there are many other foods that can substitute for corn.

As time passes, more substitutes become available and so the demand for a particular good becomes more elastic. As an example, if the price of gasoline permanently doubled overnight, you would have few ways of changing your gasoline consumption in the very short term. For instance, you might walk to class instead of drive, run all of your errands at one time, or car pool with friends. Over time you have more ways to substitute for driving and you have more ways of adjusting your gasoline consumption. For example, you could move closer to work or school or buy a more fuel-efficient car.

☞ While it may be true that there are no or few good substitutes for a particular good, such as insulin, if multiple stores sell that good, buyers do have substitutes. Insulin purchased from one pharmacy is a very close, almost perfect, substitute for insulin purchased at another pharmacy. As a result, each pharmacy will face a very elastic demand curve for insulin purchased from that pharmacy.

Price elasticity also depends on the fraction of a person's income that they spend on a good. People will respond more to a change in the price of housing than they will to a change in the price of light bulbs.

The demand for necessities is usually less elastic than the demand for luxuries.

5.2 [20.2] Using Price Elasticity to Predict Changes in Quantity

If we know the price elasticity, we can forecast how a change in price will affect the quantity demanded. By rearranging the elasticity formula, we have:

☑ Key Equation

percentage change in quantity demanded = percentage change in price x E_d

For example, if the price elasticity of demand is 0.7 and we want to know what impact a 10% increase in the price of shoes will have in the market, we calculate:

percentage change in quantity = 10 x 0.7 = 7%.

So, with a 10% increase in price we expect the sales of shoes to decrease by 7%.

🖹 Remember

If you know any two of the pieces to the elasticity formula, you can solve for the third. So if you know the percentage changes in price and quantity, you can solve for elasticity. If you know the percentage change in price and the elasticity, you can solve for the percentage change in quantity. If you know the percentage change in quantity and the elasticity, you can solve for the percentage change in price.

Let's review two Applications that answer key questions we posed at the start of the chapter:

1. How does the elasticity of demand vary over time?

    APPLICATION 1:
    A CLOSER LOOK AT THE ELASTICITY OF DEMAND FOR GASOLINE
    This application examines the elasticity of demand in both the short-run and the long-run. The short-run elasticity of traffic volume is .1. This means that a 10% increase in gasoline prices leads to a short term reduction in traffic volume of 1%. Over time demand should be more elastic. In this case, the long-run elasticity of demand is .3, indicating that a 10% increase in price will lead, in the long-run, to a 3% decrease in traffic volume.

    Similar results can be seen in the impact of changes in the price of gasoline on fuel efficiency.

2. How can we use the price elasticity of demand to predict the effects of public policies?

APPLICATION 2: SMOKING, DRINKING AND ELASTICITY
This application examines the how young adults adjust their consumption of cigarettes and alcohol to higher taxes. It is estimated that the elasticity of demand for beer for young adults is 1.3. This means a 10% increase in the price of beer will lead to a 13% reduction in beer consumption. This will also lead to a reduction in highway deaths for young adults as highway deaths among young adults are roughly proportional to their beer consumption.

Teenagers have relatively elastic demands for cigarettes. The 1997 federal tobacco settlement increased the price of cigarettes increased by roughly 25%. What does this mean for teenage cigarette consumption? The price elasticity of demand is estimated to be 1.3 which suggests that:

1.3 = (percentage change in quantity) / 25.
Or,

Percentage change in quantity = 25(1.3) = 32.5.

5.3 [20.3] Price Elasticity and Total Revenue

Total revenue is the money that a firm gets from selling its product. For any product, total revenue equals the price per unit times the number of units sold. The price elasticity of demand determines whether revenue increases or decreases as price changes. Remember that price and quantity move in opposite directions along a demand curve.

If demand is elastic, the change in quantity (in percentage terms) is greater than the change in price (in percentage terms). For a price decrease, this means that we will sell more than enough additional units to make up for the lower price per unit. When demand is elastic, price and revenue move in opposite directions so a decrease in price increases revenue.

If demand is inelastic, the change in quantity (in percentage terms) is less than the change in price (in percentage terms). For a price decrease, this means that we won't sell enough additional units to offset the lower price per unit. When demand is inelastic, price and revenue move in the same direction so an increase in price increases revenue.
If demand is unit elastic, the price and quantity changes exactly offset each other and there is no change in revenue.

🗒 Remember

Revenue is simply the measure of how much money a firm earns from selling its product. An increase in revenue does not mean that profits have increased. To calculate how profits change, we would need to know how costs change as well.

When demand is elastic, price and revenue move in opposite directions. When demand is inelastic, price and revenue move in the same direction.

Agriculture provides a nice example of elasticity and revenue. A bumper crop is the result of favorable weather conditions during a growing season and refers to a larger than expected harvest. This means a shift to the right in the supply curve of agricultural products. As you recall, this will lower prices and increase quantity. Should farmers be happy with bumper crops? If the bumper crop is market wide and all farmers produce more, the answer is no. Since the demand for agricultural products is inelastic, lower prices lower the revenue that farmers receive from selling their crops. Because of the inelastic nature of the demand curve, farmers as a whole are better off with a drought which shifts supply to the left.

💣 Caution!

You need to realize that these results only hold if the bumper crop or drought affects the entire market. If only a portion of the market is affected (say one state) there may not be a significant impact on the market price. In those cases, if farmers in Kentucky have a bumper crop while the rest of the nation experiences normal growing conditions; farmers in Kentucky will be better off, they will sell more at roughly the same price, while other farmers will be unaffected.

Let's review an Application that answers a key question we posed at the start of the chapter:

3. If demand is inelastic, how does an increase in price affect total expenditures?

APPLICATION 3: VANITY PLATES AND THE ELASTICITY OF DEMAND

For an extra fee a driver can choose a "vanity" plate as opposed to the standard license plate of their state. Virginia has both the highest proportion of vanity plates among the fifty states as well as a very low fee for vanity plates. Should Virginia increase the price of vanity plates? What would be the impact on revenue from vanity plate sales?

The price elasticity for vanity plates in Virginia is estimated to be .26, clearly inelastic. If Virginia wished to raise more revenue from the sales of vanity plates, they should increase the price. While this would lead to fewer vanity plates being sold, the total revenue from those sales would increase.

4. If demand is inelastic, how does a decrease in supply affect total expenditures?

APPLICATION 4: DRUG PRICES AND PROPERTY CRIME

If government succeeds in lowering the supply of illegal drugs, the price of those drugs will increase. However, since the demand for illegal drugs is inelastic, this will increase the amount spent on those drugs. If drug habits are funded by criminal activity, restricting the supply of drugs could lead to an increase in property crimes as users need to steal more to pay for their drugs.

📄 Remember

Keep in mind that total revenue and total expenditures by consumers are the same thing. When we look from the firm's perspective, revenue is the money they receive for selling their product. When we look from the consumer's perspective, expenditures are the money they spend to buy products. One dollar in revenue to a firm is then equal to one dollar in expenditure by consumers.

5.4 [20.4] Elasticity and Total Revenue for a Linear Demand Curve

We often represent demand using a linear demand curve. While the slope is constant on a linear demand curve, elasticity is not. Above the midpoint demand is elastic. At the midpoint demand is unit elastic. Below the midpoint demand is inelastic. This means that if we start at the vertical intercept on the demand curve, lowering the price increases revenue until we reach the midpoint. Below the midpoint, lowering price lowers total revenue.

The reason for this is straightforward. Look at Figure 5.2 [20.2]. At point e, we have a relatively low quantity on the demand curve (10 units) and relatively high prices ($80). Thus, any price change will be small in percentage terms (since we are starting at a high price) and any quantity change will be large in percentage terms (since we are starting at a low quantity). This will lead to elastic demand. At point i, we have a relatively high quantity (40 units) and a relatively low price ($20). As a result price changes will be large in percentage terms, quantity changes will be small in percentage terms, and demand will be inelastic. You can see this in Table 5.6 [20.6].

☀ Caution!

Don't confuse slope and elasticity. While slope is constant on a linear demand curve, elasticity is not.

5.5 [20.5] Other Elasticities of Demand

The **income elasticity of demand** is a measure of how responsive quantity demanded is to changes in income. If the income elasticity is positive, we have a normal good; if the income elasticity is negative we have an inferior good. To calculate this we assume the price of the good and all demand factors other than income remain constant.

$$E_i = \frac{\text{percentage change in quantity demanded}}{\text{percentage change in income}}$$

The **cross-price elasticity of demand** is a measure of the responsiveness of the quantity demanded to changes in the price of a related good. If the cross-price elasticity of demand is positive, we have substitutes. If the cross-price elasticity of demand is negative, we have complements. To calculate this we assume the price of the good and all demand factors other than the price of the related good remain constant.

$$E_{x,y} = \frac{\text{percentage change in quantity of } X \text{ demanded}}{\text{percentage change in price of } Y}$$

✍ Study Tip

In general, elasticity measures the percentage change in quantity in response to a percentage change in some other demand or supply related factor. Typically the other factor will be a part of the name of the elasticity (so the price elasticity measures the response of quantity to a change in price).

5.6 [20.6] The Price Elasticity of Supply

The **price elasticity of supply** is a measure of the responsiveness of the quantity supplied to changes in price. Since the supply curve is upward sloping, the price elasticity of supply will always be positive. If the price elasticity of supply is greater than one, supply is elastic. If the price elasticity of supply is less than one, supply is inelastic.

$$E_s = \frac{\text{percentage change in quantity supplied}}{\text{percentage change in price}}$$

What determines the price elasticity of supply? In part, when production costs increase rapidly with output supply will be relatively inelastic. This is an application of diminishing returns:

Principle of Diminishing Returns

Suppose output is produced with two or more inputs, and we increase one input while holding the other input or inputs fixed. Beyond some point—called the *point of diminishing returns*—output will increase at a decreasing rate.

If we can quickly produce more output, without increasing costs very much, supply will be relatively elastic.

☞ Time is an important factor in the elasticity of supply. Suppose that your college suddenly enrolls an additional 1,000 students, all of whom are seeking rental housing. Since it takes time to build housing, the short-run supply of housing is relatively inelastic. Even with large increases in market rents, not very many additional units of housing can be supplied to the market. As time passes, say six months, the high prices will attract new rental housing to the market as new apartments and houses are built. After a year, even more houses will be added to the market. Over a longer time period more houses can be offered in response to the higher prices. So, the quantity change is small in the immediate time frame, but larger over the period of a year or two. This shows that the supply of housing is more elastic in the long run than in the short run. This is true for most products.

Figure 5.4 [20.4] shows a perfectly inelastic supply curve and a perfectly elastic supply curve. **Perfectly inelastic supply** means the price elasticity of supply is equal to zero and the supply curve will be a vertical line – no matter what the price the quantity produced will be the same. **Perfectly elastic supply** means the price elasticity of supply is infinity and the supply curve will be a horizontal line – if price falls even a little bit the quantity produced will fall from infinite to zero.

We can use the elasticity of supply to predict changes in the quantity supplied, just as we did with quantity demanded. We simply use:

$$\text{percentage change in quantity supplied} = E_s \times \text{percentage change in price}$$

5.7 [20.7] Using Elasticities to Predict Changes in Equilibrium Price

We know from Chapter 4 that when supply and/or demand change, the equilibrium price and quantity changes and we can forecast the direction of those changes. Using elasticities we can forecast the magnitude of those changes.

When demand changes, we can use:

$$\text{percentage change in equilibrium price} = \frac{\text{percentage change in demand}}{E_S + E_D}$$

Similarly for supply changes:

$$\text{percentage change in equilibrium price} = \frac{\text{percentage change in supply}}{E_S + E_D}$$

Let's review two Applications that answer key questions we posed at the start of the chapter:

5. How does a change in demand affect the equilibrium price?

APPLICATION 5: METROPOLITAN GROWTH AND HOUSING PRICES
It is expected that the population of the Portland (Oregon) area will grow by 12% over the next decade. We would like to know what impact this will have on housing prices. Let's assume that the demand for housing is proportional to population so it will also increase by 12%. At the metropolitan level, the price elasticity of supply is about 5.0 and the price elasticity of demand is 1.0. Given this we can find:

percentage change in equilibrium price = 12% / (5.0 + 1.0) = 12 / 6 = 2%

So, the 12% increase in population will lead to a 2% increase in housing prices.

6. How does a change in supply affect the equilibrium price?

APPLICATION 6: AN IMPORT BAN AND SHOE PRICES
Suppose that we restrict imports of shoes. This has the effect of shifting the supply curve to the left. We know that this will increase price. If the elasticity of supply is 2.3 and the elasticity of demand is 0.7, we can estimate the impact of a 30% reduction in supply as:

percentage change in equilibrium price = 30% / (2.3 +0.7) = 30 / 3 = 10%.

The import ban will increase prices by 10%.

Activity

Think about two different types of goods. The first is gasoline, the second Italian restaurant meals.

    a. Is the demand for gasoline likely to be elastic or inelastic?

        _____ Why?

    b. Is the demand for Italian restaurant meals likely to be elastic or inelastic?

        _____ Why?

    c. Suppose the price of crude oil, an input to gasoline, increases. What will this do in the market for gasoline? _____

    d. Suppose the price of milk, an input for cheese, an important component of an Italian dinner, increases. What will this do in the market for Italian restaurant meals?

        _____

    e. Using the results from section 5.7, which market is likely to see the larger increase in price, gasoline or restaurant meals? _____ Why?

Answers
    a. The demand for gasoline is likely to be inelastic. Very few substitutes.
    b. The demand for Italian restaurant meals is likely to be elastic. Many substitutes.
    c. This will decrease supply, reducing quantity and increasing price.
    d. This will decrease supply, reducing quantity and increasing price.
    e. Gasoline. Markets with less elastic demand curves have larger price impacts and small quantity impacts than markets with more elastic demand curves.

Key Terms

Cross-price elasticity of demand: A measure of the responsiveness of the quantity demanded to changes in the price of a related good; equal to the percentage change in the quantity demanded of one good (X) divided by the percentage change in the price of another good (Y).

Elastic demand: The price elasticity of demand is greater than 1.

Income elasticity of demand: A measure of the responsiveness of the quantity demanded to changes in consumer income; equal to the percentage change in the quantity demanded divided by the percentage change in income.

Inelastic demand: The price elasticity of demand is less than 1.

Perfectly elastic demand: The price elasticity of demand is infinite.

Perfectly elastic supply: The price elasticity of supply is infinite.

Perfectly inelastic demand: The price elasticity of demand equals zero.

Perfectly inelastic supply: The price elasticity of supply equals zero.

Price elasticity of demand: A measure of the responsiveness of the quantity demanded to changes in price; equal to the absolute value of the percentage change in quantity demanded divided by the percentage change in price.

Price elasticity of supply: A measure of the responsiveness of the quantity supplied to changes in price; equal to the percentage change in quantity supplied divided by the percentage change in price.

Total revenue: The money that a firm gets from selling its product.

Unit elastic demand: The price elasticity of demand equals 1.

Practice Quiz

(Answers are provided at the end of the Practice Quiz.)

1. How is the responsiveness of the quantity demanded to a change in price measured?
    a. By dividing the percentage change in the product's price by the percentage change in the quantity demanded of a product.
    b. By multiplying the percentage change in the product's price by the percentage change in the quantity demanded of a product.
    c. By dividing the percentage change in the quantity demanded of a product by the percentage change in the product's price.
    d. By multiplying the percentage change in the quantity demanded of a product by the percentage change in the product's price.

2. Suppose that the initial price of pizza is $2, and the initial quantity demanded is 100 pizzas. If the price increases to $2.20 and the quantity demanded falls to 80, using the midpoint formula what is the price elasticity of demand (in absolute value)?
    a. 0.22
    b. 10
    c. 2.33
    d. 0.10
    e. 0.43

3. If you know the value for price elasticity of demand, then which of the following can you compute?
    a. The effect of a price change on the quantity demanded.
    b. The responsiveness of the quantity supplied to changes in price.
    c. The price elasticity of supply.
    d. The effect of a price change for Good X on the quantity of Good Y sold.

4. Refer to the graphs below. Which demand curve has a value of elasticity equal to zero?

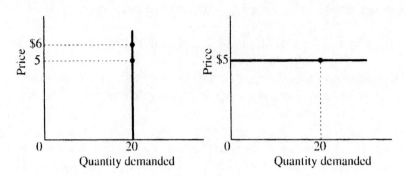

a. The graph on the left.
b. The graph on the right.
c. Both graphs.
d. Neither graph.

5. Refer to the figure below. This demand curve is perfectly elastic because:

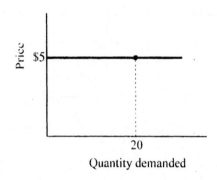

a. Quantity demanded is fixed at 20 units.
b. Total revenue does not change, regardless of quantity demanded.
c. An infinitesimal increase in price above $5 brings quantity demanded down to zero.
d. All of the above.

6. Refer to the figure below. Using the initial value formula, the value of price elasticity of supply between points *s* and *t* equals:

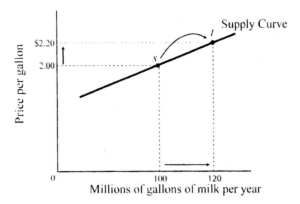

a. 0.5
b. 10
c. 1.0
d. 2.0

7. Which of the following expressions correctly states the version of the elasticity formula to predict the change in quantity demanded?
   a. percentage change in quantity demanded divided by percentage change in price equals price elasticity of demand.
   b. percentage change in price divided by the value of elasticity equals the percentage change in quantity demanded.
   c. elasticity value divided by the percentage change in price equals the percentage change in quantity demanded.
   d. none of these correctly state the version of the elasticity formula needed to predict the change in quantity demanded.

8. If the price elasticity of supply is 0.4, then a 20% increase in price will _____ the quantity supplied by _____ %.
   a. increase; 8.0
   b. decrease; 8.0
   c. increase; 80.0
   d. decrease; 0.8

9. The current price of wheat is $1.00 per bushel, and the price elasticity of demand for wheat is known to be 0.50. A bad harvest causes the supply of wheat to decrease, and as a result, the price of wheat rises by 20%. What will be the percentage change in the quantity demanded of wheat, and will farm revenues rise or fall?
   a. 20%, rise
   b. 10%, rise
   c. 20%, fall
   d. 10%, fall

10. This question tests your understanding of Application 2 in this chapter: Smoking, Drinking and Elasticity. How can we use the price elasticity of demand to predict the effects of public policies?

Under the 1997 federal tobacco settlement, if smoking by teenagers does not decline by 60 percent by the year 2007, cigarette makers will be fined $2 billion. Before the settlement, a pack of cigarettes sold for $2.48 and the elasticity of cigarette demand for teenagers is about 1.3. In order to achieve the target reduction of 60 percent, the new price of cigarettes should rise to approximately:
   a. $3.62.
   b. $4.08.
   c. $4.76.
   d. $3.97.

11. Refer to the figure below. If the elasticity of supply is 2.0 and the elasticity of demand is 1.5, what is the percentage change in price resulting from the increase in demand?

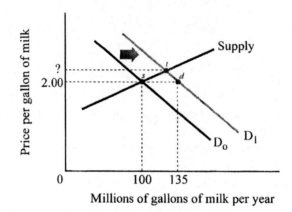

   a. 10%
   b. 35%
   c. 3.5%
   d. 20%

12. Refer to the figure below. Price elasticity of demand is:

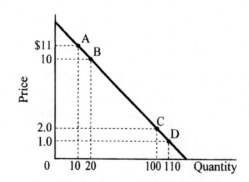

   a. Lower between points A and B than between points C and D.
   b. Lower between points C and D than between points A and B.
   c. The same between points A and B than between points C and D.
   d. The same as the value of the slope, thus constant along this linear demand curve.

13. Refer to the figure below. The relationship elasticity in this graph and total revenue is as follows:

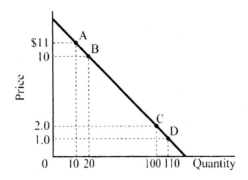

a.   A price increase along the elastic range of demand will result in an increase in total revenue.
b.   A price increase along the inelastic range of demand will result in an increase in total revenue.
c.   A price change anywhere along the line does not alter revenue because demand is linear.
d.   All of the above.

14. This question tests your understanding of Application 4 in this chapter: Drug prices and property crime. If demand is inelastic, how does a decrease in supply affect total expenditures?

   What is the consequence of higher drug prices on the (inelastic) demand for illegal drugs?
a.   A higher price will cause a decrease in total spending on illegal drugs.
b.   Drug consumption will decrease, but property crime is likely to increase.
c.   Despite the increase in the price of drugs, total drug consumption is likely to increase.
d.   There are no consequences because there is no trade off between drug prices and drug consumption.

15. In the short run, the price elasticity of demand for gasoline is estimated to be about 0.11. In the long run, studies suggest that it is about 0.9. How can you best explain this difference?
a.   The supply of gasoline is likely to increase in the long run.
b.   Consumers will have more income in the long run.
c.   Consumers will adapt and find substitutes as time goes by.
d.   The government is more likely to subsidize gasoline in the long run.

16. Refer to the figure below. Which of the statements below is entirely correct?

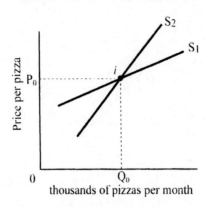

a. Over time, supply rotates from S_1 to S_2, that is, it becomes more elastic.
b. Over time, supply rotates from S_2 to S_1, that is, it becomes more elastic.
c. Over time, supply rotates from S_1 to S_2, that is, it becomes more inelastic.
d. Over time, supply rotates from S_2 to S_1, that is, it becomes more inelastic.

17. Refer to the figure below. Assume that after the increase in demand from D_1 to D_2, the market moves along the elastic supply curve. Which of the following statements is entirely correct?

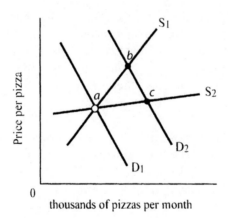

a. The market moves to equilibrium at point b, where the increase in quantity is proportionally greater than the increase in quantity from point a to point c.
b. The market moves to equilibrium at point c, where the increase in quantity is proportionally less than the increase in quantity from point a to point b.
c. The market moves to equilibrium at point b, where the increase in quantity is proportionally less than the increase in quantity from point a to point c.
d. The market moves to equilibrium at point c, where the increase in quantity is proportionally greater than the increase in quantity from point a to point b.

18. Refer to the figure below. Which of the following relationships best describes income elasticity of demand for an inferior good?

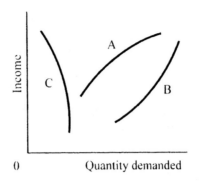

a. A
b. B
c. C
d. None of the above.

19. If the cross elasticity of demand between two products is -3.0, then:
    a. the two products are substitutes.
    b. the two products are complements.
    c. the two products are unrelated.
    d. both of the products are inferior.

20. Describe the similarities and differences between the concept of elasticity and the concept of the slope of a linear demand curve.

21. Compare the elasticity of demand for a single brand of tennis shoes to the elasticity of demand for all brands of tennis shoes combined.

Answers to the Practice Quiz

1. c. The responsiveness of the quantity demanded to a change in price, measured by dividing the percentage change in the quantity demanded of a product by the percentage change in the product's price.

2. c. Elasticity is equal to the percentage change in quantity demanded divided by the percentage change in price. The percentage change in quantity is (80-100)90 = -22.2%; the percentage change in price is (2.20-2)/2.10 = 9.5%. Elasticity is thus 2.3 in absolute value, elastic.

3. a. For this reason, elasticity is an important concept for managers and policy makers.

4. a. When demand is perfectly inelastic, the quantity demanded is the same at every price, so the price elasticity of demand is zero.

5. c. When demand is perfectly elastic, an infinitesimal increase in price will cause the quantity demanded to disappear.

6. d. First, calculate the percentage change in quantity supplied; next calculate the percentage change in price; then, divide the percentage change in quantity supplied by the percentage change in price. A 10% increase in the price of milk (from $2 to $2.20) increases the quantity supplied by 20% (from 100 million gallons to 120 million), so the price elasticity of supply is 2.0 = 20%/10%.

7. a. The elasticity formula states that price elasticity of demand equals the percentage change in quantity demanded divided by the percentage change in price. Solving for the percentage change in quantity yields percentage change in price multiplied by price elasticity of demand.

8. a. The percentage change in quantity supplied is equal to the elasticity of supply multiplied by the percentage change in price and quantity supplied moves in the same direction as price.

9. b. Elasticity of demand = (percentage change in quantity)/(percentage change in price). Thus, since elasticity is known to be 0.5, a 20% change in price must result in a 10% change in quantity demanded. Since demand is inelastic, a rise in price will cause total revenues to increase.

10. a. The required percentage change in quantity demanded is 60%. Given an elasticity value of 1.3, the required percentage change in price equals 0.6/1.3 = 0.4615 or approximately 46% increase in price. If the current price of a pack of cigarettes is $2.48, then the new price should be $2.48(1 + 0.46) = $3.62.

11. a. The increase in demand shifts the demand curve to the right, increasing the equilibrium price. In this case, quantity demanded goes from 100 to 135 as we move from D_0 to D_1 while keeping price at $2; this represents a 35% increase in demand. Given the elasticities of supply and demand, we have: 35%/(2.0 + 1.5) = 10%.

12. b. The upper portion of this downward sloping, linear demand curve is elastic, and the lower portion is inelastic.

13. b. As price increases along the inelastic range of demand, there is a move upward along the demand curve (i.e., from D to C), which corresponds to an upward move along the total revenue curve.

14. b. Drug consumption will decrease, but drug addicts who continue to use drugs will have to spend more on illegal drugs. Many drug addicts support their habits by stealing personal property—robbing people, stealing cars, and burglarizing homes. This means that drug addicts will commit more property crimes to support the higher total spending level associated with pricier drugs.

15. c. In the short run, it is difficult to make different choices about transportation. However, in the long run, consumers can adapt to changing gas prices in a number of ways, such as choice of a different car or a different place to live. Thus elasticity increases dramatically in the long run (though it is still inelastic).

16. b. As time goes by, producers have more time to make adjustments in output rather than price. Therefore, supply becomes more elastic over time.

17. d. S_2 is relatively more elastic than S_1 so that quantity changes proportionately more from point a to c than it does from point a to b. Over time, the market supply would have greater time to respond to the increase in demand by increasing quantity rather than price.

18. c. As income rises, the quantity demanded of this good decreases.

19. b. The cross elasticity of demand measures the percentage change in the quantity demanded of good X relative to the percentage change in the price of good Y. A negative relationship indicates the two goods are complements.

20. The slope of a demand curve measures the change in quantity demanded given a change in price. In other words, the slope measures the rate at which quantity demanded changes, given changes in price. Elasticity is not a measure of the rate of change in variables. Elasticity measures proportional changes, or magnitudes of change. Elasticity is a measure of comparison between the initial values and the new values of the variables. For these reasons, the value of elasticity along a linear demand curve changes, while the slope remains constant.

21. The main determinant of elasticity is the availability of substitute goods. The larger the number of substitutes available, the higher the value of elasticity. When the price of a single brand of tennis shoes increases, consumers can easily find substitutes. They simply switch to another brand. Now, if the price for all brands of tennis shoes goes up at once, consumers are less able to find close substitutes (i.e., cowboy boots are not a good substitute for tennis shoes). Therefore, the elasticity of demand for a single brand of tennis shoes is higher than the elasticity of demand for all brands of tennis shoes combined.

6 [21]
Market Efficiency and Government Intervention

Chapter Summary

This chapter discusses the efficiency of markets and the consequences of government intervention in perfectly competitive markets. Here are the main points of the chapter:

- The total surplus of a market equals the sum of consumer surplus and producer surplus.
- In a market that meets the four efficiency conditions (no external cost, no external benefits, perfect information, perfect competition), the market equilibrium maximizes the total surplus and is therefore efficient.
- Price controls reduce the total surplus of a market because they prevent mutually beneficial transactions.
- Quantity controls (such as licensing and import restrictions) decrease consumer surplus and the total surplus of the market.
- A tax on a good may be shifted forward onto consumers and backward onto input suppliers.
- Because a tax causes people to change their behavior, the total burden of the tax exceeds the revenue generated by the tax.

This chapter takes a closer look at the benefits from voluntary exchange and makes use of the principle of voluntary exchange:

 Principle of Voluntary Exchange

A voluntary exchange between two people makes both people better off.

In this chapter, we develop the concept of **efficiency**, the situation in which people do the best they can, given their limited resources.

𝒢𝒮 Study Tip

You may have an easier time measuring the gains to trade for sellers since we are familiar with the idea of profit, which means selling something at a higher price than we paid for the good. The same concept applies for consumers. Consumers "profit" when they can buy an item for less than the amount they value the item.

Applying the Concepts

After reading this chapter, you should be able to answer these five key questions:

1. How does a minimum price (floor price) affect the market?
2. Who bears the cost of import restrictions?
3. What is the role of prices in allocating resources?
4. How does a tax cut affect prices?
5. How do taxes affect behavior?

6.1 [21.1] Consumer Surplus and Producer Surplus

In earlier chapters you learned that voluntary trade benefits both parties. On the buyer's side, the **willingness to pay** is the maximum amount a consumer is willing to pay for a product. As long as the price of a product is less than the buyer's **willingness to pay**, the consumer will not only buy the product, but will gain from the trade. The gain will be the difference between the buyer's willingness to pay and the price actually paid for the good.

☞ For instance, if you are willing to pay $75 to see Kenny Chesney in concert and you are able to buy a ticket for $40, you have gained from the trade. You have traded something you valued at $40 (the money) for something you value at $75 (the ticket). In fact, you have gained $35 in value. We call this gain your consumer surplus.

Consumer surplus is calculated as the consumer's willingness to pay for a product minus the actual price the consumer paid. Graphically, consumer surplus is the area under the demand curve, above the market price. See Figure 6.1 [21.1] in the text.

Sellers gain from trade as well. If you are willing to sell an hour of babysitting services for $5, and you are actually paid $10 for babysitting, you have gained $5. You have traded something you valued at $5 (one hour of time) for something you value at $10 (the money). A seller's **willingness to accept** is the minimum amount a producer is willing to accept as payment for a product and is equal to marginal cost of production. When a good is sold for more than the willingness to accept, the sellers will gain from the trade. We call this gain producer surplus. **Producer surplus** is calculated as the price a producer receives for a product minus the marginal cost of the product. Graphically the producer surplus is the area below the price and above the supply curve.

6.2 [21.2] Market Equilibrium and Efficiency

We have shown that both buyers and sellers gain from trade. If we add the gains to the consumers and the gains to the producers, we have a measure of the gains from the trade. **Total surplus** is simply the sum of consumer surplus and producer surplus in a market.

When trades take place at the equilibrium price in the market total surplus is as large as possible. To see why, suppose that a price ceiling or a price floor exists in the market. A **price ceiling** is a maximum price set by the government. A **price floor** is a minimum price set by the government. If you look at Figure 6.4 [21.4] you see the results of price ceilings and price floors in the market.

In Panel A, the maximum price prevents trades between Cecil and Thurl as well as Forest and Dee. This is true even though Thurl and Forest are willing to pay more than enough to induce Cecil and Dee to mov their lawn. The gains to both the buyer and the seller from these trades are not realized because these trades won't happen with a price ceiling.

In Panel B, even though Thurl and Forest are willing to pay more than enough to compensate Cecil and Dee for mowing the lawn, the minimum price is higher than Thurl and Forest are willing to pay and thus they won't have their lawns cut.

In both cases trades which would benefit both parties do not happen because of the market restrictions. As a result total surplus is less than it would be if trades were allowed at the market price.

By guaranteeing that all mutually beneficial trades will take place, the market equilibrium maximizes the total surplus of the economy. While there are times when government activity in the economy is justified, in most cases government involvement reduces total surplus in the economy. We will study cases where government involvement is justified later in this book.

6.3 [21.3] Controlling Prices—Maximum and Minimum Prices

Maximum prices, or price ceilings, lead to excess demand in the market as demanders want to buy more goods at the controlled price than sellers are willing to sell. As you can see in Figure 6.5 [21.5], when this happens:

- Surplus that once belonged to producers now belongs to consumers. This is the area between prices of $300 and $400 and quantities 0 to 700. This is the result of the price ceiling being $100 less than the market price. Consumers are better off by $100 for each of the 700 units still purchased.
- Total surplus in the market is reduced. The triangle *abc* represents surplus that would exist at the market price but does not exist with the price ceiling. This lost surplus is called the deadweight loss. **Deadweight loss** is the decrease in the total surplus of the market that results from a policy such as rent control. Notice that some of this (*cad*) comes from lost surplus to consumers while some (*adb*) comes from lost surplus to producers.

📄 Remember

The lost surplus (triangle *abc*) represents the potential gains from trade which would occur at the market price, but which don't occur at the price ceiling.

When the government sets a minimum price, a price floor, we also reallocate and reduce surplus. Look back at Figures 6.3 [21.3] and 6.4 [21.4] to see this reallocation. In the market for lawn mowing, the market price was $10 as seen in Figure 6.3 [21.3]. When a price floor of $19 is set, as seen in Figure 6.4 [21.4], you can see that Abe and Bea are better off. Some of the consumer surplus that belonged to Juan and Tupak now belongs to Abe and Bea as they receive $9 extra per lawn mowed. You can also see that the gains that would have been created by the third, fourth, and fifth lawns being mowed will not exist as these trades will not be made at the higher price.

Let's review an Application that answers one of the key questions we posed at the start of the chapter:

1. How does a minimum price (floor price) affect the market?

APPLICATION 1: MILK MOUNTAINS

The U.S. government has established a minimum price of $9.90 per hundred pounds for powdered milk. The problem is that this is above the market price. As a result, more powdered milk is offered for sale than is desired by consumers. To keep the price at the floor, the U.S. government buys and stores any excess supply of milk at the $9.90 price. In essence, the government agrees to buy enough powdered milk to force the market price to $9.90.

☞ Why store the milk? First, draw a graph for the market for powdered milk showing the market price below the $9.90 floor. The government agrees to demand the excess supply at the price floor. In essence this shifts the demand curve to the right and forces the price to be $9.90. What would happen in the market if the government gave away the milk they purchase? Now more milk would be available in the market at any price, the supply curve would shift to the right, and market forces would push the price below $9.90. To keep the price floor effective, the government must buy and then store (or destroy) the excess milk production.

6.4 [21.4] Controlling Quantities—Licensing and Import Restrictions

Suppose that government doesn't control price, but instead controls quantity. The results in the market are the same as if the government set prices.

To see this, look at Figure 6.6 [21.6]. If the market for taxi services is allowed to set prices, we will have a price per mile of $3 and 10,000 miles of taxi services per day. Suppose instead we allow only 8,000 miles of taxi service to be provided. Now consumers are willing to pay $3.60 for that quantity of taxi service. We can see that:
- Some consumer surplus is reallocated to producers. For the 8,000 miles provided, producers now receive an additional $0.60 from consumers.
- The gains from trade that could have been realized from the 2,000 additional miles provided at the market price are lost to the economy. This deadweight loss is the triangle *abc* in Panel B.

☞ Look again at Panel B of Figure 6.6 [21.6]. Suppose that the government had set a price floor of $3.60 per mile on taxi cab services. With this price floor, 8,000 miles would have been provided. Producers would receive an additional $0.60 from consumers for those miles, and the market would lose the gains from trade on the last 2,000 miles of taxi cab service that would no longer be offered. This is the same result as the quantity restriction.

 Remember

Restricting the price through a price floor and setting a maximum quantity have the same effect on the market.

One important category of quantity restrictions is import quotas. An import quota limits the amount of a good that can be sold in the market. An import restriction does this by reducing the supply of a good in a market. Sugar offered for sale in the United States comes from two sources, U.S. producers and imports.

If we limit the amount of imports, there will be less sugar offered for sale at any price, and the supply curve will shift to the left.

Figure 6.7 [21.7] illustrates this shift. The minimum price at which U.S. sugar will be sold in the market is $0.26 per pound. In Panel A, we see that because of sugar imports the market price in the United States is $0.12 per pound and no U.S. sugar is offered for sale. Notice that the consumer surplus all flows to U.S. consumers, while the producer surplus all flows to foreign producers.

Panel B shows an extreme case, the United States bans all sugar imports leaving only U.S. suppliers in the market. The new market price is $0.30 and the market quantity falls from 360 million pounds per day to 160 million pounds per day.

Clearly U.S. producers are better off. Before, they received none of the producer surplus since the market price was too low for U.S. producers to offer any sugar for sale. Just as clearly, U.S. consumers are worse off. First because they are paying $0.18 more for each of the 160 million pounds of sugar still traded. Second, because U.S. consumers are now unable to buy the additional 200 million pounds of sugar that had been available before. U.S. producers gain at the expense of U.S. consumers.

Let's review two Applications that answer key questions we posed at the start of the chapter:

2. Who bears the cost of import restrictions?

APPLICATION 2:
U.S. AND EUROPEAN CUSTOMERS PAY FOR IMPORT RESTRICTIONS
We saw in Figure 6.7 [21.7] that domestic producers gain with import restrictions. You can see in that figure that workers in the U.S. sugar industry will be better off as a result of the import ban. One 1993 study estimated that import restrictions protected roughly 60,000 jobs in the U.S. textile and automobile industries. The cost of protecting these jobs was quite high, between $178,000 and $271,000 per job. This cost comes out of the pocket of consumers.

☞ Is there a better way? Import restrictions are supported because they protect U.S. jobs. What if instead of protecting the jobs we took other steps to compensate those who lose their jobs due to imports? At the most basic level, instead of spending $178,000 to save the job of a textile worker, what if we allowed the job to disappear but gave the worker a cash payment of $150,000? What do you think?

3. What is the role of prices in allocating resources?

APPLICATION 3: SUPPLY AND DEMAND FOR HUMAN ORGANS
There is an excess demand for human organs for transplant in the United States. Each year thousands die waiting for organ transplants. There is a price ceiling of $0 in the market for organs as it is illegal to buy or sell human organs. Nobel-prize winner Gary Becker suggested that allowing people to buy and sell organs would ease the shortage. Concerns over ethics and distribution have kept policymakers from embracing this plan.

6.5 [21.5] Who Really Pays Taxes?

Let's follow the book example with a $100 tax on apartments as shown in Figure 6.8 [21.8]. Suppose you are the landlord and you are willing to rent an apartment as long as you get $300 per month for the apartment. If a tax of $100 has to be paid then in order for you to keep $300 per month, the renter must pay $400. Then, $100 will go for the tax and you will keep the $300 you need to offer the apartment.

As Figure 6.8 [21.8] shows, if the price of apartments increased by $100, there would be an excess supply. Why? At the $400 price, suppliers would still be willing to offer 900 apartments, since they still keep $300 per unit. Demanders only want 900 apartments if the price is $300 and they will reduce their quantity demanded as the price increased above $300. In the figure, the new equilibrium quantity is 750. Demanders will be willing to rent 750 apartments if the price of apartments is $360. If demanders pay $360, sellers keep $260, since $100 of the rent is the tax. At $260 sellers are willing to offer 750 apartments so we have equilibrium.

In this case demanders pay $60 of the tax (in the form of higher rent) and sellers pay $40 of the tax (in the form of lower rent received per unit). There is a deadweight loss which comes from the 150 apartments that would have been rented at the market price of $300 which are not rented due to the tax.

Remember in the last chapter we saw that elasticity determined the magnitude of price changes when supply and demand curves shifted. Elasticity will also determine who bears the burden of a tax in the market. If demand is very inelastic, so quantity doesn't adjust very much to price changes, then more of the tax will be paid by demanders. This is illustrated in Panel A in Figure 6.9 [21.9]. If demand is very elastic, more of the tax will be paid by suppliers as illustrated by Panel B in Figure 6.9 [21.9].

The tax on apartments in Figure 6.9 [21.9] raises $75,000 in revenue, $100 dollars on each of the 750 units rented. This tax revenue comes from what previously had been consumer and producer surplus. However, the total loss in surplus is not just this $75,000. The triangle *abd* is the deadweight loss of the tax and it accounts for $7,500. This $7,500 is the deadweight loss from taxation. The **deadweight loss from taxation** is defined as the difference between the total burden of a tax and the amount of revenue collected by the government. This is also sometimes called the **excess burden of a tax**.

ᏸᏸ **Study Tip**

Since an inelastic demand leads to a smaller reduction in trades when a tax is imposed, the deadweight loss of a tax is smaller the less elastic the demand.

📄 **Remember**

The less elastic side of the market will bear the larger burden of a tax.

Let's review two Applications that answer key questions we posed at the start of the chapter:

4. How does a tax cut affect prices?

APPLICATION 4:
RESPONSE TO LOWER TAXES IN FRENCH RESTAURANTS

To encourage lower restaurant taxes, French restaurants promised that they would pass on savings from lower costs to both customers, in the form of lower prices, and employees, in the form of higher wages. The chapter points out that higher taxes get shifted to consumers and workers. The argument of the restaurants is that just as tax increases are shifted to consumers and workers, tax cuts will be as well.

5. How do taxes affect behavior?

APPLICATION 5: TAXES AND DECEMBER BABIES

If a baby is born at 11:55pm on December 31, the parents can claim the child as a dependent on their income taxes for the entire year. This means that a child born on December 31 reduces the income tax liability for that year. As a result, you would rather have a child on December 31 than on January 1. Data suggests more babies than would normally be expected are born during the last week of the year and fewer babies than expected are born during the first week of the previous year. Not only that, but increasing the tax benefits of having a baby in late December relative to having a baby in early January increases the number of December babies. Even babies respond to incentives provided by the tax code!

Activity

Let's think about kidney donation a bit more. Draw a demand and supply diagram for kidney transplants. The demand should be downward sloping and the supply upward sloping. To think about supply, realize that most people have two kidneys and can live with just one. Would you donate your kidney to someone? What if you were offered a large sum of money? That people would be willing to donate a kidney for money suggests that supply is upward sloping.

Currently the maximum price at which a kidney can be traded is $0. Suppose that we raise the price ceiling by some amount, it doesn't have to be to the market price:

   a.   What happens to the number of kidneys transplanted?

        ————————————————————

   b.   What happens to producer surplus, consumer surplus, and deadweight loss?

        ————————————————————

   c.   Would buying and selling kidneys conform to our principle of voluntary exchange?

        ————————————————————

   d.   What ethical or distributional issues might arise in this market?

        ————————————————————

Answers

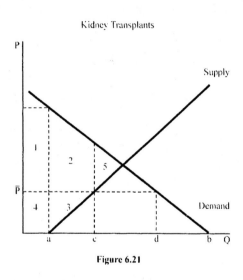

Figure 6.21

   a.   It increases from the quantity at point a to the quantity at point c.

   b.   Producer surplus increases and becomes areas 3 and 4. Consumer surplus changes from areas 1 and 4 to areas 1 and 2. The deadweight loss shrinks from 2, 3, and 5 to only area 5.

   c.   Yes, as long as trade is voluntary, both parties would trade only if they were both better off.

   d.   Under the current system organs are rationed by medical need, under the new system organs would be rationed to some extent by price and less sick, but wealthier, patients might receive organs instead of more sick, less wealthy patients.

Key Terms

Consumer surplus: The amount a consumer is willing to pay for a product minus the price the consumer actually pays.

Deadweight loss: The decrease in the total surplus of the market that results from a policy such as rent control.

Deadweight loss from taxation: The difference between the total burden of a tax and the amount of revenue collected by the government.

Efficiency: A situation in which people do the best they can, given their limited resources.

Excess burden of a tax: Another name for deadweight loss from taxation.

Price ceiling: A maximum price set by the government.

Price floor: A minimum price set by the government.

Producer surplus: The price a producer receives for a product minus the marginal cost of production.

Total surplus: The sum of consumer surplus and producer surplus.

Willingness to accept: The minimum amount a producer is willing to accept as payment for a product; equal to the marginal cost of production.

Willingness to pay: The maximum amount a consumer is willing to pay for a product.

Practice Quiz

(Answers are provided at the end of the Practice Quiz.)

1. For market equilibrium to generate the largest possible surplus and thus be efficient, which condition(s) must be met?
   a. There must be no external benefits.
   b. There must be no external costs.
   c. We must have perfect competition.
   d. We need perfect information.
   e. All of the above.

2. Refer to the figure below. How much is the total consumer surplus in this market?

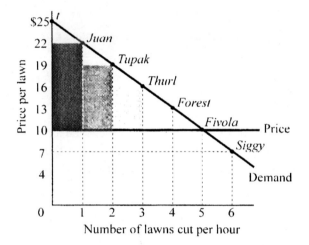

   a. $10
   b. $40
   c. $30
   d. $80

3. Refer to the figure below. Who earns the least amount of consumer surplus in this graph?

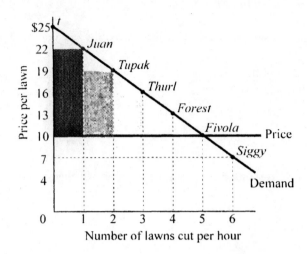

a. Juan
b. Fivola
c. Siggy
d. None of the above. They all pay the same and earn the same amount of consumer surplus.

4. Refer to the figure below. What can be said about the participation of Efrin in the market?

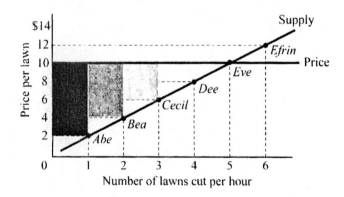

a. Efrin is the producer that receives the greatest amount of producer surplus.
b. Efrin's participation is insignificant because he earns the least amount of consumer surplus.
c. Efrin does not participate in the market at all.
d. Efrin earns the same amount of consumer surplus as Eve.

5. Refer to the figure below. What is the impact of imposing a minimum price of $16 in this market?

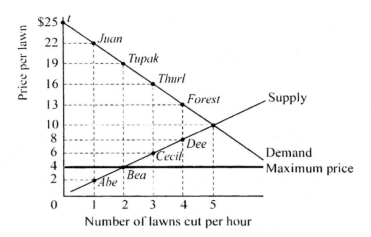

a. Forest will no longer participate in the market..
b. JBea stands to benefit the most from the minimum price IF she is able to sell the good.
c. The minimum price benefits all producers, but some more than others.
d. All producers benefit from the minimum price equally.

6. Refer to the figures below. In which case do some producers gain at the expense of consumers?

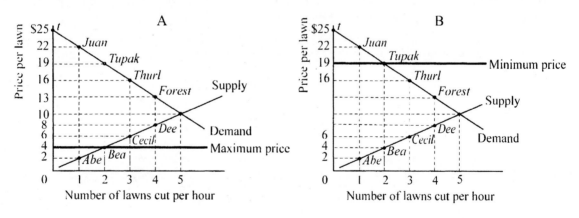

a. In case A.
b. In case B.
c. In both cases.
d. In neither case.

7. *Producer surplus*:
    a. is the difference between market price and the average cost of production.
    b. is the difference between market price and the marginal utility of the consumer.
    c. is the difference between market price and the marginal cost of production.
    d. is the difference between market price and the average utility of the consumer.

8. Refer to the figure below which demonstrates a $300 maximum price allowed. The triangle *des* is called:

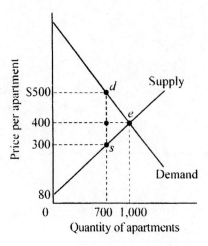

a. A rent control.
b. A maximum price area.
c. A deadweight loss.
d. A shortage.

9. This question tests your understanding of Application 1 in this chapter: Milk mountains. How does a minimum price (floor price) affect the market?

Refer to the figure below. Which of the graphs best describes this minimum price on milk?

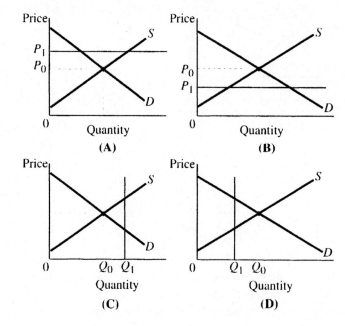

a. A.
b. B.
c. C.
d. D.

10. Refer to the figure below. After a taxi medallion policy is imposed:

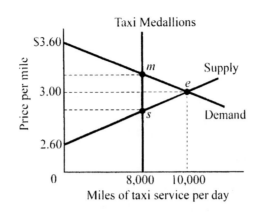

a. there is a shortage of demand for taxi service, and a decrease in the total surplus of the taxi market.
b. there is an excess demand for taxi service, and an increase in the total surplus of the taxi market.
c. there is a shortage of demand for taxi service, and an increase in the total surplus of the taxi market.
d. there is an excess demand for taxi service, and a decrease in the total surplus of the taxi market.

11. Refer to the figure below. How much is domestic supply at the $0.12 price under free trade?

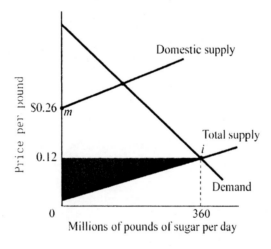

a. 360 million pounds.
b. Zero.
c. Some amount greater than zero but less than 360 million pounds.
d. None of the above.

12. Refer to the figure below. If the government stops sugar imports, then:

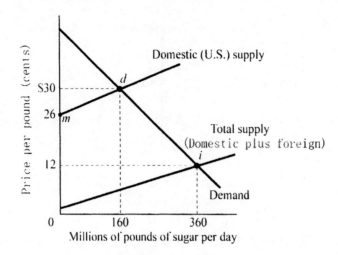

a. domestic producers in the sugar market earn a smaller surplus than before the ban.
b. domestic consumers in the sugar market earn a smaller surplus than before the ban.
c. both domestic consumers and domestic producers in the sugar market are made worse off.
d. both domestic consumers and domestic producers in the sugar market are made better off.

13. Refer to the figure below. The loss of producer surplus after the tax is imposed is represented by area:

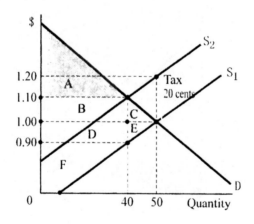

a. F
b. D
c. D+E
d. D + E + F

14. Refer to the figure below. The deadweight loss from the tax is represented by area:

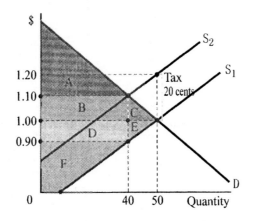

    a. B + D
    b. C + E
    c. B + C + D + E
    d. A + F

15. Refer to the figure below. Only one statement is entirely correct. In which market will the government raise a larger amount of revenue?

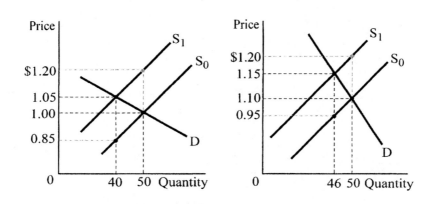

    a. In the market with the more elastic demand curve, or market A.
    b. In the market with the more inelastic demand curve, or market A.
    c. In the market with the more elastic demand curve, or market B.
    d. In the market with the more inelastic demand curve, or market B.

16. Refer to the figure below. In which of the markets do consumers bear a larger proportion of the tax?

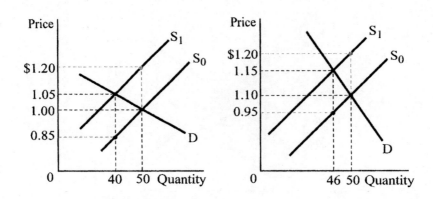

a. In market A.
b. In market B.
c. In both markets.
d. In neither of the two markets.

17. Refer to the figure below. The tax in this scenario is:

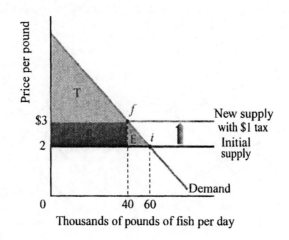

a. partially paid by producers.
b. partially passed on to consumers.
c. entirely paid by producers.
d. entirely passed on to consumers.

18. This question tests your understanding of Application 3 in this chapter: Supply and demand for human organs. What is the role of prices in allocating resources?

    What is the economist's solution to the shortage of human organs for transplants?
    a.   To solve the organ shortage, the economist would focus primarily on an appeal to people's generosity, urging them to commit their organs to the transplant program.
    b.   The economist would suggest offering monetary incentives for organ donors.
    c.   The economists would establish a commission of policy makers and health experts to decide how to best deal with the shortage of organs in the long run.
    d.   The economists would prefer to impose price ceilings in the market for organs, which would probably increase economic efficiency.

19. Assume that domestic producers cannot enter a domestic market because foreign producers can produce and sell the same good at significantly lower prices. Would you support an import ban to help domestic producers? You may refer to the illustration in the textbook as an example.

20. Suppose that you are the authority in charge of imposing taxes on selected goods and services. Your goal is to raise the largest amount of revenue possible from the tax. Would you target goods that have elastic demands, or those that have inelastic demands? Explain.

Answers to the Practice Quiz

1. e. A market equilibrium will generate the largest possible surplus when four conditions are met:
    - No external benefits: The benefits of a product (a good or service) are confined to the person who pays for it.
    - No external costs: The cost of producing a product is confined to the person who sells it.
    - Perfect information: Buyers and sellers know enough about the product to make informed decisions about whether to buy or sell it.
    - Perfect competition: Each firm produces such a small quantity that the firm cannot affect the price.

2. c. The market consumer surplus equals the sum of the consumer surpluses obtained by all the consumers in the market. Consumer surplus equals: $12 + $9 + $6 + $0 = $30.

3. b. Fivola is willing to pay $10 and actually pays $10 so her consumer surplus is $0.

4. c. Price dictates who participates in a market. Efrin is not willing to accept $10. He wants $12, so he does not participate in the market.

5. a. Forest is only willing to pay $13. If the minimum price is $16 he will not participate in the market.

6. b. A minimum price of $19 reduces the total surplus of the market as production drops from 5 to 2 lawns. Two producers gain at the expense of the consumers.

7. c. Producer surplus is the difference between what a firm is willing to accept (their MC) and what they are actually paid (the market price).

8. c. A maximum price of $300 per apartment decreases the total surplus of the market by the amount of the triangle *des*. This loss is called a deadweight loss. It represents a loss of output, as well as the availability of fewer apartments, rented at higher prices than before.

9. a. The price floor in the Application set a minimum price above the equilibrium price, which created an excess of quantity supplied over quantity demanded.

10. d. The medallion policy creates an excess demand for taxi service, and decreases the total surplus of the taxi market.

11. b. Domestic suppliers do not supply any output at $0.12. The minimum price they need in order to start producing any output at all is $0.26 per pound.

12. b. The price of sugar rises and the quantity traded decreases, resulting in a loss of consumer surplus.

13. c. Producer surplus is the area below the price level and above the supply curve. Before the tax, that area equals D + E + F. After the tax, the area is reduced to F.

14. b. The deadweight loss from taxation refers to the area that results from the resulting decrease in quantity and increase in price after the tax is imposed. Area C is a loss to consumers that is not a gain to anyone else. Area E is a loss to producers that is not a gain to anyone else.

15. d. In order to raise the largest amount of revenue, the government should tax goods that have more inelastic or steeper demand curves.

16. b. In market A the 20 cent tax increases consumer prices by five cents. In market B the 20 cent tax increases consumer prices by fifteen cents.

17. d. Producers pass the entire amount of the tax on to consumers. This occurs because the supply curve is perfectly elastic.

18. b. The failure of the conventional approach to reduce organ shortages led Nobel-winning economist Gary Becker to suggest monetary incentives for organ donors. Under his proposal, the federal government would pay donors and their survivors for the organs they donate and would distribute the organs to hospitals for transplanting.

19. An import ban would certainly help domestic producers. However, since they are able to offer the good only at much higher prices, the ban would also hurt domestic consumers. In the textbook example, the gain of producer surplus is minimal compared to the loss of consumer surplus because of the ban. The reason for the decrease in consumer surplus is that the quantity of output decreases substantially, while the price of the output increases. After the ban, many buyers, as well as the previous foreign sellers, are prevented from executing mutually beneficial transactions. Since the gain of domestic producer surplus is smaller than the loss of domestic consumer surplus, you should not support the import ban. In addition, if we ban imports from their economies, other countries are likely to ban imports of our goods. Domestic producers that export are likely to suffer as well.

20. The largest amount of revenue would be raised by taxing goods that have more inelastic demands. An inelastic demand is less responsive to price changes. Taxes are passed on to consumers in the form of higher prices. As price increases, the quantity demanded of a good that has a relatively inelastic demand curve changes little. If the demand curve is perfectly inelastic, the quantity demanded would not change at all. These consumers would be willing to absorb the entire burden of the tax. On the other hand, consumers that have highly elastic demand curves would respond to the tax by decreasing consumption of the good significantly. If the good does not sell well, the government can't expect to raise too much revenue by taxing that good.

7 [22]
Consumer Choice Using Utility Theory

Chapter Summary

In this chapter, we introduce the theory of consumer choice and show the logic behind the downward sloping demand curve. Here are the main points of the chapter:

- The law of diminishing marginal utility says that as the consumption of a good increases, utility increases at a decreasing rate.
- The theory of consumer choice has two steps: First, identify the affordable combinations of goods. Second, pick the affordable combination that maximizes utility.
- The equimarginal rule tells us to pick the combination of two activities at which the marginal benefit per dollar for the first activity equals the marginal benefit per dollar for the second.
- The individual demand curve is negatively sloped, reflecting the substitution effect and income effect of a change in price. A decrease in price decreases the relative price of the good, and consumers substitute the good for other goods (the substitution effect). A decrease in price also increases the consumer's real income, increasing the consumption of all normal goods (the income effect).

Applying the Concepts

After reading this chapter, you should be able to answer these five key questions:
1. How does a tax on one good affect the demand for substitute goods?
2. Why do consumers dislike the bundling of goods?
3. How do consumers respond to offsetting changes in taxes?
4. How do consumers respond to free goods?
5. How does product branding affect consumers' brain activity?

In this chapter, we will assume that:
- Consumers receive utility from consumption
- Consumers face a limited choice set based on their income and prices
- Consumers choose consumption which maximizes their utility given the constraints they face.

7.1 [22.1] Total and Marginal Utility

Utility is the satisfaction experienced from consuming a good. To help understand the concepts in this chapter we assume we can measure the benefit of some action by the number of utils generated. A **util** is one unit of utility. When a consumer buys one more song download, the consumer is better off, meaning they have a higher number of utils after they download the additional song than they did before. **Marginal utility** is the change in total utility from one additional unit of a good. **The law of diminishing marginal utility** states that as the consumption of a particular good increases, marginal utility decreases.

Ꮬ Study Tip

The law of diminishing marginal utility is an application of the principle of diminishing returns.

☞ Think about eating doughnuts. If you are hungry, eating a doughnut may bring a great deal of satisfaction, and in fact you may be willing to pay $1 for one doughnut. Eating a second doughnut may also bring satisfaction, but since you are not as hungry as you were before you ate the first doughnut, it will not bring the same amount of satisfaction as the first doughnut. You may only be willing to pay $0.50 for the second doughnut. You might think about eating a third doughnut, but because you are almost full you may only eat a third doughnut if it is given to you at no charge. Eating doughnuts is subject to the law of diminishing marginal utility; you receive less additional satisfaction from each additional doughnut you eat.

7.2 [22.2] Consumer Choice

A consumer wants to maximize her utility (make herself as well off as possible) subject to the limits of her income. To do this she:
- figures out her menu of options, what she can afford, then
- chooses the option that provides her highest level of utility.

A consumer's **budget line** shows all the combinations of two goods that exhaust a consumer's budget. The **budget set** is defined as the set of affordable combinations of two goods. Graphically, the budget set is the area under the budget line.

To graph the budget line (see Figure 7.2 [22.2]):
- Draw a graph with one of the two goods on the horizontal axis, the other on the vertical axis. In the graph movies are on the horizontal axis and books are on the vertical axis.
- Find the intercepts by dividing the consumer's income by the price of the good on that axis. This tells you the amount of that good the consumer could purchase if she spent all of her income on that good. So, when Maxine has $30 in income and movies cost $3 each, she can buy $30/$3 = 10 movies if she spends all her income on movies. Since books cost $1 each, Maxine could buy $30/$1 = 30 books if she spends all her income on books. You can see these as points *a* and *k* in Figure 7.2 [22.2] in the text.
- Draw the budget line as the line connecting the two intercept points.

We find the optimal combination of two goods by using the equimarginal rule. The **equimarginal rule** states that we pick the combination of two activities where the marginal benefit per dollar for the first activity equals the marginal benefit per dollar for the second activity.

☑ Key Equation

$$\frac{\text{marginal utility of activity one}}{\text{price of activity one}} = \frac{\text{marginal utility of activity two}}{\text{price of activity two}}$$

☞ Why does this work? Suppose that Maxine is at point *f* in Figure 7.2 [22.2] in the text. According to Table 7.1 [22.1], at this point the marginal utility per dollar of movies is 10 while the marginal utility per dollar for books is 18. Could Maxine do better? Suppose that Maxine spends one less dollar on movies. She will lose 10 utils by doing this. If she takes that dollar and buys a book, she will gain 18 utils. By purchasing fewer movies and spending the money on books Maxine's net gain is 8 utils.

🗎 Remember

When using the equimarginal rule, we always substitute away from the good with the smaller marginal utility per dollar and toward the good with the larger marginal utility per dollar.

Let's review two Applications that answer key questions we posed at the start of the chapter:

1. How does a tax on one good affect the demand for substitute goods?

    ### APPLICATION 1: NEW ZEALAND'S TAX ON LIGHT SPIRITS
    In this Application we measure utility by the alcohol content of a drink. The government of New Zealand wanted to reduce teenagers' consumption of light spirits and imposed a tax on beverages with alcohol content between 14 and 24 percent. The tax increased the price of light spirits and reduced the marginal utility per dollar. As we would expect, consumers substituted away from the lower marginal utility per dollar good and towards other goods with higher marginal utility per dollar. In this case, the higher marginal utility per dollar good was a new "super-light" beverage with alcohol content just below the tax threshold.

☞ You might ask if the tax accomplished its policy goal. Remember the tax was instituted because of concern over teen drinking. Is it likely the tax cut teen drinking or just shifted drinking to non-taxed beverages? The application does not give enough information to adequately address this issue. If a larger number of teens reduced their overall alcohol consumption by switching from higher to lower alcohol content drinks then those who increased their overall alcohol consumption by switching to nontaxed drinks with higher alcohol content, then the policy was successful to some degree. Policy makers at times forget that consumers will respond to changed incentives and sometimes fail to properly anticipate how the changed incentives will affect the desired policy outcome.

2. Why do consumers dislike the bundling of goods?

    ### APPLICATION 2: ONLINE MUSIC STORES AND PIRACY
    This Application shows how bundling limits consumer choice. We assume that each song Sam purchases costs $1, and initially Sam is limited to buying CDs containing 15 songs at a price of $15 each. In this situation Sam's available choices are points *a*, *c*, and *d* in Figure 7.3 [22.2]. If Sam could buy individual songs, he would have more options. Now, if he chooses he could buy only 10 songs (an option that a CD doesn't allow) and use the rest of his money on arcade games. Allowing

Sam to buy songs one at a time increases his budget set and makes Sam better off. In the diagram point *b* is Sam's optimal choice, but this choice is only available if he can buy songs one at a time.

7.3 [22.3] The Individual Demand Curve

Lessons from consumer choice allow us to understand why individual demand curves are downward sloping. Let's look at how consumers respond to a change in prices. We break the response to a price change into two pieces:

- The **substitution effect** is the change in quantity consumed caused by a change in the relative price of a good, with real income held constant. At the original prices Maxine had to give up three books in order to see one move (since a movie cost $3 and a book cost $1). If the price of movies falls to $2, Maxine now needs to only give up 2 books to see a movie. The relative price of a movie has fallen.
- The **income effect** is the change in quantity consumed caused by a change in real income with relative prices held constant. If the price of movies falls, Maxine's budget set becomes larger, she can afford more combinations of books and movies than before. To see this, at the old prices if Maxine saw 10 movies she had no money left over for books. Now, at the lower dollar price of movies Maxine can see 10 movies and still have money to buy 10 books.

As we change the price of movies, we observe how Maxine's optimal quantity of movies changes. This is how we trace out Maxine's demand curve for movies. Maxine is originally at point *e* from Figure 7.1 [22.1] of your text. She is consuming 4 movies and 18 books when the price is $3 for a movie and $1 for a book. At this point we have:

Marginal Utility of Movies / Price of Movies = 36/$3 = 12
Marginal Utility of Books / Price of Books = 12/$1 = 12

and the equimarginal rule is satisfied.

Would this be an optimal point if the price of movies fell to $2? No, because now the price of movies would fall and we would have:

Marginal Utility of Movies / Price of Movies = 36 / 2 = 18
Marginal Utility of Books / Price of Books = 12/$1 = 12

If Maxine spent one fewer dollar on books, she would lose 12 utils. If she spent that dollar on movies she would gain 18 utils, leaving a net gain of 6 utils. Maxine will want to buy more movies and fewer books as a result of the price change. Notice that she has substituted away from the good with the smaller ratio toward the good with the larger ratio.

Let's review an Application that answers one of the key questions we posed at the start of the chapter:

3. How do consumers respond to offsetting changes in taxes?

APPLICATION 3:
THE SUBSTITUTION EFFECT OF A GAS TAX DECREASES GAS CONSUMPTION

What would happen if the government increased taxes on gasoline, but cut income taxes in such a way that the average taxpayer paid the same amount in taxes after the changes as they paid before? This example is written so that after the tax adjustments the consumer could still buy the same amount of gasoline as before the tax adjustment. The question is, will the consumer buy the same amount of gasoline? The answer is no. If the consumer starts at an optimal point according to the equimarginal rule, the increase in the gas tax will effectively increase the price of gasoline. As a result the marginal utility per dollar for gasoline will become less than the marginal utility per dollar of other goods and the consumer will substitute away from gasoline, thus consuming less. This represents the substitution effect.

☞ This Application shows the usefulness of our two-good model. When we are concerned with changes that affect just a single good (such as gasoline), we can always use "all other goods" as the second good. Since we don't care how consumers change spending among other goods, only between gasoline and other goods, we can lump all other goods together. By setting the price of other goods to be $1 we eliminate needless complexity in the model and can analyze how price changes affect the good of interest.

7.4 [22.4] Consumer Puzzles—Free Goods and Branding

Let's review two Applications that answer key questions we posed at the start of the chapter:

4. How do consumers respond to free goods?

APPLICATION 4: THE BIG DIFFERENCE BETWEEN $0.20 AND FREE!

This Application points out that Amazon's U.S. offer of free shipping with orders over $25 led to a large increase in sales, while their French offer of low price (roughly twenty cents) shipping led to a much smaller increase in sales. It is a puzzle why consumers respond to "free" to a greater degree than a low, almost free, price.

5. How does product branding affect consumers' brain activity?

APPLICATION 5: NEUROSCIENCE AND THE COLA CHALLENGE

This Application illustrates that branding can affect consumer choice by impacting brain activity. When consumers knew they were drinking Coke and not Pepsi the portion of their brain involved in higher order functions was stimulated. This suggests that branding affects consumer preference through brain activity.

Activity

Ross enjoys two activities, downloading music and eating pizza. A music download costs $1 while a slice of pizza costs $2. Ross has $40 per week to spend on the two activities.

a. What is the price of pizza in terms of music downloads? What about the price of music downloads in terms of pizza?
b. Draw the budget line for Ross.
c. Ross is currently in equilibrium and is eating 15 slices of pizza and downloading 10 songs per week. The last song provided 5 utils of utility for Ross. What is the marginal utility of pizza for Ross?
d. Suppose the price of a download increases to $2. Show what happens to Ross' budget line.
e. If the price of a download increases to $2, will the marginal utility per dollar of pizza for Ross increase/decrease/stay the same? What about the marginal utility per dollar of music downloads for Ross? Will they increase/decrease/stay the same? The substitution effect will cause Ross to consume more _____ and fewer _____.
f. On your graph, illustrate whether Ross' purchasing power increases or decreases as a result of the increased price of music downloads.
g. Starting from the original prices and income levels, suppose that all prices and income double. Show that Ross will be no better off or worse off as a result.

Answers

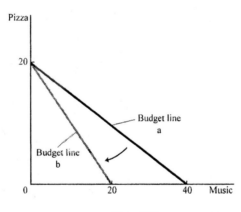

Figure 22.1

a. A slice of pizza costs 2 music downloads. A music download costs ½ of a slice of pizza.
b. The intercepts will be at 20 slices of pizza and 40 music downloads.
c. Since the MU/P ratio for music downloads is 5, the MU/P ratio for pizza must also be 5. Since the price of pizza is $2, the MU for the last slice of pizza must be 10.
d. The intercept for pizza is unchanged, the intercept for music downloads falls to 20.
e. Since the price of pizza is unchanged, the MU/P for pizza will stay the same at 5.
   Since the price of downloads has increased, the MU/P for downloads will decrease to 2.5. Ross will consume more pizza and fewer downloads.
f. Ross' purchasing power falls, there are fewer combinations of pizza and music downloads in his consumption set.
g. Ross' budget line is unchanged and so the combinations of downloads and pizza that he can buy are unchanged.

Key Terms

Budget line: The line connecting all the combinations of two goods that exhaust a consumer's budget.

Budget set: A set of points that includes all the combinations of two goods that a consumer can afford, given the consumer's income and the prices of the goods.

Equimarginal rule: Pick the combination of two activities where the marginal benefit per dollar for the first activity equals the marginal benefit per dollar for the second activity.

Income effect: The change in quantity consumed that is caused by a change in real income, with relative prices held constant.

Law of diminishing marginal utility: As the consumption of a particular good increases, marginal utility decreases.

Marginal utility: The change in total utility from one additional unit of a good.

Substitution effect: The change in quantity consumed that is caused by a change in the relative price of the good, with real income held constant.

Util: One unit of utility.

Utility: The satisfaction experienced from consuming a good.

Appendix: Consumer Choice with Indifference Curves

Appendix Overview

In this chapter, we introduce the theory of consumer choice and show the logic behind the downward sloping demand curve. We assume that:

- The theory of consumer choice has two steps: first, identify the affordable combinations of goods. Second, pick the affordable combination that maximizes utility.
- To maximize utility, the consumer finds the bundle of goods at which an indifference curve is tangent to the budget line.
- At the utility-maximizing combination of two goods, the marginal rate of substitution (the consumer's own trade-off between the two goods) equals the price ratio (the market trade-off).
- The individual demand curve is negatively sloped, reflecting the substitution effect and income effect of a change in price. A decrease in price decreases the relative price of the good, and consumers substitute the good for other goods (the substitution effect). A decrease in price also increases the consumer's real income, increasing the consumption of all normal goods (the income effect).

Applying the Concepts

After reading this appendix, you should be able to answer these four key questions:
1. To determine whether a consumer is making the best choice, what single question can you ask?
2. Why do consumers dislike the bundling of goods?
3. How do consumers respond to free goods?
4. How do consumers respond to offsetting changes in taxes?

In this appendix, we assume that:
- Consumers receive satisfaction from consumption.
- Consumption bundles which provide equal satisfaction can be shown using indifference curves.
- Consumers face a limited choice set based on their income and prices.
- Consumers choose consumption which maximizes their satisfaction given the constraint they face.

7A.1 [22A.1] Consumer Constraints and Preferences

A consumer wants to maximize her satisfaction (make herself as well off as possible) subject to the limits of her income. To do this, our consumer:
- figures out her menu of options, what she can afford, then
- chooses the option that provides her highest level of satisfaction.

A consumer's **budget line** shows all the combinations of two goods that exhaust a consumer's budget. The **budget set** is defined as the set of affordable combinations of two goods. Graphically, the budget set is the area under the budget line. The budget line shows the rate at which our consumer can trade one good for another in the market. The slope of the budget line is the trade-off between the goods and is equal to the price ratio. The **price ratio** is calculated as the price of the good on the horizontal axis divided by the price of the good on the vertical axis.

To graph the budget line (see Figure 7A.1 [22A.1]):
- Draw a graph with one of the two goods on the horizontal axis, the other on the vertical axis. In the graph, movies are on the horizontal axis and books are on the vertical axis.
- Find the intercepts by dividing the consumer's income by the price of the good on that axis. This tells you the amount of that good the consumer could purchase if she spent all her income on that good. So, when Maxine has $30 in income and movies cost $3 each, she can buy $30/$3 = 10 movies if she spent all her income on movies. Since books cost $1 each, Maxine could buy $30/$1 = 30 books if she spent all her income on books. You can see these as points *a* and *k* in Figure 7A.1 [22A.1].
- Draw the budget line as the line connecting the two intercept points.

Consumers have preferences between combinations of goods. An **indifference curve** shows the different combinations of two goods which provide the same level of utility or satisfaction to the consumer. **Utility** is the satisfaction experienced from consuming a good.

An indifference curve separates combinations of goods into three categories:
1. *Superior combinations.* These are preferred to any combination of goods on the indifference curve. An example would be point *j* in Figure 7A.2 [22A.2].
2. *Inferior combinations.* These are combinations that are viewed by the consumer as worse than those on the indifference curve. An example would be point *k* in figure 7A.2 [22A.2].
3. *Equivalent combinations.* These are combinations of goods which leave the consumer just as well off as their current choice. Any point on the indifference curve would be an equivalent combination.

In the figure, the consumer would be indifferent between points *b*, *i*, *m*, or *n*. The consumer would prefer point *j* to any of these points and would prefer any of the points *b*, *i*, *m*, or *n* to point *k*.

ᘓᘓ Study Tip

A consumer is indifferent between two combinations of goods if they would be willing to let someone else choose between the two combinations for them.

The slope of the indifference curve is called the **marginal rate of substitution** and is the rate at which a consumer is willing to trade or substitute one good for another without changing the level of satisfaction.

Each possible consumption point lies on an indifference curve. Figure 7A.3 [22A.3] in the text shows an **indifference curve map**, a set of indifference curves, each with a different utility level. As we move toward the upper right corner of the map, we move to higher levels of utility.

7A.2 [22A.2] Maximizing Utility

The consumer wants to reach the highest possible level of utility, or the highest possible indifference curve, subject to the budget constraint. This occurs at point e in Figure 7A.4 of the text, the point where the indifference curve is tangent to the budget constraint. At this point the slope of the budget constraint is equal to the slope of the indifference curve. Notice that point e is the only point on this indifference curve that the consumer can afford.

📄 Remember

The slope of the budget constraint tells us the rate at which the consumer is able to trade one good for another in the market. The slope of the indifference curve tells us the rate at which the consumer is willing to trade one good for another. Where they are equal the rate at which the consumer is willing to trade one good for another equals the rate at which she can trade one good for another.

You can see why other points in Figure 7A.4 [22A.4] would not be the optimal point:

- At point i our consumer is not spending all her income. She can purchase more books, more movies, or more of both before she reaches her budget line.
- From point b the indifference curve tells us how many movies the consumer would need to receive to stay just as well off as she is if she were to give up some books. So she would be willing to trade 9 books for one movie along her indifference curve. In the market she is actually able to trade 9 books for three movies. As a result, she will be better off after this trade and would choose to give up the books for movies.
- Point w lies outside Maxine's budget set and thus she cannot afford this combination of books and movies.

The **utility-maximizing rule** is to pick the combination of goods which sets:

$$\text{Marginal Rate of Substitution} = \frac{\text{price of good on horizontal axis}}{\text{price of good on vertical axis}}$$

Let's review three Applications that answer key questions we posed at the start of the appendix:

1. To determine whether a consumer is making the best choice, what single question can you ask?

APPLICATION 1: WHAT'S YOUR *MRS*?

To find the best combination of goods, we simply need to find the point where the price ratio is equal to the marginal rate of substitution. In this Application, we know that one cup of punch costs two cookies given the dollar prices of each. We also assume that all employees have identical tastes for cookies and punch. We can find the optimal combination by asking employees, "How many cookies would you give up to get another cup of punch?" If the answer is two, you have the right combination. If employees are willing to give up more than two cookies for another cup of punch, you have too many cookies. If employees are willing to give up less than two cookies for another cup of punch, you have too few cookies.

2. Why do consumers dislike the bundling of goods?

APPLICATION 2: ONLINE MUSIC AND PIRACY
This Application shows how bundling limits consumer choice. We assume that each song Sam purchases costs $1, and initially Sam is limited to buying CDs, each containing 15 songs, at a price of $15 each. In this situation Sam's available choices are points *a*, *c*, and *d* in Figure 7A.5 [22A.5]. If instead Sam could buy individual songs, he has more options. Now, if he chooses, he could buy only 10 songs, an option that a CD doesn't allow, and use the rest of his money on arcade games. You notice that point *b* is tangent to Sam's budget constraint and represents his highest possible utility. You also notice that at point *c* the indifference curve is not tangent to the budget line and thus can't be a maximizing point. Allowing Sam to buy songs one at a time increases his budget set and makes Sam better off. In the diagram point *b* is Sam's optimal choice, but this choice in only available if he can buy songs one at a time.

3. How do consumers respond to free goods?

APPLICATION 3: THE BIG DIFFERENCE BETWEEN $0.20 AND FREE!
This Application points out that Amazon's U.S. offer of free shipping with orders over $25 led to a large increase in sales, while their French offer of low price (roughly twenty cents) shipping led to a much smaller increase in sales. It is a puzzle why consumers respond to "free" to a greater degree than a low, almost free, price.

7A.3 [22A.3] Drawing the Individual Demand Curve

Consider what happens to the consumption of a good when its price changes. In Figure 7A.6 [22A.6] in the text we show two budget lines, one when the price of movies is $2 and the other when the price of movies is $3. The number of movies consumed falls from 7 to 4 as the price of movies increases.

When the price of movies changes, two things occur:
*   Substitution effect. This measures the change in quantity consumed caused by a change in the relative price of the good, with real income held constant.
*   Income effect. The change in quantity consumed that is caused by a change in real income, with relative prices held constant.

We find the substitution effect by keeping the consumer on the same indifference curve and finding how consumption of the two goods would change as relative prices change. This is the movement from point *s* to point *e* in Figure 7A.8 [22A.8]. We find the income effect by starting at point *e* and asking how the change in purchasing power affects consumption. This is the movement from point *s* to point *t* in Figure 7A.8 [22A.8].

💣 Caution!

Figure 7A.8 [22A.8] shows the substitution and income effects. The intuition of the substitution effect is to ask, "if we keep the consumer on the same indifference curve, would they consume the same bundle of goods?" Many students have trouble with this concept. Keep in mind that this is only a thought exercise to find the substitution effect and the entire impact of the price change includes both the substitution and income effects.

Let's review an Application that answers one of the key questions we posed at the start of the appendix:

4. How do consumers respond to offsetting changes in taxes?

APPLICATION 4:
THE SUBSTITUTION EFFECT OF A GAS TAX DECREASES GAS CONSUMPTION
This Application illustrates an increase in the gasoline tax offset by a reduction in income taxes. Originally the consumer was at point *a* in Figure 7A.9 [22A.9]. When the price of gasoline increases, the slope of the budget line changes, however, the reduction in income taxes allows the consumer to still afford point *a*. The question is, will this still be the point chosen by consumers? You can see in the diagram that the answer is no. The consumer will substitute away from the now more expensive gasoline and will consume at point *b* which lies on a more preferred indifference curve.

Activity

Ross enjoys two activities, downloading music and eating pizza. A music download costs $1 while a slice of pizza costs $2. Ross has $40 per week to spend on the two activities.

a. What is the price of pizza in terms of music downloads? What about the price of music downloads in terms of pizza?
b. Draw the budget line for Ross.
c. Ross is currently at an equilibrium point and is eating 15 slices of pizza and downloading 10 songs per week. Draw an indifference curve which shows this equilibrium point.
d. Suppose the price of pizza decreases to $1. Show what happens to Ross' budget line.
e. Suppose we require Ross to consume on the same indifference curve as his initial point, his consumption of pizza would increase/decrease/stay the same and his consumption of downloads would increase/decrease/stay the same.
f. On your graph, illustrate whether Ross' purchasing power increases or decreases. This will cause Ross to consume more/less/the same amount of pizza and more/less/the same amount of downloads starting from your answer in part e.
g. Starting from the original prices and income levels, suppose that all prices and income double. How can you show that Ross will be no better off or worse off as a result?

Answers

Use this graph as you work through the answers:

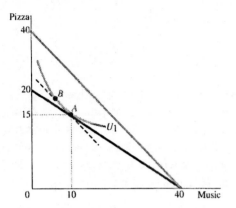

a. A slice of pizza costs 2 music downloads. A music download costs ½ of a slice of pizza.
b. The intercepts will be at 20 slices of pizza and 40 music downloads as shown above.
c. Since the MU/P ratio for music downloads is 5, the MU/P ratio for pizza must also be 5. Since the price of pizza is $2, the MU for the last slice of pizza must be 10.
d. The intercept for downloads is unchanged, the intercept for music downloads increases to 40, as shown above.
e. Since pizza now costs only one download, Ross will increase his consumption of pizza and decrease his consumption of downloads on the same indifference curve. This is a movement from A to B on indifference curve U_1.
f. Ross' purchasing power increases. This will lead him to consume more pizza and more downloads from the point in e.
g. Ross' budget line is unchanged and so the combinations of downloads and pizza that he can buy are unchanged.

Key Terms

Budget line: The line connecting all the combinations of two goods that exhaust a consumer's budget.

Budget set: A set of points that includes all the combinations of two goods that a consumer can afford, given the consumer's income and the prices of the goods.

Income effect: The change in quantity consumed that is caused by a change in real income, with relative prices held constant.

Indifference curve: A curve showing the different combinations of two goods that generate the same level of utility or satisfaction.

Indifference curve map: A set of indifference curves, each with a different utility level.

Marginal rate of substitution (*MRS*): The rate at which a consumer is willing to trade or substitute one good for another.

Price ratio: The price of the good on the horizontal axis divided by the price of the good on the vertical axis.

Substitution effect: The change in quantity consumed that is caused by a change in the relative price of the good, with real income held constant.

Utility: The satisfaction experienced from consuming a good.

Utility maximizing rule: Pick the combination that makes marginal rate of substitution equal to the price ratio.

Practice Quiz

(Answers are provided at the end of the Practice Quiz.)

1. According to the law of diminishing marginal utility, as the consumption of a particular good increases:
   a. total utility increases at a faster rate.
   b. marginal utility increases.
   c. total utility decreases at a slower rate.
   d. marginal utility decreases.

2. Refer to the figure below. The figure shows the total utility derived from consuming specific quantities of burgers. This graph of total utility is also related to specific values of marginal utility, as follows: Marginal utility is:

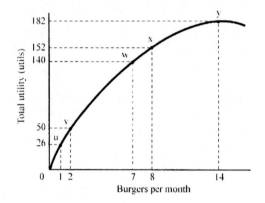

   a. greater at points *u* and *v* than at points *w* and *x*.
   b. greater at points *w* and *x* than at points *u* and *v*.
   c. the same at points *u* and *v* than at points *w* and *x*.
   d. greatest at point *y*.

3. Refer to the graph below. Along this budget line, what do points *j, e,* and *x* have in common?

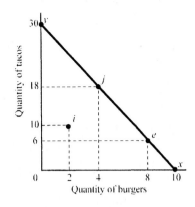

    a. At all three points total utility is maximized.
    b. At all three points the price of burgers is the same as the price of tacos.
    c. All three combinations can be obtained with the same amount of income.
    d. All of the above.

4. What is a budget set?
    a. A line that shows all the combinations of two goods that exhaust the consumer's budget.
    b. The set of utility values associated with a particular budget constraint.
    c. The set of affordable combinations of two goods.
    d. The set of combinations that lie outside of the budget line.

5. Refer to the graph below. The budget line will shift from AB to AE if:

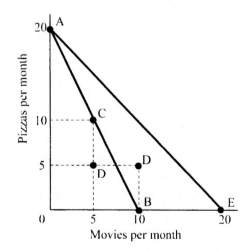

    a. income increases.
    b. the price of movies decreases.
    c. the price of pizza increases.
    d. the preference for movies increases.

6. A devoted student of economics spends all of her income on pencils and pads of graph paper. She buys 10 pads and 50 pencils. The price of a pad is $2; the price of a pencil is $0.50. The marginal utility of the tenth pad is 100; the marginal utility of the fiftieth pencil is 400. Has she maximized utility (or should she study more to find out how to do it)?
    a. She should buy more pencils and more pads.
    b. She should buy more pads and fewer pencils.
    c. She should buy more pencils and fewer pads.
    d. She should buy fewer pencils and fewer pads.

7. A consumer maximizes total utility when:
    a. choosing more of one good and less of another increases utility.
    b. choosing more of one good and less of another no longer increases utility.
    c. marginal utility is maximized.
    d. marginal utility per dollar spent on each good is highest.

8. This question tests your understanding of Application 1 in this chapter: New Zealand's tax on light spirits. How does a tax on one good affect the demand for substitute goods?

    The government imposed a special tax on light spirits (those with alcoholic content between 14 and 24%), nearly doubling the price of teens' favorite beverages, from $8 to $14. How did teenagers in New Zealand respond to the special tax on their favorite alcoholic beverage?
    a. Teens significantly reduced drinking because of the tax.
    b. The tax increased the bang per buck of light spirits.
    c. Producers responded by increasing the alcohol content and offered more potent beverages below the prices of the original light beverages to avoid the tax.
    d. As predicted by the equimarginal rule, the tax caused many teens to reduce their consumption of these beverages, often switching to other super light beverages or high alcohol content beverages.

9. Fill in the blanks. The change in the quantity demanded of a good that results from _____, holding all other factors (including real income) constant, is known as the *substitution effect*.
    a. the effect of a change in price on consumer purchasing power
    b. a change in price making the good more or less expensive relative to other goods
    c. an increase in the usefulness of a product as the number of consumers who use it increases
    d. the tendency of people to be unwilling to sell something they own

10. The move from one point to another along a consumer's demand curve is the result of:
    a. diminishing marginal utility and constant prices.
    b. changes in a determinant of demand, other than the price of the good in question.
    c. combining the substitution and income effects.
    d. permanent deviations from the equimarginal rule.

11. This question tests your understanding of Application 3 in this chapter: The substitution effect of a gas tax decreases gas consumption. How do consumers respond to offsetting changes in taxes? According to the substitution effect, when the government combines a gas tax with an income tax, so that consumers still have the same amount of money to spend on other goods, which of the following happens?
   a. Real income decreases.
   b. After the even exchange of gas taxes for income-tax cuts, the consumer is likely to choose the same consumption bundle as before.
   c. Despite the even exchange of gas taxes for income-tax cuts, the consumer is likely to cut back on gasoline spending and spend more on other goods.
   d. Gas consumption will actually increase as the relative price of gasoline increases.

12. (APPX) The rate at which a consumer is willing to substitute one good for another is called:
   a. an indifference curve.
   b. the marginal rate of substitution.
   c. the marginal rate of transformation.
   d. the total utility function.

13. (APPX) Refer to the figure below. In the theory of consumer behavior, which point is preferred to the others?

   a. Point *h* is preferred to points f,e and g.
   b. Points *f* and *e*, along the indifference curve, are preferred to points outside, such as *h* and *g*.
   c. Point *g* is preferred to points f,e and h.
   d. All these points are equally preferred.

14. (APPX) This question tests your understanding of Application 1 in the appendix to this chapter: What's your *MRS*? What is the marginal rate of substitution?
   a. The value of the slope of the consumer's budget line.
   b. The value of the slope of the consumer's indifference curve.
   c. The point at which the equimarginal principle holds.
   d. The ratio of prices that yields maximum marginal utility.

15. (APPX) Refer to the figure below. What happens if the price of good X increases, all else the same?

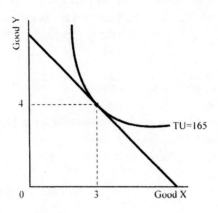

a. The indifference curve shifts to the left.
b. The indifference curve shifts to the right.
c. The budget line shifts inward along the horizontal axis, while the value of the Y-intercept remains the same.
d. The budget line shifts inward along the vertical axis, while the value of the X-intercept remains the same.

16. (APPX) Refer to the figure below. Which points on the graph are points of consumer equilibrium?

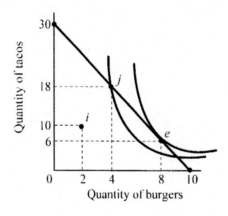

a. Points e and j.
b. Point i only.
c. Point e only.
d. Point j only.

17. (APPX) Refer to the figure below. Given the existing budget line, the consumer maximizes utility:

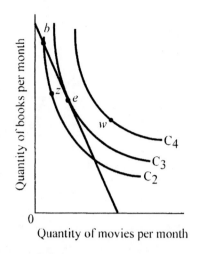

a. at point b.
b. at point z.
c. at point e.
d. at point w.

18. (APPX) Refer to the figure below. Which graph is more closely associated with the derivation of two or more points on the individual's demand curve for movies?

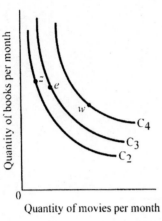
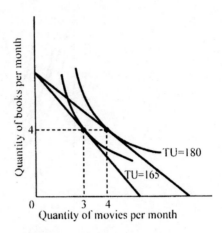
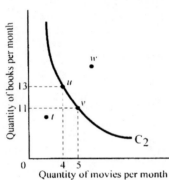
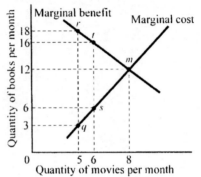

    a. The graph on the top left.
    b. The graph on the top right.
    c. The graph on the bottom left.
    d. The graph on the bottom right.

19. (APPX) This question tests your understanding of Application 4 in the appendix to this chapter: How do consumers respond to offsetting changes in taxes?

    The reason why an increase in the gas tax and a decrease in the income tax will lower gas consumption is:
    a. As income and prices rise, the budget line stays in place.
    b. There is no way to give consumers enough additional income to enable them to purchase the same amount of gasoline as before.
    c. The higher price of gasoline makes gasoline relatively more expensive and leads to a smaller quantity purchased.
    d. The increased income leads consumers to purchase less gasoline.

20. Explain the relationship between total utility and marginal utility based on the concept of diminishing marginal utility.

21. (APPX) How are the concepts of the budget line and the indifference curve combined to explain consumer equilibrium?

22. (APPX) Assume that good X is the good on the horizontal axis and good Y is the good on the vertical axis. Using your knowledge of indifference curves, explain how goods X and Y are related when an indifference curve is relatively steep versus when the indifference curve is relatively flat. In each case, which good is preferred to the other?

Answers to the Practice Quiz

1. d. Total utility is the total satisfaction derived from consuming a given number of units of a good, while marginal utility is the additional utility derived from consuming an additional unit of a good. As the quantity of a good consumed increases, total utility increases at a decreasing rate because marginal utility decreases.

2. a. As total utility increases, marginal utility decreases.

3. c. The consumer exhausts his or her entire budget when he or she obtains any one of these combinations.

4. c. A consumer's budget set is the set of affordable combinations of two goods. The budget set includes the budget line—combinations that exhaust the budget—as well as combinations that cost less than the consumer has to spend, leaving the consumer with leftover money.

5. b. As the price of movies decreases, the consumer can afford more movies with the same income as before.

6. c. Consider the utility-maximization marginal condition. Consumers maximize utility when the marginal utility of each good divided by its price is equal for all goods. (100/2), the marginal utility per dollar spent on the last pad, is less than (400/.50), the marginal utility per dollar spent on the last pencil. Thus more pencils should be bought, which requires buying fewer pads, since she is spending all her income.

7. b. When a consumer maximizes utility, the marginal utility of the last dollar spent on each good is the same.

8. d. That's exactly what happened. Consumers responded as expected to changes in taxes and prices. The tax decreased the bang per buck of light spirits and teens responded by cutting back on light spirits. In addition, some teens went the other direction, switching to beverages that were too potent to be subject to the light-spirits tax.

9. b. The substitution effect is the change in quantity consumed that is caused by a change in the relative price of the good, with real income held constant.

10. c. The net effect of a price change on quantity demanded equals the substitution effect *plus* the income effect.

11. c. Using the equimarginal rule we conclude that, when the price of gasoline increases, the bang per buck of gasoline is now lower than the bang per buck for the other good, so the citizen will cut back on gasoline and spend more on the other good. Therefore, when a gas tax is combined with an offsetting cut in income taxes, the quantity of gasoline consumed will decrease because of the substitution effect.

12. b. The marginal rate of substitution is the slope of the indifference curve, or the rate at which a consumer is willing to substitute one good for another, such that total utility remains the same.

13. a. Point *h* yields the highest total utility.

14. b. At any point along the indifference curve, the slope equals the marginal rate of substitution, or the ratio of marginal utilities associated with a particular combination of the two goods consumed.

15. c. As the price of good X increases, the maximum amount that the consumer can buy of good X decreases.

16. c. At point e, the indifference curve is tangent to the budget line, and the marginal utility of the last dollar spent on each good is the same.

17. c. The consumer maximizes utility at the tangency of an indifference curve and a budget line (point e).

18. b. The individual demand for movies shows the quantity of movies demanded at each price level. To derive the individual's demand curve for movies, we change the price of movies and look at what happens to consumer equilibrium. The effects of the price change take us to a new budget line and indifference curve, where the quantity of movies demanded has changed as a result of the price change.

19. c. Notice in Figure 7A.9 that even though the new budget line passes through the original consumption point (point a) the increase in the relative price of gasoline leads the consumer to reduce their consumption so that the budget line is tangent to the indifference curve.

20. Total utility is the amount of satisfaction (measured in utils) obtained from the consumption of a total number of units of a given good. Marginal utility is the additional satisfaction obtained from the consumption of an additional unit of a good. The law of diminishing marginal utility states that as the consumption of a particular good increases, marginal utility decreases. In other words, as consumption increases, total utility derived from all units of a good consumed increases, but by less and less each time. This means that an increase in consumption increases total utility but decreases marginal utility. And vice versa, a decrease in consumption decreases total utility and increases marginal utility.

21. A budget line shows the combinations of two goods that a consumer can afford, given his or her income, and the prices of the two goods. The slope of the budget line is equal to the ratio of the prices. An indifference curve shows the combinations of two goods that yield the same level of total utility. The slope of the indifference curve is called the marginal rate of substitution, or the ratio of marginal utilities. Consumer equilibrium is found where the slope of the budget line is tangent to the slope of an indifference curve. At that point, the utility-maximizing rule takes effect, that is, the marginal utility of the last dollar spent on each good is the same.

22. Indifference curves are downward sloping. Along a relatively steep indifference curve, a small increase in the quantity of X requires a large decrease in the quantity of Y. If a consumer is willing to give up a lot of Y in order to obtain a little of X, such that utility remains constant, then X must be preferred to Y. Along a flat indifference curve, a large increase in X requires only a small decrease in Y. This means that in order to take away some of Y, the consumer must be compensated by a large increase in X, so that total utility remains the same. Y must be preferred to X.

8 [23]
Production Technology and Cost

Chapter Summary

In this chapter, we explore the cost side of a firm and explain the shapes of the firm's short-run and long-run cost curves. Here are the main points of the chapter:

- The negatively sloped portion of the short-run marginal-cost curve (*MC*) results from input specialization that causes increasing marginal returns.
- The positively sloped portion of the short-run marginal-cost curve (*MC*) results from diminishing returns.
- The short-run average-total-cost curve (*ATC*) is U-shaped because of the conflicting effects of (a) fixed costs being spread over a larger quantity of output and (b) diminishing returns.
- The long-run average-cost curve (*LAC*) is horizontal over some range of output because replication is an option, so doubling output will no more than double long-run total cost.
- The long-run average-cost curve (*LAC*) is negatively sloped for small quantities of output because (a) there are indivisible inputs that cannot be scaled down and (b) a smaller operation has limited opportunities for labor specialization.
- Diseconomies of scale arise if there are problems in coordinating a large operation or higher input costs in a larger operation.

Applying the Concepts

After reading this chapter, you should be able to answer these five key questions:
1. What are the cost components for electronic products?
2. How do indivisible inputs affect production costs?
3. What are the sources of scale economies in production?
4. What is the cost structure for information goods?
5. How does technological innovation affect production cost?

8.1 [23.1] Economic Cost and Economic Profit

Principle of Opportunity Cost

The opportunity cost of something is what you sacrifice to get it.

The objective of the firm is to maximize its **economic profit**, the difference between total revenue and economic cost. **Economic cost** is the opportunity cost of the inputs used in the production process; equal to explicit costs plus implicit costs. **Explicit cost** is the actual monetary payment for inputs. **Implicit cost** is the opportunity cost of inputs that do not require a monetary payment.

Economic cost and profit are different than accounting cost and profit. The accounting cost measures the explicit costs of production. The accounting profit is found as total revenue minus accounting cost.

☞ You can think about explicit costs as those costs for which you write a check to somebody. Implicit costs are typically foregone opportunities to receive money.

📄 Remember

The difference between economic profit and accounting profit is implicit cost.

☞ To see the difference between economic and accounting profit, consider the following example. Brian owns 1,500 feet of store space and has $20,000 in the bank. He decides to open a business using the space he owns and uses his own $20,000 as start-up capital. Tom rents 1,500 square feet of store space next to Brian for $2,000 per month and borrowed $20,000 at 10% interest for start-up capital. Over the course of a year an accountant would record $26,000 more in costs for Tom than Brian. Why? Each month Tom writes a check for $2,000 for rent, and each year he writes a check for $2,000 in interest expense. Brian doesn't write a check for his store space, and he didn't borrow money.

You should see though that Brian and Tom face the same economic costs. For Brian the costs of store space and capital are opportunity costs, not explicit costs. By choosing to use his store space he has given up the opportunity to rent that space to someone else. This opportunity is worth $2,000 per month as that is what Tom is paying for space next to Brian. By using his own money for capital he has given up the opportunity to earn interest on that money. If we assume he could have loaned the money at 10%, he has given up $2,000 in interest per year.

Even though both will make the same economic profits, Brian will always make $26,000 per year more in accounting profits than Tom.

8.2 [23.2] A Firm with a Fixed Production Facility: Short-Run Costs

In the short run, we assume that a firm is producing output with at least one fixed input. A fixed input is one that does not change as the level of production changes; it might be factory size, or the level of capital. If you own a pizza shop and have only one oven, that is your fixed input.

The table in Figure 8.1 [23.1] of the text shows the relationship between labor inputs used and total output produced. The third column shows the **marginal product of labor**, the change in output from one additional unit of labor. While marginal product increases early in the production process, at some point the production function begins to exhibit diminishing returns. **Diminishing returns** means that as one input increases while other inputs are held fixed, output increases at a decreasing rate. The total product curve shown in Figure 8.1 [23.1] is the graphical representation of the production function. The **total-product curve** shows the relationship between the quantity of labor and the quantity of output produced, *ceteris paribus*.

Recall from Chapter 2 that one of our key principles was the principle of diminishing returns:

Principle of Diminishing Returns
Suppose that output is produced with two or more inputs and we increase one input while holding the other inputs fixed. Beyond some point—called the point of diminishing returns—output will increase at a decreasing rate.

✍ Study Tip

All output measures, such as total product, marginal product, and average product, are functions of input variables, such as labor and capital.

We define costs in the short run as one of two types:
- **Fixed costs** are costs which do not vary with the level of output. These are costs that you pay whether you produce or not. Rent on factory space would be a fixed cost. The reason? You pay a fixed amount per month regardless of how much you produce.
- **Variable costs** are costs which vary with the quantity produced. Materials costs would be an example; the more you produce, the more raw materials you need.

Short-run total cost is the sum of fixed cost and variable cost.

✍ Study Tip

Since fixed costs do not change in the short run, they are ignored in most short-run decisions.

☞ Think about starting a coffee shop. Which costs would be fixed? Clearly the rent on your location would be a fixed cost. The cost of capital (coffee machines, display cases, interest on loans) would be a fixed cost. Regardless of whether you ever sell a cup of coffee, you need to pay rent and have coffee machines and display cases if you are going to open a coffee shop. What about the cost of coffee beans, pastries, and workers? These are examples of variable costs. As you sell more coffee, you will need to purchase larger amounts of coffee beans and cups. The busier your coffee shop, the more workers you will be interested in hiring.

🔗 Study Tip

Cost measures such as total cost, marginal cost, and average costs, are functions of quantity produced.

When we divide our output measures by quantity, we create average cost measures:

Average fixed cost = Fixed cost / quantity

Average variable cost = Variable cost / quantity

Average total cost = Total cost / quantity

In addition, since total cost is the sum of fixed and variable costs,

Average total cost = average fixed cost + average variable cost

Short-run marginal cost is defined as the change in short-run total cost resulting from a one-unit increase in output.

📄 Remember

Marginal cost is the cost measure used by a firm to determine the quantity of output to produce. We will make extensive use of marginal cost in the rest of the course. In many ways, it is the most important cost concept from this chapter.

Figure 8.3 [23.3] shows the relationship between average cost and marginal cost. You notice that when marginal cost is below average cost, average cost is falling. When marginal cost is above average cost, average cost is rising. The marginal cost gives us the cost of producing one more unit. The average cost gives us the average of all the previously produced units. If the next unit costs more to produce than the average of the previous units, the average will increase. If the next unit costs less than the average of the previous units, the average will fall. The text in Table 8.3 [23.3] has a very nice example of this principle using grade point averages.

8.3 [23.3] Production and Cost in the Long Run

The long run is defined as the period of time over which a firm is perfectly flexible in its choice of all inputs. In other words there are no fixed inputs, or fixed costs, in the long run. Another key difference between the short run and the long run is that there are no diminishing returns in the long run. Remember, diminishing returns require a fixed quantity of some input, and in the long run, the level of all inputs is variable.

The **long-run total cost** of production is the total cost of production when a firm is perfectly flexible in choosing its inputs. The **long-run average cost** is the long-run total cost divided by the quantity of output. When long-run average cost is constant over increasing ranges of output, we have constant returns to scale in production. **Constant returns to scale** is the situation in which the long-run total cost increases proportionately with output, so average cost is constant. The **long-run marginal cost** is the change in long-run cost resulting from a one-unit increase in output.

When production uses an indivisible input, costs do not change proportionately with output. An **indivisible input** is one that cannot be scaled down to produce a smaller quantity of output. The text gives several examples:

- A railroad company must lay a complete set of tracks to transport any goods by rail.
- A hospital must buy a CT scanner or MRI machine if it wishes to do any diagnostic scans. The hospital can't buy half a scanner if it anticipates a small number of scans.
- To make pizza, a pizzeria must have a pizza oven.

Economies of scale describes a situation in which the long-run average cost of production decreases as output increases. The **minimum efficient scale** is the output at which scale economies are exhausted. **Diseconomies of scale** describe a situation in which the long-run average cost of production increases as output increases.

Figure 8.6 [23.6] shows examples of actual long-run cost curves for aluminum production, truck freight, and hospital services. You notice that all of these are downward sloping over early ranges and become flat as output continues to increase. Long-run average costs become flat because firms are not subject to diminishing returns in the long run as they are able to vary the amounts of all input. In some cases firms may experience decreasing returns to scale as output increases which will cause the long-run average cost curve to have an upward-sloping segment.

💣 Caution!

The difference between the short run and the long run is not calendar time! The difference is the existence of a fixed input. A large manufacturing facility may have a short run that is years long, while a small landscaping company may be able to vary the level of all of its inputs in a matter of weeks.

8.4 [23.4] Applications of Production Cost

Let's review five Applications that answer key questions we posed at the start of the chapter:

1. What are the cost components for electronic products?

APPLICATION 1: THE PRODUCTION COST OF AN iPOD TOUCH
Table 8.4 [23.4] in the text shows the cost components for an iPod nano. Because of the quantity of inputs purchased by Apple, they are able to pay $40 for flash memory which would cost other companies much more. This is an illustration of economies of scale, at higher output levels, the cost per unit falls. In this case it is true because input prices fall at high output levels.

2. How do indivisible inputs affect production costs?

APPLICATION 2:
INDIVISIBLE INPUTS AND THE COST OF FAKE KILLER WHALES
This Application considers how an indivisible input affects the average cost of production. To prevent sea lions from eating certain fish species, Rick Funk has offered to build a fake killer whale to scare off the sea lions. In order to produce the fake killer whale, a mold must be created at a cost of $11,000. This is an indivisible cost. Additional fake killer whales would cost only $5,000 each as the existing mold could be reused.

☞ There are many situations where the first unit of a good has a very high cost due to indivisible costs. If you have ever ordered T-shirts for a campus group you were likely charged a "set-up" fee to cover the costs of designing the T-shirt in addition to charges for materials and labor. Most stores charge the set-up fee only once and so the next time you order that same T-shirt you would pay only the actual material and labor cost for the T-shirt.

💣 Caution!

Indivisible costs place a wedge between average cost and marginal cost. Economic decision making is based on marginal cost. Failing to recognize the presence of indivisible costs can lead to poor decision making.

---

3. What are the sources of scale economies in production?

APPLICATION 3: SCALE ECONOMIES IN WIND POWER
This Application illustrates one source of scale economies. Installing a large turbine windmill is proportionately less expensive than installing a smaller turbine windmill. (This means that doubling the capacity of the turbine does not double the purchase and installation cost.) Table 8.5 [23.5] in the text shows that a large turbine can generate 4 times the energy as a smaller turbine at less than 4 times the cost. As a result the long-run average cost curve would be downward sloping from an output level of 5 million kilowatt hours to an output level of 20 million kilowatt hours.

4. What is the cost structure for information goods?

APPLICATION 4: THE AVERAGE COST OF A MUSIC VIDEO
A music video typically has a high first-copy cost, but additional copies are very inexpensive. This is because to produce the first copy we must pay a director ($28,000), a producer ($10,000), filming ($81,000) and editing ($81,000). These costs however are only paid once and any additional copies of the video can be produced at very low cost. As a result, the average cost of producing the video continues to fall as output increases.

5. How does technological innovation affect production cost?

APPLICATION 5: THE FALLING COST OF SOLAR POWER
This application highlights how technology has reduced the cost of solar energy. In particular this application focuses on how improved technology has reduced the capital cost of solar cells from about $20 per watt of electricity generated in 1980 to less than $5 in 2007.

Activity

A firm in the short run faces labor costs of $50 per unit of labor, which is the only variable cost, and has fixed costs of $100. Given this information and the relationship between labor and output, fill in the following table. The table contains columns for average product (*AP*), marginal product (*MP*), variable cost (*VC*), total cost (*TC*), marginal cost (*MC*), average cost (*AC*), average variable cost (*AVC*), and average fixed cost (*AFC*). Note: there will be some rounding error and averages do not exist for 0 units of output since one cannot divide by zero.

Labor	Output	AP	MP	VC	TC	MC	AC	AVC	AFC
0	0								
1	5								
2	14								
3	27								
4	40								
5	50								
6	54								
7	56								

Answer

Labor	Output	AP	MP	VC	TC	MC	AC	AVC	AFC
0	0			0	100				
1	5	5	5	50	150	10	30	10	20
2	14	7	9	100	200	5.55	14.29	7.14	7.14
3	27	9	13	150	250	3.85	9.26	5.55	3.70
4	40	10	13	200	300	3.85	7.50	5	2.5
5	50	10	10	250	350	5	7	5	2
6	54	9	4	300	400	12.5	7.41	5.55	1.85
7	56	8	2	350	450	25	8.04	6.25	1.79

Key Terms

Accounting cost: The explicit costs of production.

Accounting profit: Total revenue minus accounting cost.

Average fixed cost: Fixed cost divided by the quantity produced.

Average variable cost: Variable cost divided by the quantity produced.

Constant returns to scale: A situation in which the long-run total cost increases proportionately with output, so average cost is constant.

Diminishing returns: As one input increases while the other inputs are held fixed, output increases at a decreasing rate.

Diseconomies of scale: A situation in which the long-run average cost of production increases as output increases.

Economic cost: The opportunity cost of the inputs used in the production process; equal to explicit cost plus implicit cost.

Economic profit: Total revenue minus economic cost.

Economies of scale: A situation in which the long-run average cost of production decreases as output increases.

Explicit cost: The actual monetary payment for inputs.

Fixed cost: Cost that does not vary with the quantity produced.

Implicit cost: The opportunity cost of inputs that do not require a monetary payment.

Indivisible input: An input that cannot be scaled down to produce a smaller quantity of output.

Long-run average cost: The long-run cost divided by the quantity produced.

Long-run marginal cost: The change in long-run cost resulting from a one-unit increase in output.

Long-run total cost: The total cost of production when a firm is perfectly flexible in choosing its inputs.

Marginal product of labor: The change in output from one additional unit of labor.

Minimum efficient scale: The output at which scale economies are exhausted.

Short-run average total cost: Short-run total cost divided by the quantity of output; equal to *AFC* plus *AVC*.

Short-run marginal cost: The change in short-run total cost resulting from a one-unit increase in output.

Short-run total cost: The total cost of production when at least one input is fixed; equal to fixed cost plus variable cost.

Total-product curve: A curve showing the relationship between the quantity of labor and the quantity of output produced, *ceteris paribus*.

Variable cost: Cost that varies with the quantity produced.

Practice Quiz

(Answers are provided at the end of the Practice Quiz.)

1. A firm's *accounting cost*, defined as actual cash payments for inputs equals:
    a. the firm's implicit cost.
    b. the firm's explicit cost.
    c. the firm's economic cost.
    d. the sum of the costs listed above.

2. To compute a firm's economic cost, we must determine what the firm sacrifices to use inputs in the production process. Which of the following statements is consistent with this assertion?
    a. What matters to a firm is the actual monetary payment for inputs, not the implicit or implied payments.
    b. Economic cost includes opportunity cost of the inputs.
    c. Economic cost equals explicit cost.
    d. Accounting profit is always lower than economic profit.

3. The change in output resulting from one additional unit of labor is the definition of:
    a. diminishing returns.
    b. the total product curve.
    c. marginal product of labor.
    d. short-run marginal cost.

4. In the short run, the cost that is independent of the amount of output produced is called:
    a. economic cost.
    b. implicit cost.
    c. fixed cost.
    d. variable cost.

5. The vertical distance between the average total cost curve and the average variable cost curve equals:
    a. average fixed cost.
    b. fixed cost.
    c. marginal cost.
    d. the number of units produced.

6. Refer to the figure below. Which of the following components of cost is best represented by the curve labeled 1?

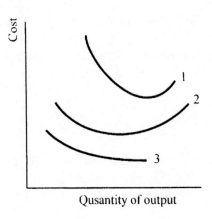

a. Total cost.
b. Average total cost.
c. Average variable cost.
d. Average fixed cost.

7. At levels of output where the firm's short-run average cost curve is rising:
    a. the marginal cost curve is above the short-run average cost curve.
    b. the marginal cost curve is below the short-run average cost curve.
    c. the marginal cost curve is equal to the short-run average cost curve.
    d. the marginal cost curve may be above or below the short-run average cost curve.
    e. None of the above is true.

8. Refer to the figure below. How much is the value of fixed cost?

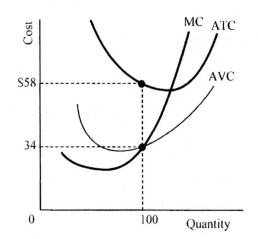

a. $5,800
b. $2,400
c. $3,400
d. None of the above. Fixed cost cannot be computed using this graph.

9. Returns to scale are measured by:
   a. long-run average cost.
   b. long-run total cost.
   c. long-run marginal cost.
   d. short-run marginal cost.

10. When a firm is subject to constant returns to scale and decides to replicate its existing operation, which of the following remains the same?
   a. The firm's profit.
   b. Total costs.
   c. Average cost.
   d. Output.

11. An *indivisible input* is:
   a. one that must be used in combination with other inputs.
   b. one that causes the average cost of production to increase as output increases.
   c. one that cannot be scaled down to produce a smaller quantity of output.
   d. an input whose cost cannot be divided by the number of units produced.

12. All other things equal, when we reduce the workforce:
   a. each worker will become more specialized and labor productivity will increase.
   b. each worker will become more specialized and labor productivity will decrease.
   c. each worker will become less specialized and labor productivity will increase.
   d. each worker will become less specialized and labor productivity will decrease.

13. The *minimum efficient scale* represents:
   a. the scale that eliminates diminishing returns.
   b. the greatest number of employees a firm can hire and still operate efficiently.
   c. the price at which all units supplied to the market will be purchased.
   d. the output at which scale economies are exhausted.
   e. the output levels for which the long-run average cost curve is downward sloping.

14. Refer to the figure below. When does the firm experience economies of scale?

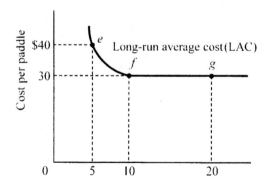

   a. As output increases from 5 to 10 rakes per minute.
   b. As output increases from 10 to 20 rakes per minute.
   c. Throughout the entire range of output, from 5 to 20 rakes per minute.
   d. When it decreases output, from 20 to 10 rakes per minute.

15. If a firm's long-run average cost curve is positively sloped:
    a. the firm experiences economies of scale, and the long-run average cost of production will rise with additional output produced.
    b. the firm experiences diseconomies of scale, and the long-run average cost of production will rise with additional output produced.
    c. the firm experiences economies of scale, and the long-run average cost of production will fall with additional output produced.
    d. the firm experiences diseconomies of scale, and the long-run average cost of production will fall with additional output produced.

16. Consider a firm that has just built a small plant, with a cost of $2,500. Labor is the only variable cost of production and each worker costs $10.00 per hour. Fill in the following table, and use it to answer the next three questions.

    After how many worker hours does diminishing returns set in?

Number of Worker Hours	Output	Fixed Cost	Variable Cost	Total Cost	Marginal Cost	Average Variable Cost	Average Total Cost
0	0				--	--	--
50	400						
100	900						
150	1300						
200	1600						
250	1800						
300	1900						
350	1950						

    a. 50
    b. 100
    c. 150
    d. 200
    e. 250

17. In the table in question 16 above, what is the marginal cost of output when 150 workers are employed??
    a. 1.15
    b. 1.25
    c. 1,500
    d. 2,500

18. In the table in question 16 above, what is the average variable cost when 1,600 units are produced?
    a. $1.67.
    b. $1.25.
    c. $1.56.
    d. 2,500 units.

19. This question tests your understanding of Application 1 in this chapter: The production cost of an iPod Touch: What are the cost components for electronic products?

If the goal is to provide the same numbers as the text example then the comment to the right is correct. Since this data is irrelevant to the following question I would simply cut the table out entirely.

Apple has sold millions of iPods. What is the impact of its large sales volume on the profit-maximizing behavior of its suppliers?
a. Suppliers have an incentive to cut costs per unit, but only if the amount of the cut is significant.
b. Suppliers have an incentive to cut costs per unit, even if the amount of the cut is small.
c. As sales of iPods rise, suppliers have an incentive to increase their prices and therefore the costs for Apple in order to increase their profits.
d. A large sales volume does not visibly affect Apple's relationship with its suppliers.

20. This question tests your understanding of Application 3 in this chapter: Scale economies in wind power: What are the sources of scale economies in production?

Table 8.5   WIND TURBINES AND THE AVERAGE COST OF ELECTRICITY

	Small Turbine (150 kilowatt)	Large Turbine (600 kilowatt)
Purchase price of turbine	$150,000	$420,000
Installation cost	$100,000	$100,000
Operating and maintenance cost	$75,000	$126,000
Total cost	**$325,000**	**$646,000**
Electricity generated (kilowatt-hours)	5 million	20 million
Average cost (per kilowatt-hour)	$0.065	$0.032

Which of the following best describes the fact that economies of scale exist in wind power?
a. The fact that a large turbine has many times the generation capacity of a small one.
b. The fact that large wind turbines are more costly than small ones.
c. The fact that the generating capacity of the higher-cost turbine more than offsets the higher initial cost.
d. The fact that the large turbine has higher operating costs than the small one.

21. Use the average height of five people plus one more person to explain the relationship between the average and marginal concepts.

22. If you examine closely the relationship between average total cost and average variable cost, you notice that, as output increases, the gap between the two narrows. Why does the gap narrow?

23. In the short run, the cost structure of a business firm is a reflection of the behavior of output under diminishing returns. Explain.

24. What is the implication of using a production process that has at least one indivisible input?

Answers to the Practice Quiz

1. b. Accounting cost includes the monetary payments for inputs, but ignores the opportunity cost of inputs that do not require an explicit monetary payment.

2. b. To compute a firm's economic cost, we must determine what the firm sacrifices to use inputs in the production process.

3. c. The marginal product of labor is the change in output from one additional unit of labor.

4. c. The cost of the production facility, which is independent of the amount of output produced, is called fixed cost.

5. a. Since average variable cost plus average fixed costs equals average cost, the vertical distance between average variable cost and average cost gives average fixed cost at that level of output. You notice that as output increases average cost and average variable cost move closer together.

6. b. Average cost is U-shaped and lies above average variable cost and average fixed cost.

7. a. If marginal cost is above average cost, the average cost must be rising. On the contrary, if marginal cost is below average cost, it pulls the average downward.

8. b. $ATC 2 AVC = AFC$, or 58 2 34 = 24. Then AFC x $Q = TFC$, or 24 × 100 = $2,400.

9. a. The firm's long-run average cost (LAC) equals the long-run cost divided by the quantity produced.

10. c. By simply replicating an existing operation, a firm can double its output and its total costs, leaving average cost unchanged.

11. c. An indivisible input is one that cannot be scaled down to produce a smaller quantity of output.

12. d. When we reduce the workforce, each worker will become less specialized, performing a wider variety of production tasks. The loss of specialization will decrease labor productivity.

13. d. The minimum efficient scale is the output at which scale economies are exhausted, which is also output level where the long-run average cost curve becomes horizontal.

14. a. As long as the long-run cost per unit decreases with an increase in output, the firm enjoys economies of scale.

15. b. If a firm's long-run average cost curve is positively sloped, the firm experiences diseconomies of scale, meaning that when the firm increases its output, the long-run average cost of production increases.

16. b. Diminishing returns occur when a given increase in inputs results in output increasing at a decreasing rate. Fifty labor hours initially produces 400 units. The next increase of 50 produces 500 units. The third increase of 50 hours (to a total of 150) produces only 400 units. Thus we would say that diminishing returns set in after the 100th labor hour.

17. b. Marginal cost is the change in cost divided by the change in output, or 500/400 = 1.25.

18. b. Average variable cost is variable cost divided by output or 2,000/1,600 = 1.25.

19. b. The large volume also provides a large reward for cost cutting. With millions of units sold, small savings per unit add up to a large increase in profit.

20. c. The scale economies occur because the cost of purchasing, installing, and maintaining a wind turbine increases less than proportionately with the turbine's generating capacity.

21. If each of five people is five feet tall, then the average height is five feet. If one additional person is taller than the average, that person will cause the average height to rise. In other words, when the marginal is greater than the average, the average will rise. If the marginal person is shorter than the average of the other five, the average of the six combined will decrease. In other words, when marginal is less than average, the average will fall.

22. The explanation of why the gap narrows involves the concept of average fixed cost. Average fixed cost equals fixed cost divided by the amount of output produced. Since fixed cost does not change with output, an increase in output results in an ever-decreasing value of average fixed cost. Now, average total cost is the sum of average fixed cost plus average variable cost. At higher levels of output, the contribution of average fixed cost is smaller (for the reasons stated above) and the contribution of average variable cost is larger. To find average total cost, the amount of average fixed cost that we stack on top of average variable cost becomes smaller and smaller.

23. The short-run total product curve shows that, initially, output increases at an increasing rate as more units of labor are added to the production process. During this stage of production, while product increases at an increasing rate (marginal product increases), cost increases at a decreasing rate (marginal cost decreases). Then, production reaches the stage of diminishing returns. During this stage, output increases at a decreasing rate (marginal product decreases), and cost increases at an increasing rate (marginal cost increases).

24. The implication is that these indivisible inputs cannot be scaled down to produce a smaller quantity of output. Therefore, the long-run average cost curve of the firm is downward sloping. A decrease in the level of output results in an increase in the cost per unit of output produced.

9 [24]
Perfect Competition

Chapter Summary

This chapter explores the decisions made by perfectly competitive firms and the implications of those decisions for the supply side of the market. Here are the main points of the chapter:

- A price-taking firm should produce the quantity of output at which the marginal revenue (the price) equals the marginal cost of production.
- An unprofitable firm should continue to operate if its total revenue exceeds its total variable cost.
- The long-run supply curve will be positively sloped if the average cost of production increases as the industry grows.
- The long-run supply curve is flatter than the short-run supply curve because there are diminishing returns in the short run, but not in the long run.
- An increase in demand causes a large upward jump in price, followed by a downward slide to the new long-run equilibrium price.

This chapter examines decisions made by firms in a **perfectly competitive market**, a market with many sellers and buyers of a homogeneous product and no barriers to entry. Because all buyers and sellers are small relative to the size of the market, they are all **price takers**, that is, they take the market price as given. The five key features of a perfectly competitive market are:

- There are many sellers.
- There are many buyers.
- The product is homogeneous.
- There are no barriers to market entry.
- Both buyers and sellers are price takers.

☞ Study Tip

To say that a product is homogeneous simply means that consumers view all goods as perfect substitutes and will buy from whichever seller offers the product at the lowest price.

Applying the Concepts

After reading this chapter, you should be able to answer these five key questions:
1. What is the break-even price?
2. How do entry costs affect the number of firms in a market?
3. How do producers respond to an increase in price?
4. Why is the market supply curve positively sloped?
5. How do supply restrictions affect the boom-bust housing cycle?

9.1 [24.1] Preview of the Four Market Structures

We are going to look at four primary market structures in the text. In a perfectly competitive market the firms are price takers while in the other market structures firms have some ability to set the price of their product.

The **firm-specific demand curve** shows the relationship between the price charged by a specific firm and the quantity the firm can sell. For a *monopoly*, a market structure with only one seller, the firm-specific and market demand curve are the same. A *perfectly competitive firm* faces a horizontal firm-specific demand curve. This means the competitive firm can sell all the output it desires at the market price, but will sell no output at any other price. A firm in *monopolistic competition* faces a downward sloping demand curve, but with no barriers to entry there are many firms, each selling a slightly different product from the others. An *oligopoly* contains only a few firms because of government regulation or economies of scale.

ᛗ Study Tip

> Study Table 9.1 [24.1] carefully. It is an excellent summary of the four market structures. Understanding why and how each element contributes to a particular structure will guide you through the next few chapters.

9.2 [24.2] The Firm's Short-Run Output Decision

The competitive firm chooses the output which will maximize its economic profit. While we can find this output level by calculating the total revenue, total cost, and profit at each output level, we are going to apply the marginal principle.

The Marginal Principle

Increase the level of an activity as long as its marginal benefit exceeds its marginal cost. Choose the level at which the marginal benefit equals the marginal cost.

For a firm, the benefit of producing a unit of output is the money they receive when they sell the unit of output. **Marginal revenue** is the change in total revenue from selling one more unit of output. For a competitive firm that can sell all the output it desires at the market price, the market price is the marginal revenue.

From the marginal principle we determine that a competitive firm will want to produce output where:

marginal revenue = marginal cost.

Since marginal revenue is the same as price, we can say that a competitive firm will produce output to the point where:

price = marginal cost.

The profit earned by the firm can be expressed as:

☑ Key Equation

economic profit = (price – average cost) x quantity produced

You can see that profits will be zero if price and average cost are equal. The **break-even price** is the price at which economic profit is zero; price equals average total cost.

🗎 Remember

Zero economic profit means that the firm is covering all of its explicit costs, and earning enough money to cover its implicit, or opportunity costs. A firm earning zero economic profits will earn positive accounting profits.

9.3 [24.3] The Firm's Shut-Down Decision

When a firm is losing money it must decide whether to stay open or shut down. The basic decision rule is:
- Operate in the short run if total revenue > variable cost
- shut down immediately if total revenue < variable cost

☞ Let's suppose that you have opened a coffee shop near your campus. You have a lease on the store space which doesn't expire for another 10 months. The lease payment is $1,000 per month. You must make this lease payment for the next 10 months whether or not you keep the coffee shop open. Currently your coffee shop is losing money each month and you are trying to decide what to do. In this case, you will operate if losses are less than $1,000 per month and shut down if losses are greater than $1,000 per month. Let's see why.

Suppose you are currently losing $1,200 per month. This means your revenue is not able to pay your variable costs. This would mean, for instance, that some workers are not being paid. If you close down you are still liable for the $1,000 per month lease payment, but all of your other costs are zero. You would rather close down and lose $1,000 per month instead of operating and losing $1,200 per month.

Suppose instead you are currently losing $800 per month. This means you are able to cover all of your variable costs, and contribute $200 per month toward your lease payment. If you were to close in this situation you would have no revenue, but would still have a $1,000 per month lease payment. Clearly you would rather lose $800 instead of $1,000 per month.

This is a short-run decision. In ten months, your lease will expire and you will have the option of signing a new lease or not. If you are still losing money, you will exit the industry at that time. You should be able to see that your decision at that time will have you face the choice of signing a lease and losing $800 per month, or not signing, exiting the market and losing $0.

The **shut-down price** is the price at which the firm is indifferent between operating and shutting down. The shut-down price is equal to the minimum average variable cost.

☄ Caution!

The decision of whether to operate or not ignores any sunk cost. A **sunk cost** is a cost that a firm has already paid or committed to pay, so it cannot be recovered. Only the relationship between revenue and variable cost is important for the short-run decision.

Let's review an Application that answers one of the key questions we posed at the start of the chapter.

1. What is the break-even price?

APPLICATION 1: THE BREAK-EVEN PRICE FOR A CORN FARMER
This Application illustrates break-even and shut-down prices. The break-even price for a corn farmer is $0.72 per bushel. At prices above this the farmer will earn a profit. At prices below this the farmer will suffer a loss. Of the $0.72 per bushel cost, $0.44 per bushel is variable. As a result, $0.44 per bushel is the farmer's shut-down price. If the price of corn is below this, the farmer will not receive enough revenue to cover the cost of growing corn.

9.4 [24.4] Short-Run Supply Curves

The **short-run supply curve** shows the relationship between the market price of a product and the quantity of output supplied by a firm in the short run. Since the firm chooses its output by finding the point where price, which is marginal revenue for the competitive firm, is equal to marginal cost, the marginal cost curve will function as the short-run supply curve. As we've already seen, if the price is below average variable cost, the firm will produce zero.

📄 Remember

The short-run supply curve for a firm is the firm's marginal cost curve above average variable cost.

The **short-run market supply curve** shows the relationship between market price and the quantity supplied in the short run. It is found by summing the quantity supplied of each individual firm at any given price.

A competitive market will reach short-run equilibrium when two conditions are met:
1. In the market the quantity demanded is equal to the quantity supplied. This is seen as point *a* in Figure 9.6 [24.6] in the text.
2. Each firm in the market chooses its profit maximizing level of output as shown by point *b* in Figure 9.6 [24.6].

In the short run, firms may earn profits, which will attract entry, or suffer losses, which will lead to exit. Long-run equilibrium is reached when no firms have an incentive to enter or exit the industry, that is, when all firms earn zero economic profits.

📄 Remember

Economic profits attract entry to the market and economic losses encourage firms to leave the market. In long-run equilibrium, firms earn zero economic profits and no firm wants to enter or exit the market.

Let's review an Application that answers one of the key questions we posed at the start of the chapter:

2. How do entry costs affect the number of firms in a market?

APPLICATION 2: WIRELESS WOMEN IN PAKISTAN
"Wireless women" in Pakistan operate in a market that can be considered perfectly competitive. They offer a standardized product, there are a large number of suppliers each taking the market price as a given, and easy entry.

☞ Suppose that you are considering becoming a wireless woman in Pakistan. You have an initial investment of $310 for equipment and will earn roughly three times the average daily wage. Entry will continue in this market until the price drops and the net income of the women is closer to the average daily wage. At this point women will be indifferent between undertaking the investment to become a wireless woman earning a wage slightly higher than the normal daily wage and simply earning the normal daily wage without the capital investment.

9.5 [24.5] The Long-Run Supply Curve for an Increasing Cost Industry

The **long-run market supply curve** shows the relationship between the market price and quantity supplied in the long run. The long run is a time period long enough that firms can enter or leave the market as they are able to adjust the quantity of all their inputs.

An **increasing cost industry** is one in which the average cost of production increases as the total output of the industry increases. The long-run supply curve will be positively sloped in this type of industry. There are two primary reasons why costs might increase as firms enter the industry:
- Increasing input prices. If firms entering the market have to compete with existing firms for inputs, we expect the price of inputs to increase as a result of entry.
- Less productive inputs. As the industry grows, firms may be forced to use less productive inputs than when the industry was smaller.

☞ Suppose profits attracted you to the home health care industry and you need to hire qualified nurses. You may find the best source of nursing labor is currently employed at the local hospital. In order for you to hire nurses, you must either attract them away from the hospital or entice nurses not currently practicing to work for you. Both of these will require you to offer higher wages to nurses than are currently being offered. This will drive up the price of labor for all employers of nurses.

Remember that in the long run, market price and average cost will be equal since all firms in the market will earn zero economic profits. To draw the long-run market supply curve for the example in the text we find the average cost of producing shirts for different levels of industry output. Connecting these points traces the long-run supply curve as shown in Figure 9.7 [24.7] in the text.

Let's review two Applications that answer key questions we posed at the start of the chapter:

3. How do producers respond to an increase in price?

APPLICATION 3: WOLFRAM MINERS OBEY THE LAW OF SUPPLY
Wolfram was used during World War II to make armor plate and armor-piercing shells. The price of wolfram increased dramatically as the Allies bid up the price of wolfram to ensure that none would be sold to the Axis nations. As the price of wolfram increased from $1,144 per ton to $20,000 per ton, miners in Spain greatly increased the amount of wolfram they brought to market. This is what we expect with an upward sloping supply curve, as the market price increases, more of the product will be offered for sale. This meant that the Allied nations bought much more wolfram than anticipated.

4. Why is the market supply curve positively sloped?

APPLICATION 4: THE WORLDWIDE SUPPLY OF COPPER
The mining industry is an increasing cost industry. This Application shows that at low prices only those mines with relatively low costs operate. As the market price increases, it becomes profitable to mine copper in areas with higher extractions costs. The example is given of a new deposit of copper in Afghanistan. Given the costs of developing the site for mining, it would only be profitable if the price of copper exceeded $7,000 per ton. At prices below this amount, no firm would have an incentive to mine copper in this area.

9.6 [24.6] Short-Run and Long-Run Effects of Changes in Demand

Figures 9.8 [24.8] and 9.9 [24.9] in the text illustrate what happens when the demand increases in a market that had been in competitive equilibrium. Notice that:
- As the demand in the market increases, the market price increases from $7 to $12.
- Firms increase their output in response to the higher market price. You can see this as the movement from point c to point d in Panel B of Figure 9.8 [24.8].
- At this higher price, existing firms earn economic profits, thus attracting entry to the market.
- Figure 9.9 [24.9] shows the result. Entry causes the market price to fall, and since this is an increasing cost industry, firms' costs rise.
- Entry continues until firms in the market once again are earning zero economic profits.
- The new market equilibrium occurs at point c in Figure 9.9 [24.9] of the text. As we would expect with an increase in demand, both the market price and quantity are higher at the new equilibrium point c than at the old equilibrium point a.
- To review: In the short run existing firms increase output in response to the higher prices, this is the movement from point a to b in Figure 9.9 [24.9]. In the long run, entry occurs in the market, driving the market price down. Entry stops when economic profits are once again zero. The new equilibrium is at point c in Figure 9.9 [24.9].

Let's review an Application that answers one of the key questions we posed at the start of the chapter:

5.   How do supply restrictions affect the boom-bust housing cycle?

APPLICATION 5:
PLANNING CONTROLS AND HOUSING CYCLES IN BRITAIN
This Application illustrates that more strict development controls lead to a steeper supply curve in the housing market. The steeper the supply curve the greater the price response to changes in demand. As a result, an increase in demand will lead to a large increase in price as the supply side can't respond well due to the development controls. When the controls are relaxed the price drops as the supply side of the market responds. The application notes that Britain has more severe development restrictions and also more frequent housing booms and busts than does the U.S.

9.7 [24.7] Long-Run Supply for a Constant-Cost Industry

In a **constant-cost industry**, the average cost of production is constant. This means the long-run supply curve is horizontal. This situation occurs when the industry uses only a small amount of the available inputs in the market. In this case new firms can purchase all the inputs they desire with no impact on input prices.

Figure 9.11 [24.11] of the text illustrates what happens in a constant-cost industry when market demand increases. Notice that:
- As the demand in the market increases, the market price increases from $1 to $5.
- Firms will increase their output in response to the higher market price. You can see this as the movement from point *a* to point *b* in Figure 9.11 [24.11].
- At this higher price, existing firms earn economic profits, thus attracting entry to the market.
- Entry causes the market price to fall. Since this is a constant-cost industry, entry has no effect on the costs of the firms.
- Entry continues until firms in the market once again are earning zero economic profits. Since costs are unchanged, this will occur at the same price as the previous equilibrium.
- The new market equilibrium occurs at point *c* in Figure 9.11 [24.11] of the text. We have an increase in market quantity, but since the long-run supply curve is horizontal the new market price is the same as the old market price.
- To review: In the short run, existing firms increase output in response to the higher prices; this is the movement from point *a* to *b* in Figure 9.11 [24.11]. In the long run, entry occurs in the market, driving the market price down. Entry stops when economic profits are once again zero. The new equilibrium is at point *c* in Figure 9.11 [24.11].

Activity

Let's see how the shape of the long-run supply curve affects outcomes. In Figure 9.9 [24.9] we have a short- and long-run supply curve for shirts. Given the long-run supply in the diagram we have a long-run equilibrium of $10 and 1,200 shirts per minute. Draw a more elastic long-run supply curve in Panel A below and a less elastic long-run supply curve in Panel B below and notice the differences in price and quantity in long-run equilibrium from those in Figure 9.9 [24.9].

Panel A: Draw a more elastic (flatter) long-run supply curve, making sure to draw the curve through point *a*. Notice that this will result in a long-run price lower than $10 and a quantity greater than 1,200.

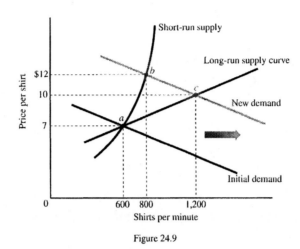

Figure 24.9

Panel B: Draw a less elastic (steeper) long-run supply curve making sure to draw the curve through point *a*. Notice that this will result in a long-run price between $10 and $12 and a quantity between 800 and 1,200.

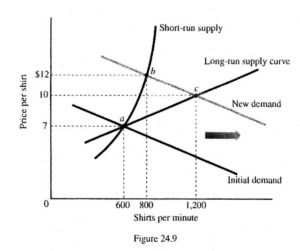

Figure 24.9

In terms of the housing Application, more restrictive zoning laws would tend to make the long-run supply less elastic. Less restrictive zoning laws would tend to make the long-run supply more elastic.

Key Terms

Break-even price: The price at which economic profit is zero; price equals average total cost.

Constant cost industry: An industry in which the average cost of production is constant; the long-run supply curve is horizontal.

Firm-specific demand curve: A curve showing the relationship between the price charged by a specific firm and the quantity the firm can sell.

Increasing cost industry: An industry in which the average cost of production increases as the total output of the industry increases; the long-run supply curve is positively sloped.

Long-run market supply curve: A curve showing the relationship between the market price and quantity supplied in the long run.

Marginal revenue: The change in total revenue from selling one more unit of output.

Perfectly competitive market: A market with many sellers and buyers of a homogeneous product and no barriers to entry.

Price taker: A buyer or seller that takes the market price as given.

Short-run market supply curve: A curve showing the relationship between market price and the quantity supplied in the short run.

Short-run supply curve: A curve showing the relationship between the market price of a product and the quantity of output supplied by a firm in the short run.

Shut-down price: The price at which the firm is indifferent between operating and shutting down; equal to the minimum average variable cost.

Sunk cost: A cost that a firm has already paid or committed to pay, so it cannot be recovered.

Practice Quiz

(Answers are provided at the end of the Practice Quiz.)

1. Which of the following is a characteristic of a perfectly competitive market?
    a. There are many buyers and sellers (hundreds).
    b. Firms can gain an advantage over others by differentiating their product.
    c. Firms cannot freely enter or leave the market.
    d. Both buyers and sellers can manipulate market price.
    e. All of the above.

2. Which of the following is a *firm-specific demand curve*?
    a. The market demand curve in a perfectly competitive market.
    b. The firm's demand curve in a perfectly competitive market.
    c. The demand curve in competitive conditions only. Monopolies don't have firm-specific demand curves.
    d. The demand curve in a market that produces a single, specific product.

3. Refer to the graph below. Which panel best describes the demand curve facing a monopolist?

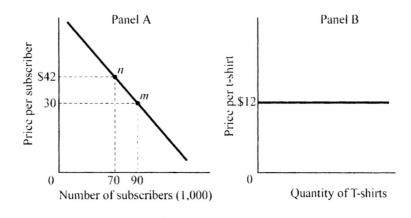

a. Panel A
b. Panel B
c. A monopolist faces both types of demand curves.
d. A monopolist is never confronted with either one of the curves depicted in the graph.

4.   Refer to the graph below. Which level of output maximizes profit?

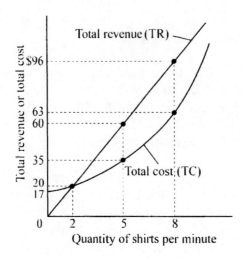

a.   2 shirts per minute.
b.   5 shirts per minute.
c.   8 shirts per minute.
d.   Either 5 or 8 shirts per minute, but not 2.

5.   In perfect competition marginal revenue is the same as:
a.   marginal benefit.
b.   price.
c.   the change in total revenue that results from selling one more unit of output.
d.   All of the above.

6.   Refer to the table below. What level of output maximizes profit?

Output: shirts per minute	Marginal Revenue	Marginal Cost
0	$12	$0
1	12	5
2	12	1
3	12	3
4	12	4
5	12	5
6	12	7
7	12	9
8	12	12
9	12	16
10	12	21

a.   Zero units of output.
b.   Four units of output.
c.   Eight units of output.
d.   Ten units of output.

7. Refer to the figure below. At what price level is *economic profit* equal to zero?

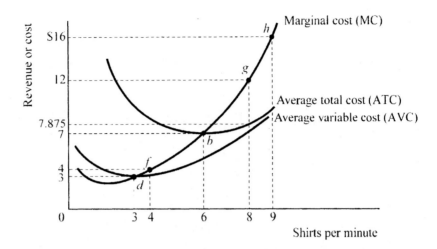

a. $3
b. $4
c. $7
d. $12

8. Refer to the table below. When price is $4, the firm would produce:

Output Shirts per Minute	Fixed Cost	Variable Cost	Total Cost	Total Revenue
0	$17	$0	$17	$0
1	17	5	22	4
2	17	6	23	8
3	17	9	26	12
4	17	13	30	16
5	17	18	35	20
6	17	25	42	24

a. zero output. The firm does not produce any output because profit is always negative.
b. two units of output, although it would suffer a loss from doing so.
c. four units of output, although it would suffer a loss from doing so.
d. six units of output, where revenue is the greatest.

9. In the short run the firm should:
a. operate if price > average variable cost.
b. shut down if price < average total cost.
c. shut down if price > average total cost.
d. operate if price > average fixed cost.

10. Refer to the figure below. The *shut-down price* corresponds to:

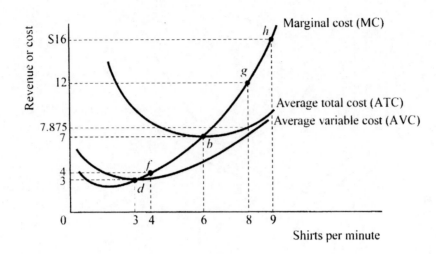

a. point *g*
b. point *b*
c. point *f*
d. point *d*

11. The perfectly competitive firm's short-run supply curve is the part of the firm's:
a. short-run average cost curve above the marginal cost.
b. short-run average variable cost curve above the shut-down price.
c. short-run marginal cost curve above the shut-down price.
d. short-run marginal cost curve above the break-even price.

12. Refer to the figure below. Which of these two curves is the *firm's short-run supply curve* as opposed to the short-run market supply curve?

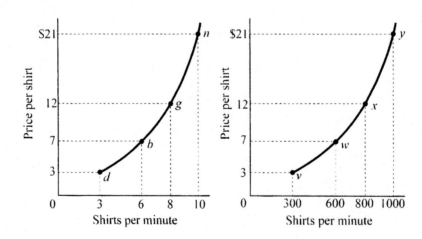

a. The one on the left.
b. The one on the right.
c. Either curve. They are one and the same.
d. There isn't sufficient information to establish which curve is the firm's supply curve and which curve is the market supply curve.

13. Refer to the figure below. Which of the following is likely to happen in this market in the long run?

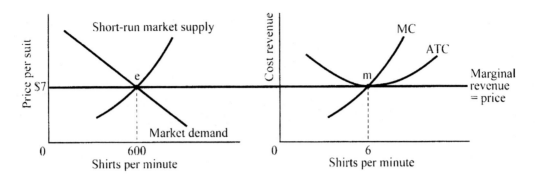

a. More firms will probably enter the market.
b. Some firms will probably exit the market.
c. Some firms might enter and others exit the market simultaneously.
d. No other firms will enter the market.

14. Refer to the figure below. At each point on this long-run market supply curve, the market price equals:

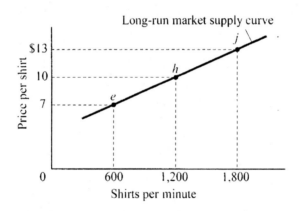

a. the short-run marginal cost of production.
b. the long-run profit per unit of output.
c. the long-run average cost of production.
d. marginal cost both in the short run and in the long run.

15. Refer to the figure below. Which supply curve best describes the long-run response to an increase in demand?

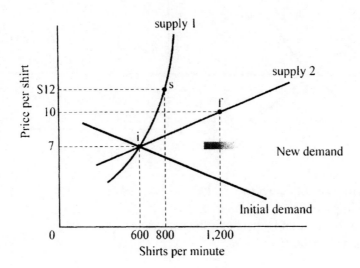

    a. Supply 1.
    b. Supply 2.
    c. Neither supply 1 nor supply 2. Supply curves cannot describe such response.
    d. Which one depends on consumer preferences.

16. Refer to the figure below. In a constant cost industry, which supply curve is the long-run supply curve in this scenario?

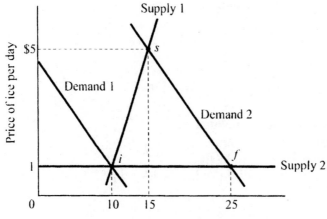

    a. Supply 1.
    b. Supply 2.
    c. Both curves appear to be long-run supply curves.
    d. It is difficult to compare the two supply curves in order to tell which one could be a short-run supply curve and which one a long-run supply curve.

17. This question tests your understanding of Application 1 in this chapter: The break-even price for a corn farmer. What is the break-even price?

    To illustrate the notions of break-even and shut-down prices, let's look at these prices for the typical corn farmer. The break-even, or zero-profit, price is $0.72 per bushel. At this price, the farmer will produce at the minimum point of the average total-cost curve, with the average cost equal to the market price of $0.72.

    In the short run, when will the farmer decide to shut down operations?
    a. When the price falls below $0.72 per bushel, or when the price is not high enough to cover all the costs.
    b. When the price is higher than $0.72 per bushel.
    c. At any price level that results in losses for the farmer.
    d. When the price level is too low to cover variable costs.

18. This question tests your understanding of Application 3 in this chapter: Wolfram miners obey the law of supply: How do producers respond to an increase in price?

    During World War II, the United States and its European allies bought up all the wolfram produced in Spain, thus denying the Axis powers—Germany and Italy—this vital military input.

    Using the framework of supply and demand, which of the following best describes what happened in the market for wolfram based on the buying strategy of the United States and its European allies and the corresponding response by suppliers?
    a. The higher demand for wolfram caused a higher price and consequently a decrease in demand, or a shift of the market demand curve to the left.
    b. Higher demand for wolfram resulted in higher prices and higher quantity supplied. Then, as more and more Spanish firms entered the market, the supply of wolfram shifted to the right.
    c. Market entry of new suppliers of wolfram resulted in a substantial increase in the price of wolfram, which forced the allies to buy wolfram at very high prices.
    d. Both the demand and the supply of wolfram increased, but since the increase in demand was greater than the increase in supply, prices rose substantially after new suppliers entered the market.

19. Use the tools you learned in this chapter to explain how the price mechanism ensures that resources are allocated toward producing the goods that people want most.

20. Compare and contrast the decisions of the business firm in the short run with those it must make in the long run.

21. Explain the process that takes a perfectly competitive industry from short-run equilibrium to long-run equilibrium. Assume that firms are suffering losses in the short run.

22. Consider the personal computer industry. Do you think the industry has an upward sloping, downward sloping, or horizontal long-run industry supply curve?

Answers to the Practice Quiz

1. a. A perfectly competitive market is a market with five features: There are many sellers (hundreds); there are many buyers (hundreds); the product is standardized or homogeneous; firms can freely enter or leave the market; and, both buyers and sellers take the market price as "given."

2. b. The firm-specific demand curve shows the relationship between the price charged by a specific firm and the quantity the firm can sell.

3. a. In panel A, the demand curve facing a monopolist is the market demand curve. In panel B, a perfectly competitive firm takes the market price as given, so its demand curve is horizontal at the market price.

4. c. To maximize profit, the firm chooses the quantity of output that generates the largest vertical difference between the two curves. The profit at 8 shirts is $33. The profit at 5 shirts is only $25.

5. d. The marginal benefit—or marginal revenue—of producing shirts is the change in total revenue that results from selling one more shirt. The marginal revenue of a perfectly competitive firm is simply its price: Marginal benefit = marginal revenue = market price.

6. c. The marginal principle tells us that the firm will maximize its profit by choosing the quantity at which marginal revenue (the market price) equals marginal cost.

7. c. The firm will have zero economic profit when the average total cost equals the price. This is at the bottom of the *ATC* curve where *ATC* and *MC* intersect.

8. c. When market price is $4, price remains above average variable cost. In this case, it makes sense for a firm to suffer a loss and still remain in operation because the firm can pay for all its variable costs and have some revenue left to pay for at least part of the fixed cost payment.

9. a. The firm should continue to operate if price exceeds the average variable cost; otherwise, it should shut down.

10. d. At point *d*, price is sufficient to pay for all of the variable cost and none of the fixed cost. If the firm shut down, the firm would not incur any variable costs but without revenue would cover none of the fixed cost. Both situations are equivalent.

11. c. The firm's short-run supply curve shows the relationship between the market price and the quantity supplied by the firm over a period of time during which one input—the production facility—cannot be changed. The firm's short-run supply curve is the part of the firm's short-run marginal cost curve above the shut-down price.

12. a. In the graph on the left, the firm's short-run supply curve is the part of the marginal-cost curve above the shut-down price ($3). In the graph on the right, there are 100 firms in the market, so the market supply at a given price is 100 times the quantity supplied by the typical firm.

13. d. Firms enter a market only if they expect to earn a profit. Firms leave the market if they expect to suffer continued losses. Because price equals average cost at the chosen quantity, economic profit is zero, and no other firms will enter the market.

14. c. The long-run market supply curve shows the relationship between the price and quantity supplied in the long run, when firms can enter or leave the industry. At each point, the market price equals the long-run average cost of production. Because this is an increasing cost industry, the market supply curve is positively sloped.

15. b. The short-run supply curve is steeper than the long-run supply curve because production facilities are fixed and there are diminishing returns in the short run. In the long run, firms can enter the industry and build more plants, so the price eventually drops.

16. b. In the short run, the supply curve is relatively steep, so the price rises by a large amount. In the long run, firms enter the industry, pulling the price back down.

17. d. At a price between the shut-down price and the break-even price ($0.72), the farmer will lose money but will continue to operate at a loss because total revenue will exceed the variable cost of growing corn.

18. b. At first, higher demand results in higher price and higher quantity supplied. Then, entry causes a shift of the supply curve to the right.

19. The material in this chapter shows how the market and the firm interact with each other. Changes in market conditions, including both determinants of supply and demand, affect market equilibrium. Changes in equilibrium price send signals to profit-maximizing firms that show how firms should adjust output in the short run, and industry size in the long run.

20. In both the short run and the long run, the firm's objective is the same: to maximize profit. In the short run, the firm must determine what level of output to produce, given its current plant size, and market price. In the long run, profit maximization is achieved by finding the most efficient scale of plant, or the one that minimizes cost per unit for a target level of output to be produced.

21. If firms are suffering losses in the short run, some of the firms will exit the industry in the long run. As firms exit the industry, the market supply curve shifts to the left, causing price to increase. As price increases, the remaining firms receive higher revenue for the sale of their output, eventually reducing the losses to zero. The exit of firms will stop once the increase in price is sufficient to guarantee a normal rate of return for the remaining firms.

22. The industry must have a downward-sloping industry supply curve. An indication of this phenomenon is revealed by computer prices. As time goes by, the industry keeps coming up with better, cheaper computers. This decrease in price over the long run is caused by specialization and innovation. Inputs continue to be more and more sophisticated, resulting in a decrease in the cost per computer produced. Calculators, VCRs, and digital watches are other examples of industries that have experienced similar progress.

10 [25]
Monopoly and Price Discrimination

Chapter Summary

This chapter explores the subtleties of monopolies and their pricing policies. Here are the main points of the chapter:

- Compared to a perfectly competitive market, a market served by a monopolist will charge a higher price, produce a smaller quantity of output, and generate a deadweight loss to society.
- Some firms use resources to acquire monopoly power, a process known as rent seeking.
- Patents protect innovators from competition, leading to higher prices for new products but greater incentives to develop new products.
- To engage in price discrimination, a firm divides its customers into two or more groups and charges lower prices to groups with more elastic demand.
- Price discrimination is not an act of generosity; it's an act of profit maximization.

Applying the Concepts

After reading this chapter, you should be able to answer these four key questions:
1. What happens when a monopoly ends?
2. What is the value of a monopoly?
3. When do firms have an opportunity to charge different prices to different consumers?
4. Does voluntary pricing work?

In this chapter, we study the decisions made by a monopoly firm. **Monopoly** refers to a market in which a single firm sells a product that does not have any close substitutes. In particular we see that a monopoly:

- exercises **market power**, the ability of a firm to affect the price of its product.
- requires **barriers to entry**, which prevent other firms from entering a profitable market, in order to keep their monopoly position.
- takes advantage of its market power when making pricing decision.

A monopoly occurs when some barrier to entry prevents firms from entering a profitable market. Some types of barriers to entry include:

- **Patents**. A patent grants a firm the exclusive right to sell a new product for some period of time. Governments may also issue licenses to a particular firm to sell a product.
- **Network externalities**. This is the situation in which the value of a product to a consumer increases with the number of other consumers who use it.

☞ Think of cell phone service. One way to make your cell phone service more valuable is to allow you to talk free (no minutes or money charged) to other subscribers on the same network. The more friends you have on your network, the more valuable your phone service becomes, and the harder it will be for a new entrant to lure you away.

- Government licensing. This occurs when government chooses a single firm to sell a particular product.
- Ownership of a key resource. The DeBeers company controls about 80% of the world's production of diamonds.
- **Natural monopoly**. This is a market in which the economies of scale in production are so large that only a single large firm can earn a profit.

10.1 [25.1] The Monopolist's Output Decision

Just as the competitive firm, the monopolist will choose to produce output to the point where marginal revenue is equal to marginal cost. For the monopolist, however, marginal revenue and price are not the same.

 The Marginal Principle

Increase the level of an activity as long as its marginal benefit exceeds its marginal cost. Choose the level at which the marginal benefit equals the marginal cost.

Figure 10.1 [25.1] in your text provides a demand schedule for a monopolist. Since the monopolist is the only firm in the market and faces the market demand curve, in order to increase output the monopolist must lower the price on all units that it sells. Lowering the price to sell an additional unit of output has two impacts:

- Good news: The firm earns new revenue by selling an additional unit of output.
- Bad news: The firm earns less revenue on all the units it would have sold at a higher price.

Suppose in Figure 10.1 [25.1] the monopolist is initially selling 3 units at a price of $10 each. To sell a fourth unit, the monopolist must lower the price to $8 for every unit that it sells. There are two ways to convince yourself that the marginal revenue from selling unit four is less than the price of unit four:

- You can see that total revenue will increase from $30 to $32, a $2 increase in revenue even though the price per unit is now $8.
- The good news of selling unit four is that we earn $8 in new revenue when we sell unit four. The bad news of selling unit four is that we lose $2 per unit on each of the first three units since we could have sold them for $10, but are now selling them for $8. The bad news means we give up $6 in revenue from the first three units. The total change in revenue is the $8 in good news minus the $6 in bad news, for marginal revenue of $2.

Remember

When a firm faces a downward sloping demand curve, marginal revenue will be less than price.

 Key Formula

marginal revenue = new price + (slope of demand curve x old quantity)

A monopolist chooses its profit maximizing output and price by:
- Finding the quantity at which marginal revenue is equal to marginal cost. This is shown as point *a* in Figure 10.2 [25.2].
- Charging the price from the demand curve which corresponds to the monopoly's desired quantity of output. This is point *b* in Figure 10.2 [25.2].
- Earning the profits shown as the shaded rectangle in Figure 10.2 [25.2] with height of $7 (the difference between the price of output at point *b* and the average cost of output at point *c*), and base of 900 units, the amount sold by the monopolist.

10.2 [25.2] The Social Cost of Monopoly

Figure 10.3 [25.3] in your text illustrates the effect of monopoly on price and output in a market. For simplicity, assume there are no fixed costs and firms produce with a constant marginal cost. If this market were a monopoly market the firm would produce 200 doses per hour, at a marginal cost of $8 per dose, and charge $18 per unit. The monopolist will earn a profit of $2,000. This is illustrated in Panel A of Figure 10.3 [25.3].

Remember from Chapter 9 [24] that in a competitive market, price and marginal cost are equal. Thus in a competitive market we will produce 400 units of output at a price of $8 per unit, the marginal cost of production. We see this in Panel B.

 Remember

A monopoly market will always have a higher price and lower output than a competitive market.

The monopoly will make consumers worse off than they would be under competition. This is illustrated in Figure 10.4 [25.4] in your text. At the competitive output level and price, consumer surplus consists of areas A, B, and D. Total surplus in the market consisted of areas A, B, and D.

With the monopoly output level and price consumer surplus decreases to area A. Area B is now producer surplus. Total surplus is the sum of areas A and B. Area D is not surplus to either producers or consumers and is called the deadweight loss from monopoly. The **deadweight loss from monopoly** is a measure of the inefficiency from monopoly; equal to the decrease in the market surplus.

To see why look at triangle D. The base of triangle D represents all the units of the good which would have been sold under competition, but which are not sold under monopoly. The value that these trades would have generated has been lost to the economy. You can see that each of these units would add value to the economy as the demand curve, which measures what consumers are willing to pay for each unit, is above the marginal cost curve, which measures the cost of producing each unit, for all of these now un-traded units. Because the monopolist will not sell these units, the surplus generated from these trades will not be realized.

The area of triangle D can be calculated by the formula:

$$area = .5(base)(height)$$

In this case the base of the triangle is the 200 doses of the drug that will not be produced. The height of the triangle is $10. This gives us a deadweight loss of:

$$area = .5(200)(10) = \$1,000$$

Rent seeking, the process of using public policy to gain economic profit, can also be considered an efficiency cost of monopoly. It could be said that monopoly profits are inefficient as they are a pool of money that can be used for rent seeking.

☞ Suppose that a monopolist can spend its profits either developing a lower cost means of producing output, or giving money to legislators to protect their monopoly standing. From society's viewpoint we would rather they spend money reducing their cost of production as this will lead to lower prices and greater output in the market. In fact, the monopoly may prefer to spend the money protecting their market position. This has no benefit to society and thus would be considered an efficiency cost to society. Faced with the choice of losing all of its profits to entrants, or spending its profits to prevent entry, the monopoly would prefer to spend money to keep entrants out.

Let's review an Application that answers one of the key questions we posed at the start of the chapter:

1. What happens when a monopoly ends?

> **APPLICATION 1:**
> **ENDING THE MONOPOLY ON INTERNET REGISTRATION**
> Are prices higher when a market is a monopoly? This Application shows that when Network Solutions lost their government-issued monopoly on registering Internet domain names, the price of a domain registration fell from $35 per year to $10 to $15 per year.

10.3 [25.3] Patents and Monopoly Power

A patent gives a firm the exclusive right to produce a product for 20 years. In exchange for the negatives associated with monopoly, higher prices, lower output, deadweight loss, the patent encourages innovation and society benefits from the introduction of new products. Thus patents may be socially efficient even though the monopolies they create are economically inefficient.

☞ Patent protection is quite important in the pharmaceutical industry. It is very expensive to develop, test, and bring to market a new drug therapy. However, it is relatively simple to mimic an existing drug.

Without patent protection many of the drugs that we rely upon in society might not have been brought to market as the companies would have been unable to recover the cost of developing those products.

Let's review an Application that answers one of the key questions we posed at the start of the chapter:

2.   What is the value of a monopoly?

APPLICATION 2: BRIBING THE MAKERS OF GENERIC DRUGS
When a patent on a drug expires, other firms introduce generic versions of the drugs. How much does a drug company lose because of generic sales? This Application suggests that in one case Schering-Plough paid $60 million to delay the introduction of a generic drug. Because Schering-Plough was willing to give up $60 million to avoid competition, the monopoly profits to be earned were at least $60 million. Bribing a generic firm to stay out of the market is an example of rent-seeking behavior. Schering-Plough was willing to spend part of their monopoly profits in an attempt to keep monopoly control over the market.

10.4 [25.4] Price Discrimination

Price discrimination is the practice of selling a good at different prices to different consumers. The most common form of price discrimination is the practice of selling goods to different groups of customers at different prices. Many businesses offer students and senior citizens discounts not available to other customers. Firms engage in price discrimination in an effort to increase their profits.

To price discriminate, three conditions must be met:
1.   The firm must have the ability to set the price for their product. For this reason a perfectly competitive firm would never be able to price discriminate.
2.   The firm must be able to identify different groups of customers based upon their willingness to pay for the product.
3.   The firm must be able to prevent resale.

🖹 Remember

To determine the output level and price in different markets, a price discriminating firm simply finds the output level at which marginal revenue is equal to marginal cost in each market. The price in each market is determined from the demand curves. Marginal revenue differs between the markets because the markets have different demand curves.

When a firm price discriminates, those with less elastic demand for the good will tend to pay higher prices.

Let's review two Applications that answer key questions we posed at the start of the chapter:

1. When does a firm have an opportunity to charge different prices to different consumers?

APPLICATION 3: PAYING FOR A COLD SOFT DRINK ON A HOT DAY
If warmer temperatures change a person's taste for cold drinks, then we would expect that the demand for cold drinks would be higher on hot days. As a result, people would be willing to pay more for a cold drink on hot days. Coca-Cola developed a vending machine to take advantage of this demand relationship. The machine would increase or decrease the price of cola as the weather changed so that on hot days, when demand would be higher, the price of a cola would also be higher. This is a situation in which it is easy to determine when consumers might have different demand curves for a product. While the ability to price discriminate is present here, the machine has yet to be used, due largely to consumer protests.

2. Does voluntary pricing work?

APPLICATION 4: RADIOHEAD LETS CONSUMERS PICK THE PRICE
The band Radiohead tried an innovative pricing strategy for their 2007 release "In Rainbows," they allowed consumers to download the music and pay what they wanted. This is a good example of price discrimination as consumers could choose how much they would pay. Was it a good idea for the band? The application points out that average revenue per download was about the same as what the band would earn from conventional CD sales. The Application points out that this might be a good strategy if it encourages some people who would have downloaded the music illegally to pay something for the music or if it encourages some people to purchase the music who would not have paid $15 for a conventional CD.

Activity

The following table gives a demand curve for a market. Assume there are no fixed costs in the market and an unlimited number of units of the product can be produced at a marginal cost of $5 per unit. As a result average cost and marginal cost are the same.

a. If the market was served by competitive firms, the price in the market would be: _____ and the market quantity would be _____.

(Bonus: the consumer surplus in the market would be _____.)

b. Fill in the table.

Price	Q	TR	MR
10	0		
9	6		
8	12		
7	18		
6	24		
5	30		
4	36		
3	42		
2	48		
1	54		

c. If this market was served by a monopolist, the monopoly would sell _____ units and charge a price of _____ dollars per unit. Monopoly profit would be _____.

d. Bonus. At the monopoly outcome, consumer surplus is _____ and the deadweight loss from monopoly is _____.

Answers

a. The price would be $5; the quantity would be 30 units. Consumer surplus would be $75. To find this, recognize that the height of the consumer surplus triangle is the difference between the vertical intercept and $5, and the base of the consumer surplus triangle is the number of units sold.

b. Complete the table.

Price	Q	TR	MR
10	0	0	
9	6	54	9
8	12	96	7
7	18	126	5
6	24	144	3
5	30	150	1
4	36	144	-1
3	42	126	-3
2	48	96	-5
1	54	54	-7

c. Monopolist would sell 18 units at $7 per unit. Profit would be (7 – 5) x 18 = $36.

d. Consumer surplus would be $27. Deadweight loss would be $12. The height of the deadweight loss triangle would be 2 units (the $7 monopoly price minus the $5 marginal cost) and the base would be 12 units (the difference between the 30 units sold in a competitive market and the 18 units sold in a monopoly market).

Key Terms

Barrier to entry: Something that prevents firms from entering a profitable market.

Deadweight loss from monopoly: A measure of the inefficiency from monopoly; equal to the decrease in market surplus.

Market power: The ability of a firm to affect the price of its product.

Monopoly: A market in which a single firm sells a product that does not have any close substitutes.

Natural monopoly: A market in which the economies of scale in production are so large that only a single large firm can earn a profit.

Network externalities: The value of a product to a consumer increases with the number of other consumers who use it.

Patent: The exclusive right to sell a new good for some period of time.

Price discrimination: The practice of selling a good at different prices to different consumers.

Rent seeking: The process of using public policy to gain economic profit.

Practice Quiz

(Answers are provided at the end of the Practice Quiz.)

1. Match one of the terms below with the following definition: The ability of a firm to affect the price of its product.
    a.   Monopoly.
    b.   Network externalities.
    c.   Patent.
    d.   Market power.

2. Select the term below that most closely approximates the following statement: When the scale economies in production are sufficiently large that a market can support only one firm.
    a.   Monopoly.
    b.   Patent.
    c.   Natural monopoly.
    d.   Barriers to entry.

3. Select the most appropriate answer based on the textbook reading. Electricity transmission is an example of:
    a.   an industry with network externalities.
    b.   a natural monopoly.
    c.   an industry with market power.
    d.   an industry where one firm is able to prevent other firms from entering.

4. Refer to the figure below. How much is the marginal revenue associated with increasing quantity sold from 3 to 4 units?

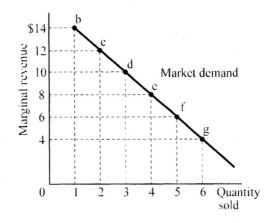

a. $2
b. $4
c. $6
d. $8

5. At a price of $30, a firm sells 150 units of output per day. The slope of the demand curve is 0.1 (in absolute value). The firm is considering cutting price to $25 to raise sales; if the marginal cost of production is $8, what should the firm do?
    a. Increase price.
    b. Keep its price the same.
    c. Decrease price.
    d. Shut down.

6. Which of the key principles of economics is used by the firm to choose how much to produce and what price to charge?
    a. The principle of opportunity cost.
    b. The principle of diminishing returns.
    c. The marginal principle.
    d. The principle of voluntary exchange.

7. Refer to the figure below. In order to maximize profit, what price should the firm charge?

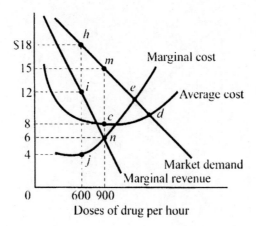

a. $18
b. $15
c. $12
d. $8

8. Refer to the figure below. How much of the total fixed cost is the monopoly able to pay when it sells 10,000 units?

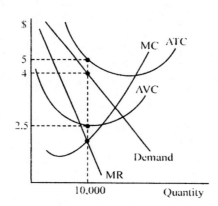

a. $15,000
b. $25,000
c. $40,000
d. $10,000

9. Refer to the figure below. Assume that the firm is producing 600 units. According to the marginal principle, what should the firm do in order to maximize profit?

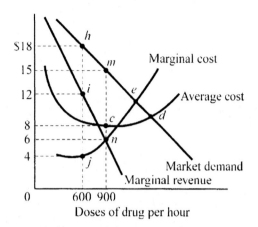

Doses of drug per hour

a. The firm should maintain the current level of output because they are making profits.
b. The firm should maintain the current level of output, because marginal revenue is greater than marginal cost, and price is the highest.
c. The firm should increase the level of output, because marginal revenue is greater than marginal cost.
d. The firm should increase the level of output to reach minimum average cost.

10. Suppose that all of the wheat farms are purchased by one firm. Relative to the current (competitive) price and quantity (and assuming that nothing else has changed), we would expect the new monopolist to:
a. sell more and charge less.
b. sell less and charge less.
c. sell more and charge more.
d. sell less and charge more.

11. Refer to the figure below. How much is consumer surplus in the monopoly case?

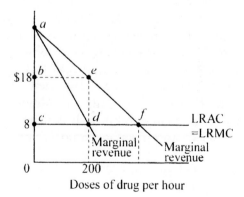

Doses of drug per hour

a. *abe*
b. *acf*
c. *edf*
d. *bcde*

12. As compared to perfect competition, monopolies:
    a. reduce consumer surplus, create positive economic profits, and generate a deadweight loss.
    b. increase consumer surplus, create positive economic profits, and generate a deadweight loss.
    c. reduce consumer surplus, create negative economic profits, and generate a deadweight loss.
    d. reduce consumer surplus, create positive economic profits, and generate a deadweight gain.

13. Refer to the figure below. What is the area of consumer surplus when the market is served by a perfectly competitive firm?

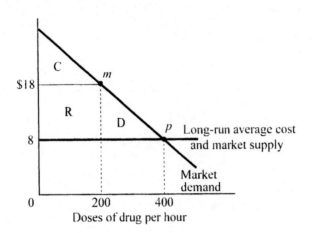

    a. C
    b. C + R
    c. C + R + D
    d. The consumer surplus area is not shown.

14. This question tests your understanding of Application 1 in this chapter: Ending the monopoly on Internet registration: What happens when a monopoly ends?

    For an illustration of the inefficiency of monopoly, we can look at what happens when a government-sanctioned monopoly ends. In February 1999, the U.S. government announced plans to end the five-year monopoly held by Network Solutions Inc. for registering Internet addresses. Network Solutions had an exclusive government contract to register Web addresses, also known as domain names, ending in .net, .org, .edu, and .com. The company registered almost 2 million names in 1998, collecting $70 for each address and charging an annual renewal fee of $35. The government's plan to introduce competition had some restrictions—an entering firm had to meet strict requirements for security and backup measures and liability insurance. Two new competitors, Register.com and Tucows.com, cut prices to between $10 and $15 per year. In addition, the new firms offered longer registration periods and permitted more characters in each domain name. Network Solutions, the original monopolist, quickly matched its competitors' lower prices and expanded service options.

    In this story, the inefficiency of monopoly refers to:
    a. the existence of a single firm in the industry.
    b. the tendency of the monopoly to charge higher prices and offer less output.
    c. the inability of new competitors to enter the industry unless the government intervenes.
    d. the tendency for average costs to rise once new competitors enter the industry.

15. Price discrimination is the practice of:
    a. dividing consumers into two or more groups, but charging the same prices to each group.
    b. dividing consumers into two or more groups and charging different prices to each group.
    c. dividing market demand among producers who will charge the same prices to consumers.
    d. discriminating against consumers on the basis of race, sex, religion, or national origin.

16. Which of the following conditions is necessary for a firm to be able to practice price discrimination?
    a. The firm must have market power.
    b. The firm must be able to separate consumers into different groups.
    c. The firm must be able to prevent resale.
    d. All of the above.

17. Which of the following is an example of price discrimination?
    a. Meals in New York City cost more than meals in a small town.
    b. The grocery store has a "buy one, get one free" sale on eggs.
    c. The local department store has special sale prices that are only good from 8 a.m. to 11 a.m.
    d. Insurance companies charge more to insure an expensive car than a cheap one.

18. This question tests your understanding of Application 3 in this chapter: Paying for a cold soft drink on a hot day: When does a firm have an opportunity to charge different prices to different consumers?

    On a hot day, are you willing to pay more than you normally would for an ice-cold can of Coke? If so, you're the type of consumer Coca-Cola Company had in mind when it developed a high-tech vending machine, complete with heat sensors and microchips, that charges a higher price when the weather is hot. The price discriminating scheme used by Coca-Cola in this case assumes that consumers have different demand elasticities for Coca-Cola. In particular:
    a. the demand for Coca-Cola becomes more elastic as the temperature rises.
    b. the demand for Coca-Cola becomes more inelastic as the temperature rises.
    c. the demand for Coca-Cola is unitary elastic regardless of the temperature.
    d. as the temperature rises, demand becomes perfectly elastic.

19. The only legal restriction concerning price discrimination is that firms cannot use it to:
    a. discriminate against the average consumer.
    b. increase the number of their customers.
    c. drive rivals out of business.
    d. discriminate against senior citizens.

20. If the demand by seniors is relatively more elastic than the demand by non-seniors:
    a. price discrimination would have seniors paying more than non-seniors for the good.
    b. price discrimination would have seniors paying less than non-seniors for the good.
    c. non-seniors will buy the same amount of the good regardless of the price.
    d. seniors will demand zero quantity at any price other than the current market price.

21. When a monopoly cuts price, there is good news and bad news, which explains why marginal revenue falls below average revenue (demand) as output increases. Expand this statement.

22. Explain the concept of deadweight loss.

23. Compare the profit-maximizing decisions of a monopoly to those of a perfectly competitive firm.

24. Explain the concept of *rent seeking*.

25. Define price discrimination and list the conditions necessary to practice it.

26. Suppose that you are the government official in charge of issuing patents. How would you use your knowledge of economics to establish a patent policy?

27. Explain why price discrimination will not work if consumers can resell the product for which price discrimination is being attempted.

Answers to the Practice Quiz

1. d. Market power is the ability of a firm to affect the price of its product. A monopolist is one type of market structure where the firm has market power.

2. c. That's the definition of a natural monopoly: When the scale economies in production are sufficiently large that a market can support only one firm.

3. b. A natural monopoly occurs when the scale economies in production are so large that only a single large firm can earn a profit. The market can support only one profitable firm because if a second firm entered the market, both firms would lose money. Some examples are cable TV service, electricity transmission, and water systems.

4. a. The total revenue of 3 units equals ($10 x 3) = $30. The total revenue of four units equals (8 x 4) = 32. Then ($32 - $30)/(4 - 3) = $2.

5. c. Marginal revenue = New Price – (Quantity x Slope of demand curve) $MR = \$25 - (150*0.1) = \$10$. Since marginal revenue exceeds marginal cost, the firm should produce more output, which requires lowering the price.

6. c. The marginal principle can be used by the firm to choose how much to produce and what price to charge. To maximize profit, the monopolist picks the output level where marginal revenue equals marginal cost.

7. b. Marginal cost equals marginal revenue when 900 units of output are produced and sold. Consumers are willing to pay $15 for 900 units.

8. a. The firm collects $40,000 of revenue, pays $25,000 of variable cost, and the rest, $15,000, pays for part of the total fixed cost.

9. c. In order to maximize profit, a monopoly sets marginal revenue equal to marginal cost, and charges the price consumers are willing to pay for that many units of output.

10. d. Relative to perfectly competitive industries, monopolies will restrict output, allowing them to charge a higher price and make a profit. This results in a net loss of benefits to society.

11. a. The perfectly competitive industry produces 200 doses, and charges $18 per dose. The area *abe* is the area above that price level and below the demand curve.

12. a. When monopolies restrict output, they reduce the consumer surplus available to consumers under perfect competition. Some of the lost consumer surplus is transferred to the monopolist as positive economic profits, while the rest become deadweight loss.

13. c. The competitive price is $8. The area above $8 and below the demand curve is the area of consumer surplus.

14. b. Monopoly inefficiency is measured by the difference in the price and quantity the monopoly offers versus those of a more competitive market. The monopolist prevents consumers from getting consumer surplus, meaning that the monopolist reduces the size of the economic pie and causes

inefficiency. The lesson is that monopoly is inefficient because it generates less output than a perfectly competitive market.

15. b. Price discrimination consists of dividing consumers into groups and charging prices based on willingness or ability to pay.

16. d. A firm has an opportunity for price discrimination if three conditions are met: Market power; different consumer groups; and, resale is not possible.

17. c. Only the early morning sale is a price discrimination scheme. Meals cost more in cities because firm costs are higher. It costs more to insure an expensive car because the company's liability is higher, and the egg sale is available to everyone.

18. b. As the temperature rises, demand becomes more inelastic, which means that quantity demanded is less responsive to the increase in price.

19. c. Firms cannot use price discrimination to drive rivals out of business.

20. b. The less elastic market segment will pay a lower price when firms are able to price discriminate.

21. The good news of a cut in price is that the firm can sell more output, thus, revenue increases. The bad news is that the firm will receive a lower price, thus, revenue decreases. When the good news outweighs the bad news, marginal revenue is positive. When the bad news outweighs the good news, marginal revenue is negative.

22. A switch from perfect competition to monopoly decreases consumer surplus by more than it increases profits, so there is a net loss or a deadweight loss to society. The deadweight loss is explained by a combination of lower output available, at a higher price. The decrease in consumer surplus is greater than the amount of deadweight loss. Some of the consumer surplus is transferred from consumers to the monopoly. The deadweight loss triangle is the portion of consumer surplus that does not represent a gain to anyone else.

23. Both the perfectly competitive firms and the monopoly use the marginal principle to determine the profit-maximizing level of output, that is, both set the level of output where marginal revenue equals marginal cost. In the perfectly competitive case, price equals marginal revenue; therefore, the competitive firm sets output where price equals marginal cost. In the monopoly case, price is greater than marginal revenue for any level of output; therefore, when the firm sets marginal revenue equal to marginal cost in order to maximize profit, the corresponding price is higher than that. The profit-maximizing decision results in a lower level of output produced and a higher price in the monopoly case.

24. A monopoly may use some or all of its positive economic profits to try to prevent others from entering the industry. This activity is called rent-seeking behavior. The firm spends money to persuade the government to erect barriers to entry and pick the firm as the monopolist. Rent seeking is inefficient because it uses resources that could be used in other ways. Such activity may yield nothing of social value. All it does is shift income from buyers to the monopoly at a cost of lost production.

25. Price discrimination is the process under which a firm divides consumers into two or more groups and picks a different price for each group. The only legal restriction on price discrimination is that a firm cannot use it to drive rival firms out of business. A firm has an opportunity for price discrimination if three conditions are met: 1) firms must have market power, 2) firms must be able to identify and divide consumers among particular groups, and 3) the products that one firm offers are not offered for resale by another firm.

26. There are trade-offs from patents that must be taken into account. It is sensible to grant a patent for a product that would otherwise not be developed but not sensible to grant one for a product that would be developed even without a patent. The purpose of the patent is to provide incentives that will cause the firm to respond by developing new products. The length of the patent should be sufficient for the monopoly to earn monopoly profits that will allow it to recover its research and development costs, but not long enough to preserve monopoly power that will result in higher prices.

27. If consumers can resell the product, those who are charged the lower price will be able to sell the product they buy to those who are charged more by the producer. The price resellers will charge is a price somewhere between the low discrimination price and the high discrimination price. Eventually, only those charged the lower price will be the ones buying from the producer. In such a case, the producer would be better off charging a uniform price.

11 [26]
Market Entry and Monopolistic Competition

Chapter Summary

This chapter is about market entry and monopolistic competition. Here are the main points of the chapter:
- The entry of a firm into a market decreases the market price, decreases output per firm, and increases the average cost of production.
- In a monopolistically competitive market, firms compete for customers by producing differentiated products.
- In the long-run equilibrium with monopolistic competition, marginal revenue equals marginal cost, price equal average cost, and economic profit is zero.
- Under monopolistic competition, the average cost of production is higher than the minimum, but there is also more product variety.
- A firm can use celebrity endorsements and other costly advertisements to signal its belief that a product will be appealing.

Applying the Concepts

After reading this chapter, you should be able to answer these four key questions:
1. How does brand competition within stores affect prices?
2. What does it take to enter a market with a franchise?
3. What are the effects of market entry?
4. What signal does an expensive advertising campaign send to consumers?

Monopolistic competition refers to a market served by many firms that sell slightly different products. This type of market has two key features:
- Each firm produces a good that is slightly different than the other firms. This means that each firm is a monopoly provider of their product.
- Products sold by different firms in the market are close substitutes for each other.

☞ For example, you can only buy a Big Mac at McDonald's. However, Wendy's, Burger King, and Hardee's all offer similar burgers which are good substitutes for the Big Mac, even though they are slightly different.

We will make two important assumptions in this chapter:
- There are no barriers to entry.
- Firms do not act strategically. Firms take the actions of other firms as given and don't consider how other firms will respond to their choice of output and price.

11.1 [26.1] The Effects of Market Entry

Firms in a monopolistically competitive market will use the marginal principle to determine how much output to produce.

 The Marginal Principle

Increase the level of an activity as long as its marginal benefit exceeds its marginal cost. Choose the level at which the marginal benefit equals the marginal cost.

When economic profits exist in a market, new entrants will be attracted to that market. In Figure 11.1 [26.1] of the text, we see in panel A, a single firm earning economic profits. These profits will attract a new entrant selling a similar, but distinct, product. Those consumers who prefer the new variety of the product will now purchase the new product. Three things will happen to the first firm as a result of entry:
- The price will fall. As the firm-specific demand curve shifts to the left due to entry, a price making firm will charge a lower price. In the figure, the price falls from $2 to $1.80.
- The quantity sold by the original firm will fall. As the firm-specific demand curve shifts left, the quantity sold by firm one falls from 300 toothbrushes to 200.
- The average cost increases. Because firm one is producing fewer toothbrushes and is on a downward sloping portion of average cost, reducing output increases the average cost.

The result is that profits fall from $330 to $160. Since positive profits still exist, entry will continue to occur until economic profits are zero for all firms.

Let's review an Application which answers a key question posed at the start of the chapter:

1. How does brand competition within stores affect prices?

APPLICATION 1: NAME BRANDS VERSUS STORE BRANDS
Many stores sell both national brand goods and generic or store label goods. Store brands serve as competition for the national brand offered in the same store. Economic theory would suggest that as store brands enter the market, the price of national brands should fall. This is exactly what happened with General Electric light bulbs in the early 1980s.

☞ You might ask why the price of General Electric light bulbs fell to only $2.00 and not to the $1.50 at which the store brands sold. In a perfectly competitive market we would expect all light bulbs to sell for the same price, but remember in a perfectly competitive market goods are perfect substitutes for one another. The fact that goods are slightly different will allow price differences to exist. For instance, you may prefer Big Macs to Whoppers, and you may be willing to pay more for a Big Mac than a Whopper. At some point, the price difference between the two will become large enough that you will choose to buy the Whopper. In this case the Big Mac and Whopper are not perfect substitutes, but they are substitutes. In the market for light bulbs, some consumers believe that General Electric light bulbs are superior to store brand light bulbs and they are willing to pay more for the General Electric bulbs.

11.2 [26.2] Monopolistic Competition

The monopolistic competition market structure can be described by the following three features:
- Many firms. Because economies of scale exist at low output levels, both small and large firms can co-exist in this market.
- Differentiated product. **Product differentiation** is the process used by firms to distinguish their products from the products of competing firms. Products can be differentiated by style, options offered, flavor, location, or many other characteristics.
- No barriers to entry. There is nothing to prevent entry from occurring in the market.

Each firm is like a monopoly in that it is the only seller of its version of the market product. The market is like competition in that goods are substitutes for each other and there is free entry into the market.

Free entry in a market will always cause economic profits to fall to zero. Entry will continue to occur until no economic profits exist. In Figure 11.1 [26.1] the impact of entry is that the firm-specific demand curve continues to shift to the left until we reach the outcome shown in Figure 11.2 [26.2] of the text. Here you see that the firm chooses its profit maximizing quantity of 80 toothbrushes and sells them for $1.40 each. At an output level of 80 toothbrushes, average cost is also $1.40. The firm is earning zero economic profits.

🖹 Remember

Economic profits attract entry into a market. With no barriers to entry, entry will occur until economic profits are zero.

☞ Product differentiation can take many forms. One important consideration is location. Think about your own purchasing decisions. Do you always buy gasoline from the same station? If so, is it because they always have the lowest price or because they are the most convenient?

Let's review an Application that answers one of the key questions posed at the start of the chapter:

2. What does it take to enter a market with a franchise?

APPLICATION 2: OPENING A DUNKIN' DONUTS SHOP
This Application provides an overview of entering a market by opening a franchise shop. If you wanted to sell donuts you could either open your own independent store, or open an outlet of a franchise store. The franchise gives you brand recognition, advertising, and training. In return you pay a fixed fee plus a percentage of your sales to the franchise holder. Can you expect to make money? If other firms can enter the market, you can expect to cover your economic costs and earn zero economic profits.

11.3 [26.3] Trade-Offs with Entry and Monopolistic Competition

While entry leads to lower prices and a larger total quantity in the market, it lowers output by firm and leads to higher average costs of production. This is the key trade-off of entry and monopolistic competition. We gain a lower market price, higher output, and more product variety, but it comes at the cost of higher costs of production.

📄 Remember

In a perfectly competitive market in long-run equilibrium, each firm is producing output at minimum average cost. Because firms in a monopolistically competitive market face a downward sloping demand curve, in long-run equilibrium, each firm will produce at higher than minimum average cost.

Figure 11.4 [26.4] of the text shows the efficiency cost of monopolistic competition. If each firm sold an identical product we would have a perfectly competitive industry as shown in Panel A. Notice that for a firm in this market marginal revenue is equal to price and the profit maximizing output of the firm occurs at point *a*. This is also the point of minimum average cost.

In Panel B, we have the firm diagram for a monopolistically competitive firm. Here the firm faces a downward sloping firm-specific demand curve and thus marginal revenue is less than price. The firm chooses price/output at point *c*, which occurs on the downward sloping portion of average cost. As a result, production costs are higher than they would be without product variety.

Let's review an Application that answers one of the key questions posed at the start of the chapter:

3. What are the effects of market entry?

APPLICATION 3: YOUTUBE VERSUS METACAFE
Metacafe entered the market for online videos, a market in which Youtube was already a key player. To differentiate itself Metacafe not only eliminated videos which received poor reviews, they also began to pay people who submitted highly rated and watched videos. In response, Youtube changed its business model offering to share advertising revenue with the producers of its popular videos.

📄 Remember

Product differentiation increases the average cost of production, but introduces new varieties of products which consumers value. Many economists believe the value consumers place on product variety outweighs the social cost of producing above minimum average cost.

11.4 [26.4] Advertising for Product Differentiation

Advertising can play a key role in markets with product differentiation. A famous study found that advertising price competition lowered eyeglass prices by about 20 percent. Advertising can also focus on different features of the product. Finally, advertising can be used to promote a brand image without conveying any real information about the product.

Advertising can also be a signal to consumers. If you are willing to pay a large sum of money to an endorser, you are signaling to the market that you believe you have a good product. Your goal with the endorser is to get people to try the product for the first time, and hopefully to continue to purchase the product. If you don't think people will like the product enough to purchase it again, you are unlikely to spend a great deal of money advertising the product.

Let's review an Application which answers one of the key questions posed at the start of the chapter:

4. What signal does an expensive advertising campaign send to consumers?

APPLICATION 4: ADVERTISING AND MOVIE BUZZ
This Application suggests that movies that viewers will like will be advertised more heavily than other movies. If advertising gets viewers to the theaters, and they like the movie, they are likely to tell their friends about the movie, and their friends are likely to go see the movie. Word of mouth increases the return to the initial advertising. As a result, movies which are likely to generate word of mouth, or buzz, are likely to be advertised more heavily.

Activity

Think of the product commercials you have recently seen on television. Answer the following questions:
a. What product was being advertised?
b. How did the advertisement attempt to differentiate its product from others?
c. Did the product use a celebrity endorser?
d. Did the advertisement attempt to create an image for the good or convey information about the product?

Key Terms

Monopolistic competition: A market served by many firms that sell slightly different products.

Product differentiation: The process used by firms to distinguish their products from the products of competing firms.

Practice Quiz

(Answers are provided at the end of the Practice Quiz.)

1. Which of the key principles of economics does the monopolistically competitive firm use to make its output decisions?
    a. The marginal principle.
    b. The principle of diminishing returns.
    c. The principle of opportunity cost.
    d. The real-nominal principle.

2. What are the characteristics of monopolistic competition?
    a. Many firms, homogeneous product, and artificial barriers to entry.
    b. Many firms, differentiated product, and artificial barriers to entry.
    c. Many firms, differentiated product, and no artificial barriers to entry.
    d. Few firms, differentiated product, and no artificial barriers to entry.

3. Monopolistic competition is similar to a perfectly competitive industry in the fact that:
    a. marginal revenue is less than price in both industries.
    b. there are no significant barriers to entry in either industry.
    c. the firm's demand is downward-sloping in both cases.
    d. there is a unique product sold in each industry.

4. Monopolistically competitive firms have some control over price because:
    a. there are no barriers to entry.
    b. there are only a few firms in the market.
    c. the products they produce are differentiated.
    d. economic profits are possible.

5. Refer to the graph below. The graph shows the revenue and cost structure of a monopolistically competitive firm. How is this graph similar or different from the graph that depicts a monopoly?

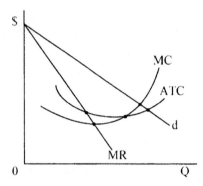

    a. There is no difference. Both graphs are identical.
    b. Marginal cost and average cost look the same as the pure monopoly's, but they are not the same concepts.
    c. The demand curve is downward sloping, but it is not the same concept as the pure monopoly's demand curve.
    d. Both graphs are entirely different. There is no similarity at all.

6. Refer to the table below. At what level of output is average total cost minimized?

Coffee Cups Sold per Week (Q)	Price (P)	Total Revenue (TR)	Marginal Revenue (MR)	Total Cost (TC)	Marginal Cost (MC)	Average Total Cost (ATC)	Profit
0	$6.00	$0.00	-	$5.00	-		
1	5.50	5.50	$5.50	8.00	$3.00		
2	5.00	10.00	4.50	9.50	1.50		
3	4.50	13.50	3.50	10.00	0.50		
4	4.00	16.00	2.50	11.00	1.00		
5	3.50	17.50	1.50	12.50	1.50		
6	3.00	18.00	0.50	14.50	2.00		
7	2.50	17.50	-0.50	17.00	2.50		
8	2.00	16.00	-1.50	20.00	3.00		
9	1.50	13.50	-2.50	23.50	3.50		
10	1.00	10.00	-3.50	27.50	4.00		

a. At 1 unit of output.
b. At 5 units of output.
c. At 6 units of output.
d. At 10 units of output.

7. Refer to the table below. What level of output should be produced in order to maximize profit?

Coffee Cups Sold per Week (Q)	Price (P)	Total Revenue (TR)	Marginal Revenue (MR)	Total Cost (TC)	Marginal Cost (MC)	Average Total Cost (ATC)	Profit
0	$6.00	$0.00	-	$5.00	-		
1	5.50	5.50	$5.50	8.00	$3.00		
2	5.00	10.00	4.50	9.50	1.50		
3	4.50	13.50	3.50	10.00	0.50		
4	4.00	16.00	2.50	11.00	1.00		
5	3.50	17.50	1.50	12.50	1.50		
6	3.00	18.00	0.50	14.50	2.00		
7	2.50	17.50	-0.50	17.00	2.50		
8	2.00	16.00	-1.50	20.00	3.00		
9	1.50	13.50	-2.50	23.50	3.50		
10	1.00	10.00	-3.50	27.50	4.00		

a. 1 unit of output.
b. 5 units of output.
c. 6 units of output.
d. 10 units of output.

8. Think back to the example in the text on deregulation and entry in trucking.

What happens when the government eliminates artificial barriers to entry? The Motor Carrier Act of 1980 eliminated the government's entry restrictions on the trucking industry, most of which had been in place since the 1930s. The market value of a firm's trucking license indicates how much profit the firm can earn in the market. The average value of a trucking license dropped from $579,000 in 1977 to less than $15,000 in 1982.

Using the graphical illustration of a perfectly competitive scenario, which of the following best describes the situation in the trucking industry after 1980?
   a. Market supply shifts to the left, causing prices to rise and consequently new firms to enter the market.
   b. Entry of new firms results in a shift of market supply to the right, causing price and profit to fall.
   c. Market supply does not change, but the entry of new firms reduces the market demand, causing prices and profit to fall.
   d. Market supply and demand shift to the right simultaneously, causing prices and profits to fall.

9. Suppose that there are currently three video rental stores in your town. Each store rents movies for $4 and has an average cost of $2 per movie. What do you expect to happen in this market in the future?
   a. More firms will enter, and the price of video rentals will rise.
   b. More firms will enter, and the price of video rentals will fall.
   c. Firms will exit the market, and the price of video rentals will rise.
   d. Firms will exit the market, and the price of video rentals will fall.

10. Suppose that the price of breakfast cereal is $4 and the average cost of producing it is $1.50. If this is a monopolistically competitive industry, what do you predict will happen in the long run?
   a. Price will increase and average cost will increase.
   b. Price will increase and average cost will decrease.
   c. Price will decrease and average cost will decrease.
   d. Price will increase and average cost will increase.

11. Which of the following contributes to a decrease in profit for the individual firm after entry of a second firm?
   a. Lower price.
   b. Lower quantity sold.
   c. Higher average cost of production.
   d. All of the above.

12. In a monopolistically competitive market, what will cause the entry of new firms to stop?
   a. An increase in the costs of producing output.
   b. A decrease in market price.
   c. A decrease in revenues.
   d. The eventual disappearance of economic profit.

13. This question tests your understanding of Application 3 in this chapter: Opening a Dunkin' Donuts shop: What does it take to enter a market with a franchise?

How much money are you likely to make in your donut shop? You will compete for donut consumers with other donut shops, bakeries, grocery stores, and coffee shops. Given the small barriers to entering the donut business, you should expect keen competition for consumers. Although your brand-name donuts will give you an edge over your competitors, remember that you must pay the franchise fee and royalties. In the monopolistically competitive donut market, you should expect to make zero economic profit, with total revenue equal to total cost.

If monopolistically competitive firms can expect to earn zero economic profit in the long run, which of the following will occur?
a. Zero economic profit does not cover the opportunity cost of being in the business, so firms will exit the market.
b. New firms will enter the market.
c. Zero economic profit means that firms earn normal profit, so they stay in the market, but there is no incentive for firms to enter.
d. For entrepreneurs, the opportunity cost of being in the industry is zero.

14. For the typical firm in a monopolisitically competitive market in long-run equilibrium:
a. the price is less than marginal cost.
b. the price is greater than average cost.
c. the price is equal to marginal revenue.
d. the price is greater than both marginal revenue and marginal cost.

15. Refer to the figure below, which shows a firm in a monopolistically competitive industry. Based on the graph, which of the following is true?

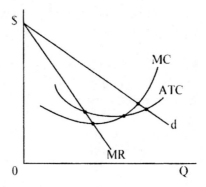

a. This industry is in long-run equilibrium.
b. We expect that more firms will enter this industry, given enough time.
c. We expect that firms will exit this industry, given enough time.
d. We expect that this firm will earn a long-run economic profit.

16. Which of the following conditions will be met in a monopolistically competitive industry in long-run equilibrium?
a. Price will be equal to marginal revenue.
b. Price will be equal to average cost.
c. Price will be equal to marginal cost.
d. Price will be equal to minimum average cost.

17. When differentiating a product by location in a market with no barriers to entry, a firm can expect to earn:
a. positive economic profit.
b. zero economic profit.
c. below normal profit.
d. losses in the short run but profits in the long run.

18. Refer to the figure below. Which statement is entirely correct? The firm in question is a monopolistically competitive firm:

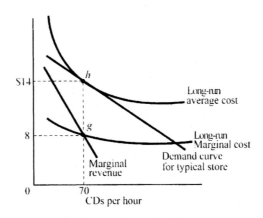

    a.   in short-run equilibrium but not in long-run equilibrium.
    b.   in short-run equilibrium and expecting new firms to enter the market.
    c.   in long-run equilibrium, as indicated by the equality of price and average cost.
    d.   neither in short-run nor in long-run equilibrium.

19. Which of the following best describes how the product differentiation of monopolistically competitive firms may benefit consumers?
    a.   Product differentiation lowers the average cost of production allowing the firms to charge a lower price than perfect competition.
    b.   Product differentiation increases the market supply curve which lowers the price of the product.
    c.   Product differentiation can locate firms more conveniently to consumers and offer versions of a product or service that better fit their needs.
    d.   All of the above.

20. As described in the textbook, by paying millions of dollars for celebrity endorsements, a firm's primary purpose is to:
    a.   comply with government regulations.
    b.   provide information about the product's characteristics and price.
    c.   send a signal to consumers that the advertised product is appealing and likely to be popular.
    d.   try to sell less appealing products.

21. Explain the concept of product differentiation by location.

22. Compare and contrast the price/output decisions of profit-maximizing firms in a perfectly competitive market versus those of a monopolistically competitive market.

23. Explain the differences in the elasticity of demand for a perfectly competitive firm, a monopolistic competitor, and a monopoly.

24. Compare and contrast the long-run equilibrium conditions that hold in a perfectly competitive market, a monopolistically competitive market, and a monopoly. Be specific by referring to the relationship between common measures such as price, marginal revenue, marginal cost, average cost, and profit.

Answers to the Practice Quiz

1. a. As long as the marginal benefit is greater than the marginal cost of production, the monopolistically competitive firm will continue to produce.

2. c. Many firms, product differentiation, and no artificial barriers to entry are characteristics of monopolistic competition.

3. b. Monopolistically competitive industries have many firms, differentiated products, and no barriers to entry. Perfectly competitive industries have many firms, identical products, and no barriers to entry. Differentiated products mean that firm demand is downward-sloping in monopolistically competitive industries, and thus marginal revenue is less than price.

4. c. Monopolistically competitive firms have some control over price because products are differentiated. Since products are not identical, demand for each firm's goods are elastic but not perfectly elastic.

5. c. The monopoly's demand curve is the entire market demand curve. The demand curve of the monopolistic competitor is only a share of market demand. Because of this the latter is more inelastic (steeper) than the former, all other things equal.

6. c. When $Q = 6$, $ATC = \$14.50/6 = 2.42$

7. b. At this level of output, marginal revenue of $1.50 equals marginal cost.

8. b. Entry of new firms results in a shift of market supply to the right, causing price and profit to fall. Each of the original firms sees a reduction in the firm-specific demand.

9. b. Since firms are earning positive economic profit, eventually more firms will enter the market. As firms enter, demand for each firm decreases and the price falls.

10. d. Positive profits will make firms enter in the long run. As firms enter, price will fall, and each firm will supply less, moving back along its average cost curve toward higher costs.

11. d. All three reasons above explain the effects of market entry on profit.

12. d. Entry will stop once the economic profit of existing firms reaches zero and revenue is just enough to cover all costs, including the opportunity cost of all inputs.

13. c. Revenue is sufficient to cover your total cost, which includes the franchise fee and royalties, as well as the opportunity cost of your time and the opportunity cost of any funds you invest in the business, but not enough to make it worthwhile for other firms to enter.

14. d. In long-run equilibrium in a monopolistically competitive market, the level of output chosen by the typical firm is where marginal revenue equals marginal cost. The price is then determined by the demand curve for the firm. This price is equal to the long-run average cost, so economic profit is zero.

15. b. This firm is making a profit. Thus, since there are no barriers to entry in a perfectly competitive industry, more firms will enter. This will cause individual demand to fall and average costs to rise, until no more firms can enter and make a positive profit.

16. b. In long-run equilibrium, profits must be equal to zero (or more firms would wish to enter). Thus, price must be equal to average cost. However, this will not be equal to minimum average cost, because there are too many firms in the market for any to reach minimum efficient scale.

17. b. As shown in the textbook example, new video stores will enter the market until each store makes zero economic profit. Each firm's revenue is high enough to cover all its costs—including the opportunity cost of all its inputs—but not enough to cause additional firms to enter the market.

18. c. When price equals average cost, the monopolistically competitive firm is in long-run equilibrium.

19. c. Consumers can choose the good or service that best fits their needs although they will pay a higher price for it. Part of that higher price might be offset by reduced travel costs since product differentiation is also based on location.

20. c. An advertisement that doesn't provide any product information may actually help consumers make decisions. By paying millions of dollars to run an advertisement, a firm sends a signal to consumers that the advertised product is appealing and likely to be popular. This is called the signaling effect of advertisement.

21. This product differentiation consists of offering the product at more locations and is one of the benefits consumers enjoy as a result of monopolistic competition. When the product is at more locations, consumers spend less time traveling to buy the product.

22. In order to maximize profit, both perfectly competitive firms and monopolistically competitive firms set output where marginal revenue equals marginal cost. In the perfectly competitive case, price equals marginal revenue; therefore, price equals marginal cost. This is one indicator that firms are efficient. In the case of monopolistic competition, the firm's demand curve is downward sloping, which means that marginal revenue is less than price. When profit is maximized, price is greater than marginal cost. This means that the amount of output produced is insufficient. Monopolistically competitive firms charge a higher price and produce less output than perfectly competitive firms.

23. The demand curve facing a perfectly competitive firm is perfectly elastic because there are perfect substitutes for the good produced by the firm. The monopolistic competitor faces a demand curve that is less elastic than the perfectly competitive firm is but more elastic than the demand curve faced by a monopoly. The reason is that the monopolistic competitor produces a good that is a close substitute for the goods produced by other firms in the market. The monopoly faces a more inelastic demand curve because the monopoly produces a good for which there are no close substitutes.

24. In perfect competition, price equals marginal revenue, equals marginal cost, equals minimum average total cost. Economic profit equals zero, that is, the amount of profit is only normal profit. In monopolistic competition, marginal cost equals marginal revenue; and price is greater than marginal revenue and marginal cost. Average cost is above the minimum average cost, and equal to price; therefore, economic profit equals zero. Firms earn only normal profit. In monopoly, marginal cost equals marginal revenue, price is greater than marginal revenue and marginal cost, and average cost is above the minimum average cost. Price is greater than average cost, so the firm may earn positive economic profit equals zero. Only in a perfectly competitive market, resources are allocated efficiently. Since price equals marginal cost, firms produce exactly what consumers want; and since average cost is minimized, firms make optimal use of their plant sizes.

12 [27]
Oligopoly and Strategic Behavior

Chapter Summary

This chapter examines markets with few firms which have an incentive to act strategically. Here are the main points of the chapter:

- Each firm in an oligopoly has an incentive to underprice the other firms, so price-fixing will be unsuccessful unless firms have some way of enforcing a price-fixing agreement.
- One way to maintain price-fixing is a low-price guarantee: One firm chooses the high price and promises to match any lower price of its competitor.
- Price-fixing is more likely to occur if firms choose prices repeatedly and can punish a firm that chooses a price below the cartel price.
- To prevent a second firm from entering the market, an insecure monopolist may commit itself to producing a relatively large quantity and accepting a relatively low price.
- The advertisers' dilemma is that both firms would be better off if neither firm advertised.

Applying the Concepts

After reading this chapter, you should be able to answer these four key questions:
1. How do firms conspire to fix prices?
2. Does a low-price guarantee lead to higher or lower prices?
3. What means—legal and illegal-do firms use to prevent other firms from entering a market?
4. How do patent holders respond to the introduction of generic drugs?

An **oligopoly** is defined as a market served by a few firms. In particular, firms in an oligopoly market
- may sell similar or differentiated products
- are concerned about how other firms in the market will react to their choices
- act strategically taking into consideration how its rivals will respond to their actions.

☞ Think of a locally owned restaurant in your city. It is unlikely that they consider how other, similar restaurants will respond to changes in their prices or menus. This is not the case with the large fast-food restaurants. When Burger King announces that they are going to shift to healthier frying oils they certainly were concerned with how McDonald's, KFC, and others would respond.

Studying oligopoly is often done using game theory. Game theory is the study of decision making in strategic situations. A strategic situation is one in which the payoff of any action depends upon the response of others to the action.

12.1 [27.1] What Is an Oligopoly?

In an oligopoly, a few firms have market power, that is, the ability to control prices. In an oligopoly market, much of the market power is concentrated in a few firms. A **concentration ratio** measures the percentage of the market output produced by the largest firms.

Most typical is the *four-firm concentration ratio*. This is simply the sum of the market shares of the four largest firms in the market.

☞ Suppose a market consists of ten firms. The largest firm has 25% of the market. The next three firms each have 15% of the market. Each of the other six firms have market share of 5%. The four-firm concentration ratio is:

$$25\% + 15\% + 15\% + 15\% = 70\%$$

Table 12.1 [27.1] in the text also contains the *eight-firm concentration ratio*. This is simply the sum of the market shares of the eight largest firms in the market.

☞ Using the numbers from our previous example, the eight-firm concentration ratio would be:

$$25\% + 15\% + 15\% + 15\% + 5\% + 5\% + 5\% + 5\% = 90\%$$

An alternative measure of market power is the *Herfindahl-Hirschman index* (HHI). To compute the HHI, we add up the squared market shares of all the firms in the industry. A monopoly will have an HHI of 10,000. This is 100^2 since the only firm in the market will have 100% market share. An industry with 100 small firms, each with 1% of the market, would have an HHI of 100.

The Justice Department classifies industries in the following ways:
- Unconcentrated: HHI less than 1,000.
- Highly concentrated: HHI greater than 1,800.

☞ Using the numbers from our first example, we have:

$$\begin{aligned} \text{HHI} &= 25^2 + 15^2 + 15^2 + 15^2 + 5^2 + 5^2 + 5^2 + 5^2 + 5^2 + 5^2 \\ &= 625 + 225 + 225 + 225 + 25 + 25 + 25 + 25 + 25 + 25 \\ &= 1{,}550 \end{aligned}$$

There are three primary reasons why an oligopoly occurs:
1. Government barriers to entry
2. Economies of scale in production
3. Advertising campaigns

12.2 [27.2] Cartel Pricing and the Duopolists' Dilemma

A **duopoly** is a market with two firms. We can use the duopoly model to understand the behavior of firms in an oligopoly market. The text considers a duopoly in air travel between two cities.

Firms in an oligopoly would like to act as a cartel. A **cartel** is a group of firms that act in unison, coordinating their price and quantity decisions. Ideally a cartel would like to charge the monopoly price for the industry product. This is shown as point *b* in Figure 12.1 [27.2] of your text. This could be done if the firms agree together to fix prices. **Price fixing** is an arrangement in which firms conspire to fix prices. Both cartels and price-fixing are illegal in the United States. It is also difficult for firms to enter a price fixing agreement unless the firms have some way to punish those who violate the agreement.

Figure 12.2 [27.2] in your text shows a more usual duopoly outcome in which firms are unable to fix prices. Each firm will sell at point *b* on their firm-specific demand curve. This translates into point *d* on the market demand curve. Notice that when firms are unable to fix prices, we have higher output and lower prices than under the cartel result (which you remember is the same as the monopoly result).

Recall the following key principle:

KEY PRINCIPLE: MARGINAL PRINCIPLE
Increase the level of an activity as long as its marginal benefit exceeds its marginal costs. Choose the level at which the marginal benefit equals the marginal costs.

We can use game theory to understand the choices facing the two firms. Figure 12.3 [27.3] in your text illustrates a **game tree**, a graphical representation of the consequences of different actions in a strategic setting. A game tree has three components:
- Decision nodes: These are the squares in the diagram and show a point at which one of the players makes a decision. In the game tree in Figure 12.3 [27.3], Jill makes the first decision, choosing a high or low price, and then Jack makes the second decision. There are two decision nodes for Jack as he faces two possible decision scenarios, one in which Jill has chosen a high price and one in which Jill has chosen a low price.
- Arrows: These show the possible paths of the game across the game tree. The game moves from left to right. The highlighted arrow shows the outcome of the game.
- Rectangles: These show the payoffs from a particular set of choices. Notice that the payoffs depend on the actions of both players. So the payoff to Jill from choosing a high price depends on whether Jack also chooses a high price.

To solve the game tree, we move from right to left. If Jill picks a high price, Jack has the choice between profits of $12,000 (with a low price) and $9,000 (with a high price). We would expect that Jack would choose the low price in this situation. If Jill picks a low price, Jack has the choice between profits of $3,000 (with a high price) and $8,000 (with a low price). Again we would expect Jack to pick the low price.

For Jack, a low price is a dominant strategy. A **dominant strategy** is an action that is the best choice for a player, no matter what the other player does.

Since Jill knows that Jack will always pick the low price, her choice is between profits of $3,000 (with a high price) or $8,000 (with a low price). She would prefer the low price. The equilibrium of the game is illustrated by the bold arrow in Figure 12.1 [27.1]. In this case Jill earns profits of $8,000 and Jack earns profits of $8,000.

If both Jack and Jill had chosen the high price, they would have each earned higher profits. This is the **duopolists' dilemma**, a situation in which both firms in a market would be better off if both chose the high price, but each chooses the low price.

The solution with both choosing the low price is the Nash equilibrium outcome for this game tree. A **Nash equilibrium** is an outcome of a game in which each player is doing the best he or she can, given the action of the other players.

Let's review an Application that answers one of the key questions posed at the start of the chapter.

1. How do firms conspire to fix prices?

APPLICATION 1: MARINE HOSE CONSPIRATORS GO TO PRISION
This Application shows how executives of marine hose companies allocated customers to different members of a cartel and fixed prices. It also illustrates that there are penalties, in this case prison time, for those caught in price fixing behavior.

⌒ Study Tip

A Nash equilibrium means that no player in a game would want to change their chosen strategy once they know what the other player has chosen.

12.3 [27.3] Overcoming the Duopolists' Dilemma

The duopolists' dilemma arises because each firm has an incentive to underprice the other to gain market share. If this incentive can be eliminated, duopolists can keep prices high.

One strategy is to ensure that there is no gain from underpricing. A **low-price guarantee**, a promise to match a lower price of a competitor, is one way to do this. Figure 12.4 [27.4] in the text illustrates that Jill's low-price guarantee eliminates Jack's ability to earn higher profits by offering a low price when Jill charges a high price. Jill does this by committing to offering a low price if Jack offers a low price. The low price guarantee essentially adds a decision node to the game tree. If Jack chooses a low price after Jill has chosen a high price, Jill automatically offers a refund to provide the same outcome as if both had chosen a low price. Jack now has the choice between earning $9,000 with a high price or $8,000 with a low price in response to Jill's high price. Jill's action has taken away the incentive for Jack to offer a low price.

If Jack and Jill make pricing decisions repeatedly it becomes easier for them to fix prices. If Jack and Jill agree to sell at the cartel price, the outcome will be at point *c* in Panel B of Figure 12.2 [27.2]. The text lists three pricing strategies:
1. A duopoly pricing strategy: If Jack violates the cartel arrangement, Jill accepts the lower profits of a low price strategy, the duopoly outcome shown as point *d*, and forever abandons the idea of cartel pricing.
2. A **grim-trigger strategy**: If Jack underprices Jill, she drops her price so low that economic profits fall to zero for both firms.
3. A **tit-for-tat strategy**: Jill decides that her pricing decision next month will be the same as Jack's pricing decision this month. This is illustrated in Figure 12.5 [27.5] in your book. Notice that Jill's choice (indicated by a square) is always the choice Jack made (indicated by a circle) in the previous period.

All three of these strategies promote cartel pricing by penalizing the firm that underprices the other firm. As with most decisions, there are benefits and costs to be considered when deciding whether to underprice:

- Benefit: If Jill chooses a high price and Jack chooses a low price, he earns $12,000 this period instead of $9,000.
- Cost: If Jill responds by charging a low price next period and in the future, Jack will earn $8,000 per period instead of $9,000.

If Jack is interested in making profits for a long period of time he would rather sacrifice the $3,000 additional dollars this period for the $1,000 additional dollars in many future periods. If Jack is unconcerned about the future, he would rather have the $3,000 now.

Explicit price fixing is illegal in the United States. The Sherman Antitrust Act of 1890 was the first of several pieces of legislation that outlawed price-fixing and cartel behavior in the United States.

🗎 Remember

Repeated interaction between oligopolists makes cooperation and cartel-like behavior more likely.

Let's review an Application that answers one of the key questions posed at the start of the chapter:

2.   Does a low-price guarantee lead to higher or lower prices?

APPLICATION 2: LOW-PRICE GUARANTEES AND EMPTY PROMISES
This Application illustrates how a low-price guarantee works to keep prices high. The incentive to lower prices is increased sales for the store that lowers its price. A low-price guarantee makes it less likely that sales will increase as a result of the lower price (since competitors will match the lower price) and as a result the guarantee eliminates the benefits of lowering the price of a product. The Application illustrates that what appears to be a guarantee of low prices actually serves to keep prices high.

12.4 [27.4] Alternative Models of Oligopoly Pricing

Price leadership is a system under which one firm in an oligopoly takes the lead in setting prices. In this model, the other firms in the market take their pricing signal from the price leader and respond accordingly.

 Frequently you will read stories in the *Wall Street Journal* about a major airline announcing a fare increase or decrease. Typically these increases will take effect far enough in the future that they can be revoked at little cost to the airline. Let's suppose that Northwest Airlines announces a 5% fare increase. If other airlines match this increase it will stay in effect. If other airlines do not match the fare increase, Northwest will revoke the increase and leave fares as they were. This is an example of Northwest Airlines attempting to be a price leader.

The text points out that a problem with price leadership is that it is difficult to determine if a firm is lowering prices because of a change in market conditions or because they are trying to increase market share.
In the **kinked demand curve model**, firms in an oligopoly match price cuts by other firms, but do not match price hikes. This is illustrated in Figure 12.6 [27.6] of your text. Notice that the demand curve is very

elastic above the current price and very inelastic below the current price. This indicates that any change from the current price will lower revenue to the firm changing price. The model suggests that price in an oligopoly market will remain relatively stable as no firm will have incentive to change their price. This model is very intuitive, but there is no evidence that firms in an oligopoly actually act in this manner.

12.5 [27.5] Simultaneous Decision Making and the Payoff Matrix

In the game tree we examined sequential decisions, games in which one player moved and then the other followed. What happens if we have a simultaneous game in which both make their decision at the same time? We can study this situation using a payoff matrix. A **payoff matrix** is a matrix or table that shows, for each possible outcome of a game, the consequences for each player.

Figure 12.7 [27.7] of your text shows a payoff matrix for Jack and Jill's pricing game. Notice that the payoffs and strategies are the same for Jack and Jill as they were in the game tree. In the matrix Jill's payoffs are in the lower left corner of each box and Jack's payoffs are in the upper right corner.

You can see the concept of dominant strategy in the matrix. Regardless of whether Jill chooses a high price or a low price, Jack is always better off with a low price. A low price is his dominant strategy. Once we know that a low price is Jack's dominant strategy, we can ignore Jack's high price column as he will never choose a strategy in that column.

Low price is also a dominant strategy for Jill. Regardless of what Jack chooses, Jill is always better off with a low price. As a result, we can ignore the high price row for Jill.

We are left with the bottom right corner with both Jack and Jill charging a low price and earning $8,000 in profits. This is the Nash equilibrium for this game matrix. With both charging a low price, neither has an incentive to change their decision. Once again you notice that both choosing a high price leads to higher profits for each.

You can see why both choosing a high price can't be a Nash equilibrium. If we somehow ended up with both charging a high price both Jack and Jill would have an incentive to change their behavior. Both in fact would want to switch to a low price strategy. Since Jack and Jill have an incentive to change their strategy once they know what the other is doing, both charging a high price can't be the equilibrium outcome.

This game is an example of a famous type of game known as the prisoners' dilemma. You notice that both Jack and Jill would be better off if they both chose a high price, and yet that outcome won't be chosen. You can see that if they started with both charging a high price that both would have an incentive to change to a low price. In a prisoners' dilemma game neither player has an incentive to choose the outcome that is best for both players.

The classic prisoners' dilemma is shown in Figure 12.8 [27.8] of your text. Bonnie and Clyde could minimize their total jail time if neither confess. You should see that if Bonnie believes that Clyde will not confess, she is better off confessing (and serving 1 year) than not confessing and serving 2 years. The same is true for Clyde, if he believes that Bonnie will not confess, he will confess and serve less jail time. While not confessing is the cooperative strategy, confess is the dominant strategy for both Bonnie and Clyde. What is in Bonnie and Clyde's joint interest is not in their individual interest.

12.6 [27.6] The Insecure Monopolist and Entry Deterrence

This section examines the choices of a monopolist in the face of potential entry. In Figure 12.9 [27.9] in the text shows the outcomes of behavior in the face of entry.

When there is no threat of entry, a monopolist will choose point c. At this point she will earn profits of $18,000. How will the monopolist act in the face of potential entry?

The monopolist could be passive, allowing the entry and then producing at the duopoly output level which is shown as point d in Figure 12.9 [27.9]. Your text shows the profit from this activity as $8,000.

Another action that Mona can take is to serve so much of the market that another firm cannot reasonably enter. In Figure 12.9 [27.9], a firm will only enter if it can serve 20 passengers. The zero profit point comes when a firm serves 120 passengers. Mona could choose point e on the demand curve. At this point she is serving 100 passengers, leaving only 20 for a potential entrant. The entry deterring quantity is calculated as:

☑ Key Equation

entry deterring quantity = zero profit quantity – minimum entry quantity

---

Notice that, for Mona, choosing point c leads to profits of $10,000. Since the profits from this strategy are greater than the profits from the duopoly outcome, we would expect Mona to price in such a way to deter potential entry. This practice is known as **limit pricing**, the strategy of reducing the price to deter entry.

Figure 12.10 [27.10] shows the game tree for this situation. Doug will choose whether or not to enter based on Mona's output. If Mona chooses a small quantity, Doug can profitably enter. If Mona chooses a large quantity, Doug can't profitably enter. If Mona chooses a small quantity and Doug enters, Mona will earn $8,000. If Mona chooses the large quantity, Doug will stay out and Mona will earn $10,000. As a result, Mona will produce the large quantity.

Your text shows that if the minimum entry quantity were only 10 passengers, Mona would not fight entry. In this case she would have to serve 110 passengers, point f in Figure 12.9 [27.9], but at this point, profits are smaller than at the duopoly outcome. As a result, Mona would allow entry with the smaller minimum entry quantity.

A **contestable market** is one with low entry and exit costs. In this situation, the threat of entry will lead a monopoly firm to choose lower prices and higher output levels, thus earning lower profits and keeping potential entrants out.

🗎 Remember

How a monopoly responds to potential entrants will depend upon which strategy leads to the highest profit for the monopolist. A monopolist will fight entry if profits from limit pricing are higher than profits with entry. If profits from fighting entry are lower than profits from allowing entry, the monopolist will take a passive approach.

Let's review two Applications that answer key questions posed at the start of the chapter:

3.   What means—legal and illegal—do firms use to prevent other firms from entering a market?

APPLICATION 3: LEGAL AND ILLEGAL ENTRY DETERRENCE
This Application illustrates two strategies chosen to deter entry. Alcoa used limit pricing to maintain its monopoly position in the aluminum market. Notice that Alcoa was willing to sacrifice some profits in the short term to prevent entry. Limit pricing is a legal means of preventing entry. Unilever provided free freezers to retailers who sold their ice cream products so long as no other brands were sold in those freezers. This meant that if a retailer wanted to sell another brand of ice cream, they would also have to pay for a freezer. As a result, many retailers would only sell Unilever brands. The European Commission ruled that this was an abuse of Unilever's market position and ordered Unilever to share their freezer cabinets with its competitors.

4. How do patent holders respond to the introduction of generic drugs?

APPLICATION 4: MERCK AND PFIZER GO GENERIC?
When the patent on a drug expires new firms are able to offer the drug for sale. This Application explores how two companies are responding to the expiration of patent rights on their drugs. Both Merck and Pfizer have agreements to produce generic versions of their branded drugs when the patents expire. In addition, the two companies are cutting the price of their branded drugs so that generic drugs are less attractive in the market.

12.7 [27.7] The Advertisers' Dilemma

Strategic behavior extends to the area of advertising as well. Figure 12.11 [27.11] of your text shows the advertising game tree for two aspirin makers. Notice that Vern's dominant strategy is "advertise." Regardless of what Adeline chooses, Vern is better off advertising. Adeline's choice then reduces to advertising and earning profits of $6, or not advertising and earning profits of $5. She will choose to advertise.

☞ With both advertising, each earns $6 in profits. If neither advertised, both would earn $8 in profits. Cigarette companies are prohibited from engaging in most forms of advertising because of the health risks of smoking and a desire to reduce smoking among teenagers. If the payoffs to advertising in the cigarette market are similar to the payoffs in this example, cigarette companies would be quite happy that the government enforces a no advertising choice on the companies. In that case the regulation also prevents cheating on the no advertising strategy.

📄 Remember

In a prisoners' dilemma, the outcome that is best for both players will not be chosen. The dilemma is that the strategy leading to the best outcome for both players is not a dominant strategy.

Activity

Suppose the advertising decision was simultaneous and not sequential.

    a.   Draw the game matrix for Adeline and Vern.
    b.   Vern's dominant strategy is to _____.
    c.   Adeline's dominant strategy is to _____.
    d.   The Nash equilibrium for this game is: _____ with Vern earning profits of _____ and Adeline earning profits of _____.
    e.   The outcome which would maximize joint profits would be _____ with Vern earning profits of _____ and Adeline earning profits of _____.

Answers

a.

	Vern	
Adeline	Advertise	Not advertise
Advertise	6 6	5 10
Not Advertise	10 5	8 8

    b.   advertise
    c.   advertise
    d.   Both choose advertise and both earn profits of $6.
    e.   Both not advertise and both earning $8.

Key Terms

Cartel: A group of firms that act in unison, coordinating their price and quantity decisions.

Concentration ratio: The percentage of the market output produced by the largest firms.

Contestable market: A market with low entry and exit costs.

Dominant strategy: An action that is the best choice for a player, no matter what the other player does.

Duopolists' dilemma: A situation in which both firms in a market would be better off if both chose the high price, but each chooses the low price.

Duopoly: A market with two firms.

Game theory: The study of decision making in strategic situations.

Game tree: A graphical representation of the consequences of different actions in a strategic setting.

Grim-trigger strategy: A strategy where a firm responds to underpricing by choosing a price so low that each firm makes zero economic profits.

Kinked demand curve model: A model in which firms in an oligopoly match price cuts by other firms, but do not match price hikes.

Limit pricing: The strategy of reducing the price to deter entry.

Low-price guarantee: A promise to match a lower price of a competitor.

Nash equilibrium: An outcome of a game in which each player is doing the best he or she can, given the action of the other players.

Oligopoly: A market served by a few firms.

Payoff matrix: A matrix or table that shows, for each possible outcome of a game, the consequences for each player.

Price-fixing: An arrangement in which firms conspire to fix prices.

Price leadership: A system under which one firm in an oligopoly takes the lead in setting prices.

Tit-for-tat: A strategy where one firm chooses whatever price the other firm chose in the preceding period.

Practice Quiz

(Answers are provided at the end of the Practice Quiz.)

1. Which of the following concepts apply to oligopoly more than to any other market structure?
    a. Differentiated product and easy entry.
    b. Homogeneous product and perfect information.
    c. Easy entry and more than one firm in the market.
    d. Economies of scale and significant barriers to entry.

2. Fill in the blanks: A *four-firm concentration ratio* is the percentage of the _____ by the four largest firms.
    a. total industry revenue shared
    b. market output produced
    c. total geographic coverage of the market
    d. market inputs purchased

3. When firms agree to act as a monopoly and set prices:
    a. they are called a cartel.
    b. they are likely to make higher profits.
    c. they have incentives to cheat on the agreement.
    d. All of the above

4. Refer to the figure below. After a close examination of the graphs on the left and the right side, you may correctly conclude that the graph on the left side is the graph of a:

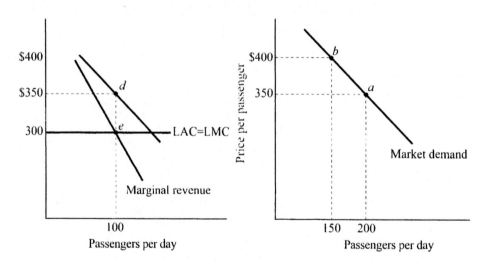

    a. monopoly.
    b. duopoly.
    c. cartel.
    d. price-fixing firm.

5. Refer to the figure below. Which of the following trajectories describes the best strategy for Jack when Jill charges the high price?

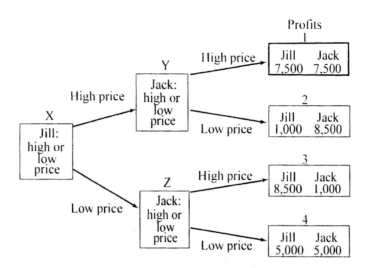

a. XY1
b. XY2
c. XZ3
d. XZ4

6. Refer to the figure below. Which trajectory describes the outcome of the prisoners' dilemma?

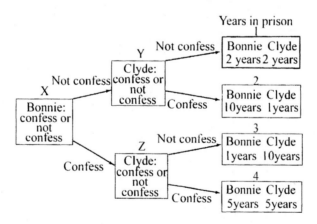

a. XZ3
b. XZ4
c. XY1
d. XY2

7. This question tests your understanding of Application 1 in this chapter: Marine hose conspirators go to prison: How do firms conspire to fix prices?

    In 2007 the U.S. government discovered a long running conspiracy to fix the price of marine hose. The activity described in this story is an example of:
    a. tacit collusion.
    b. explicit collusion.
    c. Nash equilibrium.
    d. a tit-for-tat pricing strategy.

8. When each player makes a choice without the other person knowing what that choice is, the game is called:
    a. a duopoly pricing strategy.
    b. a simultaneous decision-making game.
    c. a sequential decision-making game.
    d. a tit-for-tat strategy.

9. Which of the following is true about *guaranteed price matching*?
    a. Price matching is one of those situations that leads to the duopolists' dilemma
    b. Price matching eliminates the possibility of cartel profits.
    c. Price matching is a strategy that results in a duopoly price.
    d. None of the above.

10. In which of the following retaliation strategies does the firm drop its price to the level that will result in zero economic profit?
    a. A duopoly pricing strategy.
    b. A grim trigger strategy.
    c. A tit-for-tat strategy.
    d. None of the above.

11. Refer to the figure below. In this repeated price-fixing game, the duopoly outcome is reached:

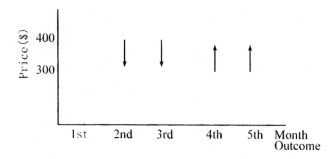

    a. in the second month.
    b. in the third month.
    c. in the fourth month.
    d. in the fifth month.

12. Refer to the figure below. Which portion of this demand curve is the elastic portion?

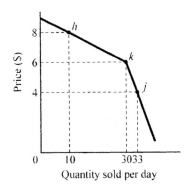

a. The portion above $6.
b. The portion below $6.
c. The entire demand curve is relatively elastic.
d. Neither portion. The entire demand curve is relatively inelastic.

13. Which of the following strategies by an insecure monopolist will lead to the duopoly outcome?
a. The passive strategy.
b. The entry-deterrence strategy.
c. Either strategy above. The duopoly outcome is always the final outcome.
d. Neither strategy above. The duopoly outcome is never the final outcome.

14. This question tests your understanding of Application 3 in this chapter: Legal and illegal entry deterrence: What means—legal and illegal—do firms use to prevent other firms from entering a market?

As explained in this story, firms use limit pricing to prevent entry. Which of the following strategies is more typical of limit pricing?
a. Producing a large quantity and charging a relatively high price.
b. Producing a small quantity and charging a relatively low price.
c. Producing a large quantity and charging a relatively low price.
d. Producing a small quantity and charging a relatively high price.

15. Refer to the figure below. Each point on this graph represents a secure monopolist, an insecure monopolist, a competitive industry with zero economic profit, and a duopoly. Which point represents the duopoly outcome?

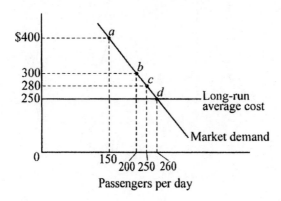

a. *a*
b. *b*
c. *c*
d. *d*

16. The strategic advertiser's dilemma states that:
   a. the relationship between advertising costs and profits is uncertain, yet firms advertise anyway.
   b. when a firm advertises, the majority of the gains are enjoyed by rival firms.
   c. although firms would be better off if they did advertise, the firms decide not to advertise.
   d. although firms would be better off if they did not advertise, the firms advertise anyway.

17. Refer to the figure below. Knowing Jill's dominant strategy, Jack's best response is to:

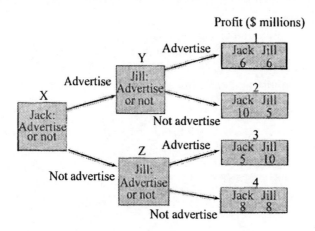

a. follow the trajectory X, Y, 1.
b. follow either X, Y, 1, or X, Z, 4.
c. follow either X, Y, 1, or X, Z, 3.
d. follow either X, Y, 2, or X, Z, 4.

18. When firms are trapped in the advertisers' dilemma:
    a. the allocation of resources in the industry actually improves.
    b. advertising results in a net increase in industry profits.
    c. advertising actually decreases the firm's cost.
    d. None of the above.

19. Briefly, explain the duopolists' dilemma and compare it to a cartel agreement.

20. Briefly explain the prisoners' dilemma.

21. Briefly, explain the concept of price leadership and explain the problems associated with implicit price agreements.

22. Most firms in an oligopoly earn economic profit, yet additional firms do not enter the market. Explain why not.

23. Explain the concept of guaranteed price matching, and explain whether it results in lower or higher prices.

24. Explain the concept of contestable markets. What is the extreme outcome of contestable markets?

Answers to the Practice Quiz

1. d. Few firms dominate the market, and the behavior of the firm depends on the reaction it expects of others.

2. b. A four-firm concentration ratio is the percentage of the market output produced by the four largest firms.

3. d. A cartel, illegal under U.S. law, consists of firms acting together to set prices and thus increase profit. However, cartels tend to fall apart due to the incentive to cheat.

4. b. The market demand curve tells us that 200 tickets will be sold at $350. The firm-specific graph tells us that the profit-maximizing firm will charge $350 and sell 100 tickets or one half of the market output. This will be a duopoly.

5. b. Jack earns higher profits when he charges the lower price once Jill decides to charge the high price—$8,500 instead of $7,500.

6. b. The duopolists' dilemma explains why Bonnie and Clyde are forced to confess when given the proper incentive to confess. Clyde and Bonnie individually are better off confessing whether the other confesses or not.

7. b. Under the Sherman Antitrust Act of 1890 and subsequent legislation, explicit price fixing is illegal. It is illegal for firms to discuss pricing strategies or methods of punishing a firm that underprices other firms.

8. b. A simultaneous decision-making game is a game in which each player makes a choice without the other person knowing what that choice is.

9. d. Guaranteed price matching is a strategy where a firm guarantees it will match a lower price by a competitor; prices are likely to end up at the monopolist level so that the firms make cartel profits.

10. b. In a duopoly pricing strategy, the firm also lowers price; abandons the idea of cartel profits, and settles for duopoly profits which are better than the profits when she is underpriced by the other firm. In a grim-trigger strategy, the firm drops the price to the level that will result in zero economic profit. In a tit-for-tat strategy, the firm chooses whatever price the other firm chose the preceding period.

11. b. This is the duopoly outcome of underpricing, both firms charging the low price.

12. a. The demand curve above $6 is elastic (use the *TR* test to check—*TR* moves with *Q* above $6 and with *P* below $6 so it is elastic above and inelastic below).

13. a. A passive strategy allows the second firm to enter the market, leading to the existence of two firms in the market.

14. c. Producing a large quantity and charging a relatively low price is a typical strategy of limit pricing. Limit pricing is pricing designed to prevent a firm from entering the market.

15. b. This is the duopoly outcome with a price between the secure monopolist (a) and the insecure monopolist (c).

16. d. If neither firm advertises, the profits of both firms would be higher.

17. a. Jill's dominant strategy is to advertise, thus Jack's best action is to advertise, giving us trajectory X,Y, 1.

18. d. Resources used in advertising may be wasted; and industry profits will likely decrease.

19. The duopolists' dilemma is a situation in which both firms in a market would be better off if they chose the high price but each chooses the low price. This occurs when firms act interdependently, or when the actions of one firm affect the actions of the other. In the duopoly situation, both firms act on their own, without price agreements. In effect, both firms behave competitively. This results in a lower price and higher output produced by the firms in the duopoly than by firms in a cartel. A cartel is an agreement whereby firms agree to coordinate price and output decisions, in effect acting as a monopoly. The outcome of a cartel agreement is the same as the outcome of a monopoly. The cartel restricts output and charges higher prices.

20. The prisoners' dilemma is the duopolists' dilemma. When two prisoners are placed in separate cells, and each prisoner is unaware of the other's decision to confess or not to confess, they end up implicating each other. Although both criminals would be better off if they both kept quiet, they implicate each other because the police reward them for doing so.

21. Price leadership is an implicit agreement under which firms in a market choose a price leader, observe that firm's price, and match it. The problem with an implicit pricing agreement is that price signals sent by the leader may be misinterpreted. Firms could interpret a price cut as being the result of a change in market conditions, in which case firms just match the lower price and price fixing continues. Or, firms could interpret the price cut as an underpricing strategy, in which case a price war may be triggered, destroying the price-fixing agreement.

22. For three reasons: 1) Economies of scale large enough to generate a natural oligopoly but not a natural monopoly. 2) Government barriers to entry preserve the existence of only a few firms in the market. 3) Entry in an oligopolistic market may require a substantial investment in an advertising campaign necessary to enter the market.

23. Guaranteed price matching is a scheme under which a firm guarantees that it will match a lower price by a competitor; also known as meet-the-competition policy. If one producer chooses the high price, the other will match the high price in which case both producers will earn maximum (cartel) profits. If one producer chooses the low price, the other will match the low price and both firms will earn minimum (duopoly) profits. Therefore, firms have no reason to choose the low price. Guaranteed price matching will result in higher prices. Price matching eliminates the duopolists' dilemma and makes cartel profits and pricing possible, even without a formal cartel. Guaranteed price matching ensures that consumers pay the higher price!

24. A contestable market is a market in which the costs of entering and leaving are low, so the firms that are already in the market are constantly threatened by the entry of new firms. In the extreme case of perfect contestability, firms can enter and exit at zero cost, and the market price would be the same as the perfectly competitive price.

13 [28]
Controlling Market Power: Antitrust and Regulation

Chapter Summary

This chapter explores public policies for markets with a few dominant firms. Here are the main points of the chapter:

- A natural monopoly occurs when there are large-scale economies in production, so the market can support only one firm.
- Under an average-cost pricing policy, the regulated price for a natural monopoly is equal to the average cost of production.
- The government uses antitrust policy to break up some dominant firms, prevent some corporate mergers, and regulate business practices that reduce competition.
- The modern approach to merger policy uses price data to predict the effects of a merger.
- In most circumstances, predatory pricing is unprofitable because the monopoly power is costly to acquire and hard to maintain.
- The deregulation of the airline industry led to more competition and lower prices on average, but higher prices in some markets.

Applying the Concepts

After reading this chapter, you should be able to answer these four key questions.
1. How does a decrease in demand affect the price of a regulated monopoly?
2. What are the tradeoffs with a merger?
3. Does competition between the second- and third-largest firms matter?
4. How does a merger affect prices?

13.1 [28.1] Natural Monopoly

Natural monopolies occur when the scale of production is so large that only one firm can survive in the market. Many public utilities are natural monopolies.

☞ Think about a municipal water system. Even if you could secure a low-cost source of water, there would be a tremendous monetary cost involved in digging up streets and laying water pipe, not to mention the inconvenience to residents. In a situation like this, either the city will provide the utility service, or will allow a natural monopoly provider in the market.

If left to its own devices, a natural monopoly would choose output where marginal revenue is equal to marginal cost and set the price from the demand curve. This is illustrated at point *b* in Figure 13.1 [28.1] of your text.

The Marginal Principle

Increase the level of an activity as long as its marginal benefit exceeds its marginal cost. Choose the level at which the marginal benefit equals the marginal cost.

𝒢𝓇 Study Tip

Regardless of the market structure, a firm will always choose to produce output to the point where marginal revenue is equal to marginal cost.

Entry is not going to occur in this market, even with economic profits, because of the high fixed costs of entering the market. As Figure 13.2 [28.2] of the text shows, if two firms tried to split the market, each firm's firm-specific demand curve would lie below the average cost curve and both firms would lose money. As a result there will be no entry.

In the case of natural monopoly, government typically sets a maximum price that the monopoly can charge consumers. A typical approach is *average-cost pricing* in which the price is set at the intersection of the average-cost curve and the demand curve. This is illustrated by point *e* in Figure 13.3 [28.3] in your text. At this point, the regulated monopolist will earn zero economic profits.

Let's review an Application that answers a key question posed at the start of the chapter:

1. How does a decrease in demand affect the price of a regulated monopoly?

APPLICATION 1:
A DECREASE IN DEMAND INCREASES THE PRICE OF CABLE TV

To understand this Application, look at Figure 13.3 [28.3] in your text. Currently the market is regulated at point *e*, where average cost and demand intersect. If the population of the city, and thus the demand for cable TV, were to fall, the demand curve would shift to the left. Notice that as the demand curve shifts to the left, the price at which average cost and demand intersect increases.

Caution!

The fact that the price increased as demand decreased is a result of the price being set by a regulatory rule as opposed to the market.

13.2 [28.2] Antitrust Policy

A **trust** is an arrangement under which the owners of several companies transfer their decision-making powers to a small group of trustees. The practical effect is to limit competition among the firms and allow the firms to act more like a monopolist. Antitrust policy exists to promote competition among firms. Both the Antitrust Division of the Department of Justice and the Federal Trade Commission are tasked with enforcing the antitrust laws of the U.S.

There are three basic types of antitrust policy:
- Breaking up monopolies.
- Blocking mergers.
- Regulating business practices.

Many of today's largest tobacco companies were at one time all part of the American Tobacco Company. By 1907 the American Tobacco Company controlled 95% of the U.S. cigarette market. The Supreme Court found that the American Tobacco Company used its monopoly position to eliminate rivals and in 1911 ordered that the company be broken into several smaller tobacco companies.

A **merger** is a process in which two or more firms combine their operations. There are two basic types of mergers:
- Horizontal merger: the joining together of firms producing a similar product.
- Vertical merger: the joining together of firms at different stages of the production process.

Mergers which are expected to have little impact on the market are allowed. Mergers which will reduce competition, typically defined as giving firms more ability to raise prices, are challenged and may be prevented or allowed only with certain restrictions on the firms.

The Wonder Bread case provides a nice example of a restriction on a merger. Before the merger would be allowed, Interstate Bakeries had to sell off some of its brands and bakeries so that adequate competition would continue to exist in the market after the merger of Interstate and Continental bakeries.

Certain business practices may also reduce competition in the market. A **tie-in sale** is a business practice under which a business requires a consumer of one product to purchase another product. **Predatory pricing** occurs when a firm sells a product at a price below its production cost to drive a rival out of business and then increases the price.

Let's review three Applications that answer key questions posed at the start of the chapter:

2.   What are the tradeoffs with a merger?

APPLICATION 2: SATELLITE RADIO MERGER?
This Application examines the tradeoffs faced by the U.S. Department of Justice and the Federal Communications Commission as they evaluated the proposed merger between XM and Sirius satellite radio. Even though the firms combined to have 14 million subscribers, neither was making profits. By merging the firms hoped to reduce costs and reach profitability. The risk that regulators needed to consider was that the firms might try to raise prices now that there was no competition in the satellite radio market.

3. Does competition between the second- and third-largest firms matter?

APPLICATION 3: HEINZ AND BEECH-NUT BATTLE FOR SECOND PLACE
This Application illustrates that competition among firms leads to lower prices, even if the firms involved are not the largest in the market. A merger between Heinz and Beech-Nut, the second- and third-largest producers of baby food, was blocked by the FTC. The Application makes two key points. First, the competition between Heinz and Beech-Nut for shelf space served to hold down prices, including the price of Gerber baby food, the market leader. Had these two firms merged, it is likely that baby food prices would have increased. Second, with fewer firms it is easier to coordinate pricing, thus making cartel-like behavior more possible.

4. How does a merger affect prices?

APPLICATION 4:
XIDEX RECOVERS ITS ACQUISITION COST IN TWO YEARS
By acquiring two of its rivals in the microfilm market, Xidex was able to increase the price of microfilm by 11% for one variety and 23% for another. By reducing the number of firms, Xidex was able to exercise additional market power. To settle an antitrust lawsuit, Xidex agreed to license microfilm technology to other firms at a very low price. The rationale for this was that the other firms would provide some competition to Xidex and lead to lower prices in the market.

The following table summarizes key antitrust legislation:

Law	Date Enacted	Regulation Enacted
Sherman Act	1890	Made it illegal to monopolize a market or to engage in practices that result in a restraint of trade.
Clayton Act	1914	Outlawed specific practices that discourage competition, including tie-in sales contracts, price discrimination for the purpose of reducing competition, and stock-purchase mergers that would substantially reduce competition.
Federal Trade Commission Act	1914	Created a mechanism to enforce antitrust laws.
Robinson-Patman Act	1936	Prohibited selling products at "unreasonably low prices" with the intent of reducing competition.
Celler-Kefauver Act	1950	Outlawed asset-purchase mergers that would substantially reduce competition.
Hart-Scott-Rodino Act	1980	Extended antitrust legislation to proprietorships and partnerships.

13.3 [28.3] Deregulation: Airlines, Telecommunications, and Electricity

In 1978, entry restrictions and price controls were lifted in the airline market. It is estimated that deregulation led to 28% lower prices in these markets. In markets with a hub airport, airports with two-firm concentration ratios above 85%, fares were 23% higher than at airports with more competition.

The Telecommunications Act of 1996 was designed to promote competition among firms in video, voice, and data transmission. The act opened local telephone markets for competition, eliminated price controls on cable TV, and allowed the Baby Bells to enter long-distance markets, provided sufficient local service competition exists.

In the early 1990s, technological advances removed the natural monopoly characteristics from electricity generation. This, as well as dramatic price differences across states, led to a push to deregulate electricity markets. California partially deregulated its electricity markets in 1998 with undesirable results. Deregulation allowed wholesale prices of electricity to vary, but did not allow retail prices to vary. Since the retail price could not change, there was no way to provide incentives to consumers to change the amount of electricity they used. As a result, electricity companies were losing money on each unit sold, and one of the largest utilities filed for bankruptcy.

Activity

This activity relates back to Application 2. Recall that it was suggested that when a natural monopoly faced a lower demand for their product, the price in the market would increase. You also recall that the price was regulated to equal average cost. To see this, complete the activity.

    a.   In the graph below, draw a demand curve which represents a decrease in demand from the current level. Make sure that the new demand curve still crosses the long-run average cost curve. The point at which average cost and demand intersect is at a (choose one) higher/lower price than at point *e*.

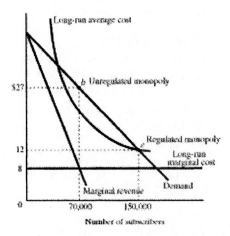

    b.   If the demand increased, the point at which average cost and demand intersect is at a (choose one) higher/lower price than at point *e*.

Answers

    a.   Since the demand curve shifts to the left, average cost and demand will intersect at a lower quantity and thus at a higher price.

    b.   Since the demand curve shifts to the right, average cost and demand will intersect at a higher quantity and a lower price.

Key Terms

Merger: A process in which two or more firms combine their operations.

Predatory pricing: A firm sells a product at a price below its production cost to drive a rival out of business, and then increases the price.

Tie-in sales: A business practice under which a business requires a consumer of one product to purchase another product.

Trust: An arrangement under which the owners of several companies transfer their decision-making powers to a small group of trustees.

Practice Quiz

(Answers are provided at the end of the Practice Quiz.)

1. If a market is a natural monopoly:
    a. the government can and often does intervene by regulating the price charged by the monopolist.
    b. the government can but does not intervene in the market.
    c. the government is prevented by law from intervening in the market.
    d. the price charged by the monopolist is close or equal to the competitive price.

2. The fact that a long-run average cost curve is negatively sloped and steep reflects:
    a. large economies of scale.
    b. diseconomies of scale.
    c. constant returns to scale.
    d. small economies of scale.

3. Refer to the figure below. When the monopolist maximizes profit, how much is the profit per subscriber?

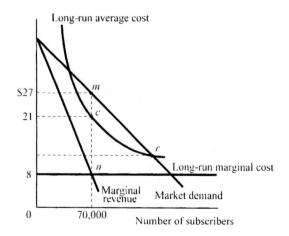

    a. $27
    b. $21
    c. $6
    d. $420,000

4. Refer to the figure below. After entry of a second firm, which demand curve is more likely to be the demand faced by a single firm?

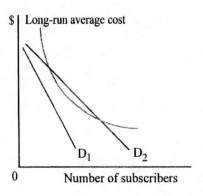

a. D_1
b. D_2
c. A demand curve outward, which equals the sum of D_1 and D_2.
d. The same as the long-run average cost curve.

5. Refer to the figure below. After entry of a second firm, what price would a single firm charge?

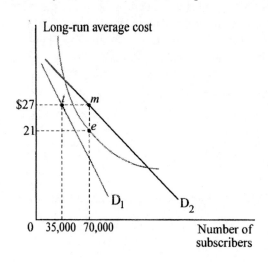

a. $27
b. $21
c. Either $21 or $27 would yield significant profit.
d. Neither $21 nor $27. A second firm would not enter.

6. What happens under an *average-cost pricing policy*?
   a. The government chooses the price at which the demand curve intersects the long-run average cost curve.
   b. The government chooses the price at which the demand curve intersects the long-run marginal cost curve.
   c. The government chooses the price at which marginal revenue equals long-run marginal cost.
   d. The government chooses the price that minimizes the long-run average cost of production.

7. A process in which two or more firms combine their operations is called:
   a. a merger.
   b. a monopoly.
   c. a cartel.
   d. a duopoly.

8. Which of the following terms refers to the practice in which a business forces the buyer of one product to purchase another product?
   a. A merger.
   b. Predatory pricing.
   c. Tie-in sales.
   d. A natural monopoly.

9. Which of the following is a type of antitrust policy?
   a. Blocking mergers.
   b. Preventing trusts.
   c. Regulating business practices.
   d. All of the above.

10. Which of the following will usually reduce competition and lead to higher prices?
    a. Trusts.
    b. Average-cost pricing.
    c. Antitrust policy.
    d. All of the above.

11. What is the name of a pricing scheme under which a firm decreases its price to drive a rival out of business and increases the price when the other firm disappears?
    a. Predatory pricing.
    b. Smart pricing.
    c. Always pricing.
    d. Rule of thumb pricing.

12. This question tests your understanding of Application 3 in this chapter: Heinz and Beech-Nut battle for second place: Does competition between the second- and third-largest firms matter?

    Which of the following arguments did the FTC use to block the merger of Heinz and Beech-Nut?
    a. The elimination of competition would lead to higher prices and a greater likelihood of price fixing.
    b. The smaller the number of firms in an oligopoly, the more difficult it is to coordinate pricing.
    c. The two remaining companies would compete vigorously and prices would fall.
    d. Significant market concentration makes it harder for firms in the market to collude.

13. Which of the following pieces of legislation made it illegal to monopolize a market or to engage in practices that result in a restraint of trade?
    a. The Sherman Act.
    b. The Robinson-Patman Act.
    c. The Clayton Act.
    d. The Federal Trade Commission Act.

14. Which piece of antitrust legislation prohibited selling products at "unreasonably low prices" with the intent of reducing competition?
    a. The Federal Trade Commission Act.
    b. The Clayton Act.
    c. The Sherman Act.
    d. The Robinson-Patman Act.

15. The Telecommunications Act of 1996 did which of the following?
    a. Enacted stiff price controls on cable TV.
    b. Opened local telephone service up to competition.
    c. Permanently removed the Baby Bells from the long distance telephone market.
    d. All of the above.

16. In the 1990s, growing pressure to deregulate the electricity market came from:
    a. innovations that reduced the economies of scale in electricity generation.
    b. substantial similarity in electricity prices across states.
    c. the positive experience of California after deregulating the industry.
    d. All of the above.

17. In some cases, the existence of monopoly is beneficial to society as a whole. Explain and give examples.

Answers to the Practice Quiz

1. a. The government usually does intervene by regulating the price charged by the natural monopolist.

2. a. The long-run average-cost curve is negatively sloped and steep, reflecting the large economies of scale that occur in the industry.

3. c. Profit per subscriber equals revenue per subscriber, or price, of $27 minus cost per subscriber, or average cost, of $21. $27 − $21 = $6.

4. a. Market demand must be shared by two firms, so each firm's demand curve is less than before. D_1 shows less demand than D_2.

5. d. After entry, the firm's demand curve lies entirely below the long-run average-cost curve. No matter what price the typical firm charges, it will lose money. Therefore, a second firm will not enter the market.

6. a. Under an average-cost pricing policy, the government chooses the price at which the demand curve intersects the long-run average-cost curve.

7. a. A merger is a process in which two or more firms combine their operations.

8. c. Tie-in sales occur when a business forces the buyer of one product to purchase another product.

9. d. The choices above summarize all of the types of antitrust regulation available today.

19. a. Trusts are created to enable firms to more easily behave as a monopoly.

11. a. Predatory pricing is a pricing scheme under which a firm decreases its price to drive a rival out of business and increases the price when the other firm disappears.

12. a. The FTC argued that "significant market concentration makes it easier for firms in the market to collude, expressly or tacitly, and thereby force price above or farther above the competitive level." In other words, in a market with two firms instead of three, it would be easier for the baby-food manufacturers to fix prices.

13. a. The Sherman Act of 1890 made it illegal to monopolize a market or to engage in practices that result in a restraint of trade.

14. d. The Robinson-Patman Act of 1936 prohibited selling products at "unreasonably low prices" with the intent of reducing competition.

15. b. Deregulation of local telephone service occurred under this act.

16. a. In the 1990s, growing pressure to deregulate the electricity market came from innovations that reduced the economies of scale in electricity generation, as well as substantial variation in electricity prices across states. The energy debacle in California may modify other states' plans to deregulate their electricity markets.

17. Society is better off when a single firm serves the entire market demand in industries that exhibit large economies of scale. When fixed costs are very high, the firm exhibits economies of scale so large that average costs continuously decline with output. In such cases, it may be efficient to have only one firm in an industry. Such an industry is called a natural monopoly. Public utilities are examples of natural monopolies. Electricity, gas, and telephone companies have large fixed costs associated with establishing and maintaining a single scale of operations. A single power plant, for example, can serve thousands of customers across various states. There is no need to have two power plants operating at the same time. Airlines, trains, and trucking are other examples of industries that face large-scale economies and are often subject to economic regulation.

14 [29]
Imperfect Information: Adverse Selection and Moral Hazard

Chapter Summary

This chapter examines what happens when one side of the market doesn't have complete information. Here are the main points of the chapter:

- The adverse-selection problem occurs when one side of the market cannot distinguish between high-quality and low-quality goods. The presence of low-quality goods pulls down the price that buyers are willing to pay, which decreases the quantity of high-quality goods supplied, which further decreases the average quality and the price. In the extreme case, only low-quality goods are sold.
- A thin market occurs when the sellers of high-quality goods have a relatively low minimum supply price, so some high-quality goods are sold.
- In a market subject to asymmetric information, buyers have an incentive to invest in information to help make better choices and sellers have an incentive to provide quality guarantees.
- Insurance markets suffer from adverse selection because compared to insurance sellers, buyers have better information about the risks they face.
- Insurance encourages risky behavior because part of the cost of an unfavorable outcome will be paid by an insurance company.

Applying the Concepts

After reading this chapter, you should be able to answer these five key questions:
1. Why does a new car lose about 20 percent of its value in the first week?
2. How can government solve the adverse-selection problem?
3. Does the market for baseball pitchers suffer from the adverse-selection problem?
4. Who benefits from better information about risks?
5. How does adverse selection affect the price of insurance?

14.1 [29.1] The Lemons Problem

The classic example of a market with imperfect information is the used-car market. The seller of the car has better information about the quality of the car, and in particular how a car has been maintained, than does the buyer. This is a case of **asymmetric information**, a situation in which one side of the market—either buyers or sellers—has better information than the other. The fact that good used cars (known as plums) and bad used cars (known as lemons) are offered in the same market will make it difficult for the market to come to an efficient outcome. The used-car market is an example of a **mixed market**, a market in which goods of different qualities are sold for the same price.

To find a consumer's willingness to pay in a mixed market, we must answer three questions:
- How much is the consumer willing to pay for a plum?
- How much is the consumer willing to pay for a lemon?
- What is the chance that a used car will be a lemon?

Suppose that a plum is worth $4,000 and a lemon is worth $2,000 and that half the cars offered are lemons. In this case, we would expect a consumer to be willing to pay the following for a used car:

$$\text{willingness to pay} = 0.5(\$2,000) + 0.5(\$4,000) = \$3,000$$

☑ Key Equation

willingness to pay =   (probability of a lemon) x (value of a lemon) +
                       (probability of a plum) x (value of a plum)

Figure 14.1 [29.1] of your text shows the supply curve for both plums and lemons. Notice that those sellers who know they have good quality cars require a higher price to sell the car than do sellers with lemons. Thus the supply curve of plums lies above the supply curve of lemons.

When buyers are willing to pay $3,000 for a used car, 80 lemons (point *b*) and 20 plums (point *a*) will be sold. This will cause buyers to re-evaluate the likelihood of buying a lemon.

Suppose that buyers now believe that 80% of used cars are lemons. The willingness to pay of buyers becomes:

$$\text{willingness to pay} = .8(\$2,000) + .2(\$4,000) = \$2,400.$$

We see in Figure 14.1 [29.1] that no plums will be offered for sale at this price of $2,400. If consumers believe that all cars are lemons, the price of a used car will fall to $2,000 and 45 cars, all lemons, will be sold.

A lemons market is an example of the adverse-selection problem. The **adverse-selection problem** is a situation in which the uninformed side of the market must choose from an undesirable or adverse selection of goods. As shown in the used-car example, adverse selection can lead to a continual reduction in quality in a mixed market. As in that market, the steps that occur in this process are:
1. The presence of low-quality goods in the market reduces the expected value of the good and the consumer's willingness to pay.
2. The lower market price reduces the number of high quality goods offered for sale, increasing the fraction of low-quality goods.
3. The decrease in the average quality of goods again reduces the expected value of the good and the consumer's willingness to pay.

Figure 14.2 [29.2] shows a less extreme case, that of the thin market. A **thin market** is a market in which some high-quality goods are sold but fewer than would be sold in a market with perfect information.

In equilibrium, the proportion of lemons in the market is equal to the expectations of the consumers concerning the proportion of lemons in the market.

☞ The problem in the lemons market is that sellers know more about the quality of the product than do buyers. This can happen in many markets. For instance if you were hiring a worker, you would never hire a lazy, unmotivated worker who is barely competent to do his or her job. However, you have probably worked with a person like that. How did that person get hired? There is asymmetric information in the labor market. The person applying for a job knows more about his or her true characteristics than does the person doing the hiring, thus leading to an adverse-selection problem, just as in the market for used cars.

📄 Remember

Adverse-selection occurs when a characteristic of a good ("quality") can't be observed equally well by both sides of the market.

The lemons model predicts that:
- The presence of low-quality goods will reduce the number of high-quality goods offered in a mixed market.
- Buyers and sellers will invest in information identifying high-quality goods.

In the market for used trucks, there is no apparent lemon effect for newer, less than ten years old, vehicles. There does seem to be evidence that older trucks which are sold tend to be of lower quality than older trucks which remain with their current owners.

14.2 [29.2] Responding to the Lemons Problem

Both buyers and sellers have incentive to solve the lemons problem. Buyers would like to increase the likelihood that they buy a plum. Sellers of plums would like to indicate that their car is a plum and receive a higher price for their higher quality car. Here are some ways that buyers and sellers respond to the lemons problem:
- Buyers invest in information. A buyer may take a used car to a mechanic for an inspection to better determine the quality of the car.
- Consumer satisfaction and ratings. Sellers may seek out consumer ratings in an effort to show that they are high quality.
- Guarantees. Sellers can indicate their belief that they have a quality product by offering refunds to unsatisfied customers or by promising to repair defective products.
- Lemons Laws: Many states have these laws that require automakers to buy back cars that have frequent repair problems in the first year.

Recall the following key principle:

KEY PRINCIPLE: THE PRINCIPLE OF VOLUNTARY EXCHANGE
A voluntary exchange between two people makes both people better off.

☞ For a while, Kia aired commercials comparing its cars to those of Toyota. After comparing features and prices, the commercial ended with the Kia owner asking the Toyota owner if the Toyota came with a ten-year warranty like the Kia. Why would Kia need to offer a ten-year warranty, and why might Toyota not feel compelled to match that offer? Think of how many people you know who have owned Toyotas. Do you feel as though you have a good sense of the quality of a Toyota vehicle? Think of how many people you know who have owned a Kia. Since Kia is a less well-known brand, buyers may have more uncertainty as to the quality of a Kia than they do about the quality of a Toyota. To overcome this adverse-selection problem, Kia offers a very long warranty to indicate to buyers that they are offering a quality product.

Let's review three Applications that answer key questions we posed at the start of the chapter:

1. Why does a new car lose about 20 percent of its value in the first week?

APPLICATION 1: THE RESALE VALUE OF A WEEK-OLD CAR

Why would someone sell a week-old car? That question in buyers' minds causes new cars to immediately lose a great deal of value. While it could be that the owner of the car changed his or her mind, it could also be that something was wrong with the car. Buyers in the used car market don't want to pay a new-car price for a bad car. Because of this asymmetric information problem, driving a car off a dealer's lot immediately reduces its market value.

2. How can government solve the adverse-selection problem?

APPLICATION 2:
REGULATION OF THE CALIFORNIA KIWIFRUIT MARKET

This Application provides a nice example of asymmetric information. Growers of kiwifruit know whether it was picked at an appropriate time for optimal sweetness, or if it was picked early, which leads to tart fruit. Buyers have no way of knowing the sweetness of a particular fruit without buying the fruit. At one time, kiwifruit from California tended to have a wide variance in sweetness and as a result, stores were unwilling to pay as much for California fruit as they were for more consistently sweet fruit from other sources. In 1987, California growers implemented a federal order setting a minimum sugar content standard for kiwifruit. This standard reduced the adverse selection problem as buyers now know the minimum quality level that they will receive. As a result of more certainty as to quality, the price of California kiwifruit increased.

3. Does the market for baseball pitchers suffer from the adverse-selection problem?

APPLICATION 3: BASEBALL PITCHERS ARE LIKE USED CARS

Why do baseball pitchers who change teams seem to be injured more than those who don't? The answer can be understood by thinking about adverse selection. In general, for a player to change teams, the new team must have offered more money to the player than the player's old team. Of course, the old team likely had better information on the health of the pitcher. Just as owners of bad cars have more incentive to sell them in the used car market than do owners of good cars, it may be the case that teams with bad (less healthy) pitchers may be more likely to let them test the free-agent market than teams with good (more healthy) pitchers. If the lemons problem exists, we would expect pitchers who change teams to have more injury problems than pitchers who choose to remain with their current team. It turns out that, on average, pitchers who switch teams spend five times longer recovering from injuries than pitchers who don't change teams.

14.4 [29.4] Uninformed Sellers and Knowledgeable Buyers: Insurance

Now consider two people buying health insurance. One is healthy and would have $2,000 in medical expenses per year. The other is unhealthy and would have $6,000 in medical expenses per year. While the buyer knows if he or she is high cost or low cost, the insurance company does not. Figure 14.3 [29.3] of your text illustrates this. As you would expect, high-cost buyers have a higher demand for insurance than do low-cost buyers.

How will the insurance company choose its price? Suppose for this example, it charges an amount equal to the expected payout and believes that half its customers are healthy. Adapting our equation for willingness to pay, we find the insurance company will charge:

$$0.5(2,000) + 0.5(\$6,000) = \$4,000$$

At this price, 25 low-cost people will buy insurance indicated by point *a*, as will 75 high-cost people indicated by point *b*. At this ratio of high-cost and low-cost consumers, the insurance company would increase the premium to:

$$0.25(\$2,000) + 0.75(6,000) = \$5,000$$

As fewer low-cost people choose insurance, the premium will continue to increase until, in the extreme case, only high-cost buyers are in the market. This is one reason why it is difficult for uninsured individuals to buy health insurance. A healthy, low-cost uninsured person will be unwilling to pay the high premium charged in the insurance market.

Insurance companies respond to this by using **experience rating**, a situation in which insurance companies charge different prices for medical insurance to different firms depending on the past medical bills of a firm's employees.

Let's review an Application that answers one of the key questions we posed at the start of the chapter:

4. Who benefits from better information about risks?

APPLICATION 4: GENETIC TESTING BENEFITS LOW-RISK PEOPLE
This Application illustrates how better information could lead to better pricing of insurance. If someone is a low-cost health insurance person, the ability to identify himself or herself as such would lead to a lower insurance premium if insurers could adjust premiums on an individual basis. Those who can be identified as high-cost people would then pay higher premiums to offset their higher expected costs. This would be good for healthy people, but not good for those who are predisposed to high health-care costs. The Application points out that most states have laws that would prevent insurance companies from acting on genetic information in setting premiums.

📄 Remember

In most insurance markets, buyers of insurance will have more information about their behavior and risks than will sellers. As a result, the adverse-selection problem exists in all insurance markets.

14.5 [29.5] Insurance and Moral Hazard

Having insurance typically causes people to take greater risks because a large part of any loss will be borne by their insurance company. This is an example of moral hazard. **Moral hazard** is a situation in which one side of an economic relationship takes undesirable or costly actions that the other side of the relationship cannot observe. In the insurance world, insurance companies can't monitor the actions of their policyholders to see that insured individuals act responsibly.

Insurance companies use deductibles, a dollar amount that a policy holder must pay before getting compensation from the insurance company, to decrease the moral hazard problem. By requiring individuals to bear some of the financial burden of risky activities, the insurance companies encourage people to take steps to avoid risk.

☞ By way of example, think of Andy, who has just purchased a new convertible. On a sunny day, Andy is late for class and is trying to decide whether to leave the top down on his vehicle even though his iPod, and two of his textbooks are in the car. Suppose that Andy will have to pay to replace these goods if they are stolen. Andy would likely decide that the benefit of putting the top up (not having his things stolen) outweighs the cost (being a few minutes late for class). Suppose that Andy was fully insured so that he would receive money to replace his stolen goods. In this case, insurance reduces the cost of leaving the top down and Andy is more likely to do this, ignoring for simplicity the administrative burden of an insurance claim. If Andy is responsible for the first $250 in losses from his car, this may be a high enough cost to motivate Andy to be late for class and put the top up on his car.

Deposit insurance for Savings and Loans (S&Ls) may have contributed to the Savings and Loan crisis of the 1980s because of the moral hazard problem. Federal insurance protected deposits up to $100,000. The insurance reduced the cost of risky investments by the Savings and Loans because the institution would not be liable for most of the lost deposits if investments went bad.

🗎 Remember

Moral hazard occurs when the actions of one party in a transaction can't be observed by the other party.

Let's review an Application that answers one of the key questions we posed at the start of the chapter:

5. How does adverse selection affect the price of insurance?

APPLICATION 5:
WHY IS CAR INSURANCE SO EXPENSIVE IN PHILADELPHIA

This Application tries to explain why car insurance in Philadelphia is much more expensive than in Pittsburgh, even though the auto theft rate is much higher in Pittsburgh. The Application illustrates that high insurance prices cause drivers to avoid buying insurance. In the case of an accident your insurance is designed to provide coverage if you are at fault in the accident. If you are involved in an accident caused by an uninsured driver your insurance will still cover the accident, however, you wind up paying higher premiums to cover the costs caused by uninsured drivers. As prices increase, fewer people buy insurance. As there are more uninsured drivers, the cost of insurance increases.

Activity

Suppose that in the used car market good quality cars are worth $10,000 and poor quality cars are worth $4,000. You believe that half the cars in the market are good and half the cars in the market are bad.
   a.   Find the expected value of a used car in this market.
   b.   Suppose that you know you are offering a good used car. Would you be willing to pay $100 to a mechanic to attest that your car is a good car?
   c.   Why might it be that car dealers can sell used cars for a higher price than a private individual?

Answers

   a.   0.5(10,000) + 0.5(4,000) = $7,000.
   b.   If you can sell the car for $10,000 with the guarantee that it is a good car, you would certainly pay $100 to increase the sales price of the car by $3,000.
   c.   If people believe that car dealers have better quality used cars than private individuals, the expected willingness to pay would increase. Suppose that you believe that 90% of used cars sold by a car dealer are good as opposed to 50% sold by private individuals (as in part a). You would be willing to pay 0.9(10,000) + 0.1(4,000) = $9,400 for a used car from a dealer.

Key Terms

Adverse-selection problem: A situation in which the uninformed side of the market must choose from an undesirable or adverse selection of goods.

Asymmetric information: A situation in which one side of the market—either buyers or sellers—has better information than the other.

Experience rating: A situation in which insurance companies charge different prices for medical insurance to different firms depending on the past medical bills of a firm's employees.

Mixed market: A market in which goods of different qualities are sold for the same price.

Moral hazard: A situation in which one side of an economic relationship takes undesirable or costly actions that the other side of the relationship cannot observe.

Thin market: A market in which some high-quality goods are sold but fewer than would be sold in a market with perfect information.

Practice Quiz

(Answers are provided at the end of the Practice Quiz.)

1. Asymmetric information means that:
    a. either buyers or sellers have better information than the other in a given market.
    b. buyers and sellers are fully informed.
    c. only sellers are informed, and buyers must obtain all their information from sellers.
    d. it is impossible for someone to hide information

2. High-quality goods will disappear from a mixed market:
    a. as a result of consumers' expectations agreeing with their actual experiences.
    b. as a result of consumers' expectations differing from their actual experiences.
    c. regardless of the difference between consumers' expectations and actual experiences.
    d. only when consumers are fully optimistic about the chances of getting high-quality goods in a mixed market.

3. The domination of the used-car market by lemons is an example of a market in which the goods left in the market are the undesirable goods. This problem is called:
    a. asymmetric information.
    b. adverse selection.
    c. moral hazard.
    d. imperfect information.

4. As the chance of getting a low-quality good increases, buyers are willing to pay _____ for a used car and the quantity of high-quality goods will tend to _____, resulting in a so-called

    _____.
    a. less, rise, thin market.
    b. more, disappear, thick market.
    c. less, fall, thin market.
    d. more, decline, thick market.

5. Refer to the figure below. According to the textbook analysis, which supply curve is the supply of lemons?

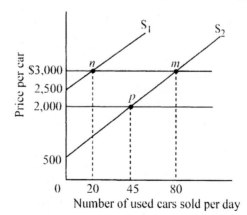

    a. S_1
    b. S_2
    c. The horizontal line setting at $3,000.
    d. The horizontal line setting at $2,000.

6. This question tests your understanding of Application 1 in this chapter: The resale value of a week-old car: Why does a new car lose about 20 percent of its value in the first week?

    A potential buyer of a week-old car might believe that a person who returns a car after only one week could have discovered it was a lemon and may be trying to get rid of it. Alternatively, the seller could have simply changed his or her mind about the car.

    The fundamental problem described in this story is what we refer to in economics as:
    a. asymmetric information.
    b. moral hazard.
    c. experience ratings.
    d. All of the above.

7. Suppose that consumers have pessimistic expectations, that is, they believe that the actual chance of getting a lemon is high. Under this scenario:
    a. the price of plums decreases and the price of lemons increases.
    b. the price of a lemon tends to equal the price of a plum.
    c. the price of used cars increases.
    d. the price of used cars decreases.

8. Suppose you are shopping for a used dishwasher. A known plum sells for $300 and a known lemon sells for $150. If you believe that the probability of purchasing a lemon is 60%, how much would you be willing to pay for a used dishwasher?
    a. $150
    b. $210
    c. $225
    d. $240

9. Suppose that buyers believe that 25% of the used computers on the market are lemons. If this market is in equilibrium and 25 lemons are sold, then how many plums are sold?
    a. 25
    b. 75
    c. 100
    d. 50

10. If the market for used stereos contains only lemons, then the market for used stereos:
    a. is an example of a monopoly.
    b. suffers from an adverse selection problem.
    c. is an example of a "thick" market.
    d. suffers from a symmetric information problem.

11. This question tests your understanding of Application 3 in this chapter: Baseball pitchers are like used cars: Does the market for baseball pitchers suffer from the adverse-selection problem?

   Professional baseball teams compete with each other for players. After six years of play in the major leagues, a player has the option of becoming a free agent and offering his services to the highest bidder. A player is likely to switch teams if the new team offers him a higher salary than his original team. One of the puzzling features of the free-agent market is that pitchers who switch teams are more prone to injuries than pitchers who don't. On average, pitchers who switch teams spend 28 days per season on the disabled list, compared to only 5 days for pitchers who do not switch teams. This doesn't mean that all the switching pitchers are lemons; many of them are injury-free and are valuable additions to their new teams. But on average, the switching pitchers spend five times longer recovering from injuries.

   All of the statements below are correct. Which one better describes the concept of adverse selection?
   a. In general, an injury-prone pitcher is more likely to switch teams. This means that, as in the used-car market, there are many "lemons" on the used-pitcher market.
   b. A player is likely to switch teams if the new team offers him a higher salary than his original team.
   c. Because the coaches, physicians, and trainers from the player's original team have more information, they know whether he is likely to suffer from injuries that prevent him from playing. In contrast, the new team has much less information.
   d. If the pitcher's team thinks he will be injury-free and productive, his team will outbid other teams and keep him.

12. Consider the market for malpractice insurance for lawyers. Suppose that a malpractice suit against a careful and a reckless attorney costs $2,000 and $20,000, respectively. Each attorney knows whether he/she is reckless or careful. Insurance companies, however, don't know but believe that 25% of the attorneys are reckless. How much do insurance companies have to charge for malpractice insurance to guarantee zero economic profit?
   a. $18,000
   b. $20,000
   c. $13,500
   d. $10,000

13. Buyers are willing to pay $5,000 for a low-quality used car and $10,000 for a high-quality used car. If the probability of getting a high-quality used car is 40%, what will the price of used cars be?
   a. $5,000
   b. $7,000
   c. $7,500
   d. $8,000

14. Thin markets can be revived by:
   a. imposing price ceilings.
   b. warranties and other devices that increase information.
   c. bringing more buyers into the market.
   d. imposing price floors.

15. A situation in which one side of an economic relationship takes undesirable or costly actions that the other side of the relationship cannot observe is called:
   a. adverse selection.
   b. moral hazard.
   c. a mixed market.
   d. asymmetric information.

16. How have health insurance companies attempted to overcome the adverse selection problem?
    a. They have switched to experience rating systems.
    b. They discourage institutions to provide group insurance in an attempt to keep high-risk individuals out of the pool of customers.
    c. They lower rates to encourage low-risk people to buy insurance.
    d. All of the above.

17. An insurance company knows less about the risks of policyholders than do the policyholders themselves. For this reason:
    a. insurance companies tend to insure only those who pose fewer risks.
    b. insurance companies tend to charge low average prices to attract more low-risk clients.
    c. insurance companies end up insuring the most undesirable group of customers.
    d. the price of insurance will tend to fall.

18. Most insurance companies today use a pricing scheme called:
    a. community rating, where the price of insurance equals the cost of providing coverage based on the medical history of the firm's employees.
    b. community rating, where the price of insurance is a different price for each firm.
    c. experience rating, where the price of insurance equals the cost of providing coverage based on the medical history of the firm's employees.
    d. experience rating, where the price of insurance is the same for each firm.

19. Define asymmetric information, and explain how the problem applies to banks.

20. Define moral hazard, and explain how the problem relates to the banking industry.

21. Explain how asymmetric information would influence your willingness to pay for a used snow blower.

22. Explain the relationship between the following concepts: asymmetric information, adverse selection, and thin market.

23. Explain how a car dealer can assure buyers that the car they are buying is a plum in a sea of lemons. What kind of protection and what problems are associated with lemon laws?

24. Summarize the concept of a mixed market and its relationship to asymmetric information.

Answers to the Practice Quiz

1. a. Asymmetric information refers to a decrease in the efficiency of markets because buyers and sellers are not fully informed.

2. a. In this case, owners of high-quality goods ask for more than buyers are willing to pay in a mixed market, so the market quantity will be comprised exclusively of low-quality goods. During the adjustment process prices fall to the point that the market consists only of low-quality goods precisely because consumers discover that their expectations are unrealistic.

3. b. Adverse selection is the result of the dynamics of asymmetric information.

4. c. A thin market is a market in which some high-quality goods are sold, but fewer than would be sold in a market with perfect information.

5. b. Owners of lemons require a lower price than owners of plums.

6. a. The problem is that buyers don't know why the car is being sold, and as long as there is a chance that the car is a lemon they won't be willing to pay the full "new" price for it. In general, buyers are willing to pay a lot less for a week-old car, and so the owners of high-quality, week-old cars are less likely to put them on the market. This downward spiral ultimately reduces the price of week-old cars by about 20 percent. In this case, imperfect information prevents people from knowing the true value of the cars, forcing them to add a risk factor that lowers how much they are willing to pay.

7. d. The willingness to pay for a used car decreases as the perceived chance of getting a lemon increases.

8. b. The probability of purchasing a plum is (1 - the probability of purchasing a lemon). The typical buyer will be willing to pay the average value of the two types of goods: (0.4 * $300) + (0.6 * $150) = $210.

9. b. In equilibrium, the expectations of the market equal the actual market outcomes. We know that if 25% of the used computers sold are lemons, then the total number of computers sold must be 100. Since 75% must be plums, 75 plums are sold.

10. b. A market that contains only lemons, or low-quality goods, offers only bad choices for consumers.

11. a. This puzzling feature of the free-agent market for baseball players is explained by asymmetric information and adverse selection. Adverse selection means that, as in the market for "lemons," the pitchers who end up in the market, or available to choose from, are those who tend to be the injury-prone pitchers.

12. b. Would careful lawyers be willing to pay the average cost of insurance? The average cost of insurance is $6,500. Since this is greater than the average cost of settling a malpractice case for careful lawyers, only reckless lawyers would purchase insurance. Thus, only a price of $20,000 guarantees zero economic profit.

13. b. .4(10,000) + .6(5,000) = $7,000

14. b. Thin markets occur due to asymmetric information. Warranties, money-back guarantees, etc., allow buyers to collect more information and thus increase their willingness to pay (and thus the market price).

15. b. Moral hazard is a situation in which one side of an economic relationship takes undesirable or costly actions that the other side of the relationship cannot observe.

16. a. Experience rating systems charge different rates to different firms, based on past experience, rather than the previous community rating systems, which were based on the average cost to the whole community.

17. c. Those who have more risk will tend to buy more insurance, regardless of price.

18. c. Each firm pays a different price based on the medical history of the firm's employees.

19. Asymmetric information occurs when one side of the market has better information than the other. In the banking industry, borrowers have better information about the likelihood that they will repay their loans than lenders. If banks cannot distinguish between good and bad customers, they will charge the same interest rates to all. To compensate for the risk of default, the bank will have to charge higher rates than the rates the bank would charge if it had only good customers. In the extreme case, the bank would end up with only the group of borrowers who were going to default on their loans anyway. Eventually, higher and higher interest rates effectively eliminate the good borrowers from the market.

20. Moral hazard is a situation that encourages risky behavior. Moral hazard causes people to take greater risks and increase the probability of a grim outcome. Moral hazard causes banks to take greater risks than are prudent. There is also a tendency for depositors to ignore the risks taken by their financial institutions because of the existence of deposit insurance.

21. In a mixed market, where high- and low-quality snow blowers are sold together, the seller has more information about the quality of the snow blower than you have. You would have to attach a probability to the possibility of buying a low-quality rather than a high-quality machine. This probability is factored into the price you are willing to pay for a used snow blower. The higher the probability that you will get a low-quality snow blower, the lower the price you are willing to pay for it.

22. The domination of the low-quality goods in a mixed market is an example of the adverse-selection problem. The quality of the goods left in the market is adverse, or undesirable. Adverse selection is the result of the dynamics of asymmetric information (one side has better information than the other), which generates a downward spiral of price and quantity. It is possible that asymmetric information generates a thin market—one in which some high-quality goods are sold, but fewer than would be sold in a market with perfect information.

23. Suppliers can identify a particular car as a plum in a sea of lemons by offering a money-back guarantee whereby the seller offers to refund the price of the car if it turns out to be a lemon. The supplier can also offer a warranty and repair guarantee whereby the seller offers to cover any extraordinary repair costs for one year. Lemons laws require automakers to buy back cars that experience frequent problems in the first year of use. A vehicle repurchased under the lemons law must be fixed before it is sold to another customer and must be identified as a lemon. A problem with enforcing these laws is that lemons can cross state lines without paper trails. However, interstate commerce laws now require the branding of cars as lemons on vehicle titles.

24. A mixed market is a market where low-quality goods and high-quality goods are mixed together. A market will break down, or the high-quality goods will tend to disappear, if either buyers or sellers are unable to distinguish between low-quality goods and high-quality goods. Asymmetric information occurs when one side of the market—either buyers or sellers—has better information about the good than the other. If buyers cannot distinguish between low-quality goods and high-quality goods, both will be sold together, in a mixed market, for the same price. In such a market, the odds of getting a plum are small. The high-quality goods will tend to disappear and, in the extreme case, will be completely nonexistent.

15 [30]
Public Goods and Public Choice

Chapter Summary

This chapter examines the role of government in providing public goods. Here are the main points of the chapter:
- When a good generates external benefits, collective decision-making generates more-efficient choices.
- A public good is available for everyone to consume (nonrival in consumption), regardless of who pays and who doesn't (nonexcludable).
- A system of voluntary contributions suffers from the free-rider problem: People do not have a financial incentive to support public goods.
- Education generates external benefits in the workplace and in elections and reduces crime.
- The median-voter rule suggests that government choices will match the preferences of the median voter, defined as the voter whose preferences lie in the middle of voter preferences.

Applying the Concepts

After reading this chapter, you should be able to answer these four key questions:
1. How can we respond to the free-rider problem?
2. What happens when external benefits spill across international boundaries?
3. What private goods generate external benefits?
4. What is the economic logic of the median-voter rule?

Government exists at many levels: federal, state, and local. At all of these levels, governments provide goods and services such as schools, utilities, fire and fire protection, libraries, social insurance, and national defense.

Governments raise money through various taxes on income, sales, and property. Figure 15.1 [30.1] graphically illustrates the major spending areas of local, state, and federal government in 2002. Figure 15.2 [30.2] illustrates the major revenue sources of local, state, and federal governments in 2002.

15.1 [30.1] External Benefits and Public Goods

Market outcomes are efficient as long as there are no external benefits or external costs involved with the transaction. A decision maker will consider the private benefit of an action, the benefit the decision maker experiences, and the private cost of the action. A private decision maker will not consider external benefits or costs of his or her actions. An **external benefit** is a benefit from a good experienced by someone other than the person who buys the good.

A **public good** is a good that is available for everyone to consume, regardless of who pays and who doesn't; a good that is nonrival in consumption and nonexcludable. Using the example from the text, even if you refuse to pay part of the costs of a dam, you can't be excluded from the benefits of the dam. This is what is meant by a public good being nonexcludable. To say that a good is nonrival in consumption means that one person consuming a good (such as watching a fireworks display, or receiving flood protection from a dam) does not prevent another person from also consuming the good, or reduce the amount of the good available for another person to consume.

In contrast, a **private good** is a good that is consumed by a single person or household; a good that is rival in consumption and excludable.

💣⃰ Caution!

Public and private goods are *not* defined by who produces the good. Public goods are goods that are nonrival in consumption. Private goods are goods that are rival in consumption.

☞ A candy bar is a rival good. If you eat a candy bar, it is no longer available for other people to eat. A candy bar is also excludable. If you don't pay for the candy bar, a store owner can refuse to give you the candy bar. In contrast, fireworks are nonrival and nonexcludable. The fact that you are watching fireworks doesn't prevent anyone else from also watching the same fireworks. Also, since fireworks explode in the sky, it is impossible to keep non-payers from watching a fireworks display.

Public goods are subject to the free-rider problem. A **free rider** is a person who gets the benefit from a good but does not pay for it. As a result of the free-rider problem, private groups are unlikely to provide a large enough quantity of public goods because everyone has an incentive to free ride. In many cases, private markets will not provide public goods at all. Governments can avoid the free-rider problem by levying taxes to pay for public goods.

☞ If you have ever done a group project for a class, you may have first-hand experience with the free-rider problem. If everyone's grade is based on the final project, it is likely that someone in the group will do less than his or her share of the work on the group project. That person knows that he or she can't be excluded from the group grade and that the other group members will likely do extra work to receive a good grade on the project.

Public television and radio stations often face the free-rider problem. People watch or listen but do not contribute. To overcome the free-rider problem, a number of tactics are used to encourage contributions, including:
- Giving token gifts, such as a coffee mug or music CD. People tend to contribute if they receive something tangible.
- Arranging matching contributions.
- Appealing to civic or moral responsibility.

Another example of the free-rider problem and the need for government involvement is public safety. What would you pay to avoid an unlikely disaster? The text uses the example of asteroid diversion. Very rarely do large asteroids hit the earth. For $250 million in initial costs plus $10 million per year, scientists believe we could divert a "doomsday asteroid." How much would you contribute to the cause? If you don't pay we can't prevent you from receiving the benefits. Even though the cost per person to avoid this is very small, few people would voluntarily contribute since they can't be excluded from the benefits.

☞ Think of the tsunami that hit Southeast Asia in December of 2004. A tsunami warning system is a public good in that it is impossible to warn some residents of affected areas without warning all residents. Large tsunamis are also very rare events. Knowing this, would you be willing to contribute to a tsunami warning system? There would be no way to keep the benefits of the warning system from you. In this case most people—especially those who live away from the coastline—would not choose to contribute, and as a result, governments typically provide these types of services.

Let's review two Applications that answer key questions we posed at the start of the chapter:

1. How can we respond to the free-rider problem?

   APPLICATION 1: FREE RIDERS AND THE THREE-CLOCK TOWER
   This Application shows how one town tried to exclude a non-payer from consuming a public good. A clock face on a tower is a public good. It is costless to provide for one more person, and it is hard to identify, let alone prevent, use of the clock tower by non-payers. In this Application, a town refused to put a clock face on the side of the tower facing the home of a wealthy non-contributor. Notice that this also penalized everyone on that side of the clock tower, even if they had contributed to the good.

2. What happens when external benefits spill across international borders?

   APPLICATION 2: GLOBAL WEATHER OBSERVATION
   Information is a public good. The cost of collecting information is the same whether one person receives the information or twenty people. This Application illustrates how the United States has encouraged cooperation and information sharing related to climate change. The Application points out that early warning of the 1997-98 El Nino prevented roughly $1.1 billion in damage to California's economy.

15.2 [30.2] Private Goods with External Benefits

Some private goods also have external benefits. Your text uses education as an example. Certainly, the person receiving the education is better off as he or she earns higher income as a result of the education. Society may also benefit in these ways:
   • A well-educated worker makes the workers around him or her more productive, which may lead to higher salaries for all of the person's co-workers.
   • A well-educated citizen makes more informed community decisions.
   • A well-educated citizen is less likely to commit crimes.

Think of the decision a high school student makes whether or not to drop out after 11th grade. A recent study suggested that the cost of one year of high school is $6,000. This cost is paid by society through the provision of public school. If a student completes year 12 of high school, he or she receives a benefit of higher earnings as a high school graduate. Society also receives a benefit from lower crime costs. For each student who graduates instead of dropping out after 11th grade, the cost of crime decreases by $1,600 per year.

☞ A classic example of a private good with an external benefit is a vaccine. If I am vaccinated against measles, not only am I unlikely to contract measles, but you benefit as well. You benefit because there is now one fewer person from whom you are likely to contract measles. I am unlikely to factor your health benefits from the vaccine into my decision to be vaccinated. This is the reason for underprovision of goods with external benefits. Individuals will make decisions concerning vaccines and other goods using the marginal principle.+

 The Marginal Principle

Increase the level of an activity as long as its marginal benefit exceeds its marginal cost. Choose the level at which the marginal benefit equals the marginal cost.

Individuals will choose the level of education, or some other activity, up to the point where the marginal benefit to the individual is equal to the marginal cost to the individual. When there are external benefits, we will have too little of an activity take place. Why? Look at Figure 16.3 [30.3] in your text. An individual will read books to the point where the marginal benefit is equal to the marginal cost. For the individual that occurs at point *a*, where the marginal private benefit equals the marginal social benefit. Reading generates an external benefit of $4 per book, so having the individual read more books is better for society. If an individual reads book 12, society gains $10 as indicated by point *d*. The individual gains only $6, indicated by point *c*. Since the cost of a book is $8, an individual won't choose to read book 12 even though society is better off by $2 if they do so, the $10 gain to society minus the $8 cost of the book. The optimal outcome occurs at point *b* with the individual reading 15 books.

📄 **Remember**

When a good provides external benefits, markets will produce too little of the good.

To encourage individuals to pursue higher levels of education, government takes various steps to lower the private cost of education. One way government does this is by providing free education through high school and greatly subsidized college education at state universities.

Let's review an Application that answers one of the key questions we posed at the start of the chapter:

3. What private goods generate external benefits?

APPLICATION 3: EXTERNAL BENEFITS FROM LOJACK

LoJack is a tracking system that makes it easier for police to recover stolen vehicles. A thief is not interested in stealing a LoJack-equipped car as it increases the likelihood that they will be caught. Since a thief can't determine which cars have LoJacks, as more people install LoJack systems we would anticipate that fewer cars will be stolen. So, installing a LoJack system provides a benefit to the owner of the car with the system as well as to other drivers. The person with the system benefits as the LoJack makes it more likely that his or her car will be recovered if stolen. Other people benefit as increased use of LoJacks lowers the likelihood that any car will be stolen. A study found that one fewer car is stolen for each three LoJack systems installed and that the dollar amount of this extra benefit is roughly $1,300 per year.

15.3 [30.3] Public Choice

Public-choice economics is a field of economics that uses models of rational choice to explore decision making in the public sector. One important result from public-choice economics is the median-voter rule. The **median-voter rule** states that choices made by government will match the preferences of the median voter.

Figure 15.4 [30.4] of your text illustrates how this model works. In the figure, we have eight possible spending levels for education, and the number of voters who prefer each level. We assume that voters will vote for the candidate, Penny or Buck, whose proposed spending on education is closest to their own.

So, if Penny proposes a budget of $3 million, everyone who wants to spend $3 million or less on education will vote for her. This is 12 votes. If Buck proposes spending $7 million, everyone who wants to spend $7 million or more will vote for him. This is also 12 votes. The other voters will cast their ballot for the candidate whose proposed spending is closest to their desired level.

The 8 voters who want to spend $6 million will then vote for Buck as his proposal is $1 million away from their preferred level while Penny's is $3 million away. The 8 voters who want to spend $4 million will vote for Penny for the same reason. This gives each candidate 20 votes, with the 10 voters who want to spend $5 million undecided.

Penny can capture those votes by increasing her spending level to $4 million. Now she will be only $1 million away from their preferred spending level while Buck will be $2 million away. In this case, 30 votes are cast for Penny while 20 votes are cast for Buck.

Buck can realize this and propose a spending level of $6 million, resulting in another tie. Both candidates are trying to appeal to the 10 voters in the middle, those wanting to spend $5 million. Penny's incentive is to continue to increase her spending level toward $5 million, while Buck's incentive is to continue to reduce his spending level toward $5 million.

At the local level, Charles Tiebout suggested that people "vote with their feet." That is, individuals choose where they will live based on the tax and spending policies of those communities. People who desire a high level of public services may choose to live in areas with high services, and correspondingly high taxes. Those who prefer fewer taxes may live in areas with very few public services, but low taxes.

Other models of government include:
- Self-interest. This suggests that politicians pursue their interest and not that of their constituents. Property tax and spending limits are attempts at correcting the self-interest motivation of politicians.
- Special interests. This suggests that small groups of people with a large individual stake in political decisions will attempt to manipulate the system at the expense of larger groups of people with smaller individual stakes in the outcome.

☞ In 2002, President Bush imposed tariffs on imported steel. (The tariffs were removed in December, 2003.) It was estimated at that time that roughly 300,000 workers in the steel industry would benefit from higher steel prices as a result. It was also estimated that 12 million workers in industries that used steel would be harmed as a result of higher steel prices. The 300,000 steel workers had a strong incentive to organize for tariffs. In an extreme case, imagine that these 300,000 workers would lose their job if the tariffs weren't implemented. In contrast, many of the 12 million other workers would be only slightly affected. In an extreme case, imagine that these workers would receive a smaller raise in pay. It would be difficult to imagine these 12 million workers effectively organizing against the tariffs. It is easy to imagine the steel workers, through their union, organizing to save their jobs. This is an example of the special-interest model.

☞ The 300,000 jobs the steel tariffs protected were primarily in West Virginia and Pennsylvania. In the 2000 Presidential election, Pennsylvania voted for Al Gore, while West Virginia voted for George Bush. The outcomes were relatively close in these states. The self-interest model of government might suggest that the steel tariffs may have been enacted in part to make voters in those states more favorable towards President Bush in anticipation of the 2004 elections.

There is evidence that all three of these models explain particular aspects of voting behavior.

Let's review an Application that answers one of the key questions we posed at the start of the chapter:

4.   What is the economic logic of the median-voter model?

APPLICATION 4: POLITICIANS ARE LIKE ICE-CREAM SELLERS

This Application extends the use of the median-voter model to seller behavior. Suppose that you have two ice-cream sellers on a beach. Where will they choose to locate? If the sellers are trying to maximize the number of people who buy from them, this Application shows that they will both locate at the center of the beach.

To understand this Application, make sure you understand the assumptions. There are 100 customers evenly distributed over the length of the beach, and each customer will choose the closest ice-cream parlor. With both ice cream stands in the middle, each will attract half the customers, and neither will have an incentive to move from that location because moving will reduce the number of customers.

Activity

Let's see how goods with external benefits can lead to inefficient outcomes. Your school student health department has issued a warning about measles outbreaks among college students and has offered to vaccinate students at a cost of $20 per vaccine.

a. What value would you have to place on a vaccine to pay $20 for the vaccine? _____

b. Suppose that you valued the vaccine at only $15; would you get the vaccine? _____

c. Explain the external benefit the vaccine provides.

d. Suppose this benefit has a marginal social value of $10, and your marginal private benefit from the vaccine is $15. If the vaccine costs $20, would you get vaccinated? _____ From society's perspective should you? _____

e. Suppose that upon receiving a vaccination you were handed a $10 bill to compensate you for the external benefit you conveyed by getting vaccinated. Would this change your decision? Why?

   _____

f. Suppose that your college reduced the price of vaccines to $10 to take account of the external benefit you conveyed by getting vaccinated. Would this change your decision? Why?

   _____

Answers

a. You would have to value the vaccine at $20 or more.
b. No, the benefit to you is less than the cost to you.
c. When you are vaccinated, there is one less person able to spread measles to others and thus the chance that other people will get measles falls.
d. No, your private benefit is less than your private cost. Yes, because the benefit to society ($25) exceeds the cost to society ($20).
e. Yes, now you receive $25 in benefits, $15 from the vaccination and $10 from the cash. Your private cost is still $20 so you will receive the vaccination.
f. Yes. Now the private cost is $10, which is less than your private benefit of $15 so you will be vaccinated.

Key Terms

External benefit: A benefit from a good experienced by someone other than the person who buys the good.

Free rider: A person who gets the benefit from a good but does not pay for it.

Median-voter rule: The choices made by government will match the preferences of the median voter.

Private good: A good that is consumed by a single person or household; a good that is rival in consumption and excludable.

Public-choice economics: A field of economics that uses models of rational choice to explore decision making in the public sector.

Public good: A good that is available for everyone to consume, regardless of who pays and who doesn't; a good that is nonrival in consumption and nonexcludable.

Practice Quiz

(Answers are provided at the end of the Practice Quiz.)

1. Select the most accurate choice in accordance with the textbook reading. Among the purposes of government is:
   a. to produce goods that generate only external benefits, not external costs.
   b. to provide goods that benefit everyone, regardless of cost, such as an asteroid-diversion system.
   c. to make decisions that people cannot make for themselves.
   d. to help people make collective decisions.

2. Which types of goods provide external benefits?
   a. Public goods only.
   b. Private goods only.
   c. Both public goods and private goods.
   d. Nonrenewable resources only.

3. Both state and local governments spend the largest percent of their money on:
   a. health and hospitals.
   b. police and corrections.
   c. education.
   d. highways.

4. Which of the following corresponds to revenues at the state level of government?
   a. Revenues that come mainly from intergovernmental grants and property taxes.
   b. Revenues that come mainly from intergovernmental grants, the sales tax, and the individual income tax.
   c. Revenues that come mainly from individual income taxes and employment taxes, including taxes collected to support Social Security and Medicare.
   d. Revenues that come mainly from other countries.

5. When is the market equilibrium said to be *efficient*?
   a. When the external benefits are greater than the external costs.
   b. When there are external benefits but no external costs.
   c. When the external costs exceed the external benefits.
   d. When there are neither external benefits nor external costs.

6. What is an external benefit?
   a. A benefit from consumption of a good that has no intrinsic value.
   b. A benefit from a good experienced by someone other than the person who buys the good.
   c. The benefit experienced by the person who buys a good.
   d. A benefit that comes from another country, in the form of imports.

7. Which statement is precisely correct? A market with external benefits:
   a. is inefficient but preferable to a market with government intervention.
   b. is efficient but could be even more efficient if the government intervened.
   c. is efficient, so there is no opportunity for government to promote efficiency.
   d. is inefficient, so there is an opportunity for government to promote efficiency.

8. *Private goods* are:
    a. rival and excludable.
    b. rival and nonexcludable.
    c. nonrival and nonexcludable.
    d. nonrival and excludable.

9. *Public goods* are:
    a. rival and excludable.
    b. rival and nonexcludable.
    c. nonrival and nonexcludable.
    d. nonrival and excludable.

10. This question tests your understanding of Application 1 in this chapter: Free riders and the three-clock tower: How do we respond to the free-rider problem?

    Back in the days before inexpensive wristwatches, most people did not carry their own timepieces. Many towns built clock towers to help their citizens keep track of time. The towns paid for the clock towers with voluntary contributions from citizens. The clock tower suffered from the free-rider problem because use of the tower produced:
    a. excludability and rivalry.
    b. nonexcludability and nonrivalry.
    c. excludability and nonrivalry.
    d. nonexcludability and rivalry.

11. Which of the following statements is entirely correct?
    a. Some private goods generate benefits for people who are not directly consuming the good.
    b. Private goods are goods that generate benefits only for those people who directly consume the good.
    c. Private goods benefit everyone except those who actually consume those goods.
    d. Private goods generate precisely the same benefits as public goods.

12. Why does the government encourage people to become educated?
    a. Because education is rival in consumption.
    b. Because education generates external benefits.
    c. Because financial aid is only a small portion of the federal budget.
    d. Because the private sector does not encourage people to become educated.

13. Suppose that the value that Nina places on a college education is $45,000, and the market price is $70,000. If the external benefit associated with Nina's attending college is $30,000. How large a subsidy would be required to get Nina to attend college?
    a. $15,000
    b. $25,000
    c. $30,000
    d. $75,000

14. Which of the following is a technique to encourage people to contribute?
    a. Giving contributors private goods in return.
    b. Arranging matching contributions.
    c. Appealing to people's sense of civic or moral responsibility.
    d. All of the above.

15. Which of the following would be considered a workplace externality of education?
   a.   A well-educated person joins a work team.
   b.   Educated citizens in a democratic society vote in elections.
   c.   Educated people earn higher legal incomes and thus commit less crime.
   d.   The benefit that a business firm obtains from the work done by an educated person.

16. This question tests your understanding of Application 3 in this chapter: External benefits from LoJack: What private goods generate external benefits?

   LoJack, a system used to recover stolen vehicles, is a private good that generates external benefits. A small, silent transmitter hidden in a vehicle allows police to track a stolen car. The name is a play on words, meant to convey the idea that LoJack will recover vehicles that are hijacked or stolen. A thief who steals a LoJack-equipped car won't keep the car for long and is likely to get caught, so LoJack is an effective deterrent to car theft. Car thieves cannot distinguish between cars with and without LoJack, so the system decreases the payoff from car theft in general, and criminals steal fewer cars. People who install LoJack systems in their cars generate benefits for themselves and external benefits for other car owners who don't have LoJack.

   Since the LoJack generates external benefits, which of the following is correct?
   a.   The marginal social benefit exceeds the marginal private benefit and the socially efficient quantity is greater than the quantity produced by the private market.
   b.   The marginal private benefit exceeds the marginal social benefit and the socially efficient quantity is greater than the quantity produced by the private market.
   c.   The marginal social benefit exceeds the marginal private benefit and the socially efficient quantity is less than the quantity produced by the private market.
   d.   The marginal private benefit exceeds the marginal social benefit and the socially efficient quantity is less than the quantity produced by the private market.

17. The *median-voter rule* is a rule suggesting that:
   a.   voters are practically indistinguishable from each other.
   b.   in theory, a perfect government is one that responds to the perfect median voter.
   c.   the choices made by government will reflect the preferences of the median voter.
   d.   the election of government officials is often a statistical dead heat.

18. Suppose one candidate proposes a $5.2 billion budget and another proposes a $9.4 billion budget, when the average voter preference is for a $8.3 billion budget and the median voter preference is $7.1 billion. The candidates are expected to move toward a budget position of:
   a. $7.1 billion.
   b.   the smaller budget $5.2 billion.
   c. $8.3 billion.
   d.   the larger budget: $9.4 billion.

19. According to the self-interest theory of government:
   a.   voters don't have much information about the costs and benefits of public services.
   b.   voters may not be able to evaluate the actions of politicians.
   c.   limitations on taxes and spending are necessary safeguards against politicians and bureaucrats.
   d.   All of the above.

20. Government is more likely to approve inefficient projects:
    a. when many people share the benefit from a project and a small number of people share the cost.
    b. when a few people share the benefit from a project and a large number of people share the cost.
    c. when those who benefit from a project are also those who pay for it.
    d. when those who pay for a project are not included in those who benefit.

21. Briefly, explain the median voter rule.

22. Theories of government behavior have been built around the concept of self-interest and special interests. The basic idea is that people manipulate government for their own gain. Expand.

Answers to the Practice Quiz

1. d. As the textbook states: "Although everyone on earth would benefit from an asteroid-diversion system, the cost of an asteroid-diversion program is so high that no single person would provide such a system. We will never have such a program—even if its benefits exceed its costs—unless we make a collective decision about what sort of diversion system to develop and how to pay for it. One purpose of government is to help make this sort of collective decision."

2. c. For example, everyone on earth would benefit from an asteroid-diversion system (a public good), including those who did not pay for it. Private goods, such as education, also generate external benefits.

3. c. Education comprises 35% of state government spending and 43% of local government spending.

4. b. At the state level, the most important revenue sources are intergovernmental grants from the federal government, the sales tax, and the individual income tax.

5. d. Neither external benefits nor external costs are desirable. They both yield inefficient results. In the case in which an external benefit exists, the market yields insufficient output; and in the case in which an external cost exists, the market yields too much output relative to the socially optimal level of output.

6. b. An external benefit is a benefit from a good experienced by someone other than the person who buys the good.

7. d. External benefits are a sign of market inefficiency. There is a chance for government to improve efficiency in both the case of external benefits and in the case of external costs.

8. a. Private goods are rival in consumption (only one person can consume the good) and excludable (it is possible to exclude a person who does not pay for the good).

9. c. A public good is available for everyone to utilize, regardless of who pays for it and who doesn't. More precisely, a public good is nonrival in consumption. Public goods are also nonexcludable: It is impractical to exclude people who don't pay.

10. b. A good that is available for everyone to consume, regardless of who pays and who doesn't is a good that is nonrival in consumption and nonexcludable.

11. a. One example of a private good that generates benefits for people who are not directly consuming the good is education.

12. b. The social benefit is greater than the private benefit derived from education. The social benefits of education may not be accounted for by the private market, in which case the market may provide an insufficient amount of education.

13. b. Market price 2 (value to consumer) = \$25,000, the subsidy required. Note that the amount of the subsidy is less than the external benefits to society.

14. d. Techniques to encourage people to contribute include: giving contributors private goods in return, arranging matching contributions, and appealing to people's sense of civic or moral responsibility.

15. a. This is called a workplace externality. In most workplaces, people work in groups and teamwork is important. A well-educated person understands instructions readily and is more likely to suggest ways to improve the production process. As a result, when a well-educated person joins a work team, the productivity of everyone on the team increases.

16. a. Refer to Figure 30.3 in the textbook for a similar example of this outcome.

17. c. If governments respond to voters, the voting public ultimately makes all the important decisions. The median-voter rule is a rule suggesting that the choices made by government will reflect the preferences of the median voter.

18. a. Both candidates will propose a budget close to the $7.1 billion, which is the preferred budget of the median voter.

19. d. The self-interest theory of government suggests that voters don't have much information about the costs and benefits of public services, and may not be able to evaluate the actions of politicians. Limitations on taxes and spending are necessary safeguards against politicians and bureaucrats who benefit from large budgets.

20. b. This is the outcome of decisions when a special-interest group manipulates the government at the expense of a larger group (all taxpayers). In general, when a few people share the benefit from a project and a large number of people share the cost, the government is more likely to approve inefficient projects.

21. The median voter rule explains how the choices made by government will tend to reflect the preferences of the average voter. When two candidates offer divergently opposed views, they will tend to move toward the preferences of the median voter. In this manner, the median, or middle of political preferences will be reflected in government decisions. If governments respond to voters, the voting public ultimately makes all the important decisions.

22. The Nobel laureate James Buchanan, among others, has suggested a model of government that focuses on the selfish behavior of government officials. The self-interest theory of government suggests that voters don't have much information about the costs and benefits of public services, and may not be able to evaluate the actions of politicians. Limitations on taxes and spending are necessary safeguards against politicians and bureaucrats who benefit from large budgets. The special-interest theory is a model of government based on the idea that small groups of people manipulate government for their own gain. When a few people share the benefit from a project and a large number of people share the cost, government is more likely to approve inefficient projects. Special-interest groups form whenever the benefits are concentrated on a few citizens but costs are spread out over many citizens.

16 [31]
External Costs and Environmental Policy

Chapter Summary

This chapter suggests the best way to control pollution and other external costs is to rely on the exchange principle. Here are the main points of the chapter:

- The optimum level of pollution abatement is where the marginal benefit equals the marginal cost.
- A tax on the emissions of electricity generators decreases total emissions as firms switch to cleaner fuels and consumers buy less electricity at the higher price.
- Compared to a pollution tax, traditional pollution regulations lead to higher production costs and higher product prices.
- Allowing firms to buy and sell pollution permits reduces the cost of abatement because low-cost firms do more of the abatement.
- Urban smog is a continuing problem, in part because the traditional command-and-control policies are less effective than an annual automobile pollution tax.
- The external cost from traffic congestion could be internalized with a tax that varies with the level of traffic congestion.
- The external cost from traffic collisions could be internalized with a tax that varies with the likelihood of causing a collision.

Applying the Concepts

After reading this chapter, you should be able to answer these six key questions:

1. How do we determine the optimum level of pollution?
2. What is the economic approach to global warming?
3. Are there different ways to reduce pollution or mitigate its effects?
4. What are the benefits of giving firms options for reducing greenhouse gases?
5. What is the external cost of young drivers?

16.1 [31.1] The Optimal Level of Pollution

As with many economic choices, finding the optimal level of pollution abatement can be done by using the marginal principle.

The Marginal Principle
Increase the level of an activity as long as its marginal benefit exceeds its marginal cost. Choose the level at which the marginal benefit equals the marginal cost.

In this chapter, we will be trying to find the optimal amount of pollution abatement. Some of the benefits of reducing pollution are:
- Better health from having cleaner air and water.
- Increased enjoyment of the natural environment.
- Lower production costs, particularly for industries that require clean water for production.

At the same time, it is costly to reduce pollution. Ideally, we would find the point where the marginal benefit of another unit of pollution reduction is equal to the marginal cost of another unit of pollution reduction.

☞ The optimal level of pollution is not zero. Achieving zero pollution would require that no one drive automobiles, trucks, or buses or fly airplanes. It is reasonable that up to some point the marginal benefit to society of driving vehicles exceeds the marginal cost to society.

> We can see this in the issue of reducing sulfur dioxide emissions. Sulfur dioxide emissions contribute to air pollution, leading to health problems and acid rain. Does that mean we should ban sulfur dioxide emissions? This Application suggests the answer is no. In Figure 16.1 [31.1], we assume a constant marginal benefit of abatement of $3,500 per million tons of pollution reduced. We can see that early units of abatement are relatively inexpensive and the marginal cost of abatement curve lies beneath the marginal benefit curve. The marginal principle would suggest that we should eliminate these units of pollution. Beyond 8 million tons of abatement, however, the cost of one more unit of pollution reduction is greater than the benefit that we would receive from eliminating that unit of pollution. The marginal principle suggests we should stop at point *a* where the marginal benefit of abatement equals the marginal cost of abatement.

Let's review an Application that answers one of the key questions we posed at the start of the chapter:

1. How do we determine the optimum level of pollution?

APPLICATION 1: REDUCING METHANE EMISSIONS
What is the optimal amount of methane reduction? It depends on the marginal costs and the marginal benefits. Early abatement is relatively inexpensive, less than $10 per ton. The abatement cost per ton increases as we try to reduce pollution more and more. This Application illustrates that the optimal amount of abatement will depend upon the benefit of reducing one more unit of pollution and the cost of reducing that unit. We will reduce pollution until the marginal benefit is equal to the marginal cost.

16.2 [31.2] Taxing Pollution

At the market level, pollution is a problem because a producer considers only the **private cost of production**, the production cost borne by a producer which typically includes the costs of labor, capital, and materials. What is not considered is the **external cost of production**, a cost incurred by someone other than the producer. From an efficiency standpoint we would like producers to consider the **social cost of production**, the private cost plus the external cost. One way that this can be done is to levy a **pollution tax**, a tax or charge equal to the external cost per unit of pollution.

In Figure 16.3 [31.3], the text illustrates how a tax changes the behavior of a firm. When faced with a $3,500 per ton tax on sulfur dioxide emissions, the firm will reduce pollution so long as it can do so at a cost of less than $3,500 per ton. So, at point a, the firm would rather pay $2,200 to reduce a unit of pollution than $3,500 in taxes to emit the unit. At point d, the firm would rather pay the $3,500 tax than pay $4,500 to reduce the unit of pollution. The optimal level of pollution abatement occurs at point c, where the marginal benefit of abatement is equal to the marginal cost of abatement.

📄 Remember

A pollution tax forces a polluter to realize some of the external cost that pollution imposes on others.

In the market for electricity, the tax on pollution effectively shifts the market supply curve for electricity to the left, as shown in Figure 16.4 [31.4]. This results in a higher price for electricity and a lower amount of electricity used. At the market level, the pollution tax reduces the quantity of pollution producing good.

In addition to reducing pollution by reducing the quantity of the pollution producing good, the tax on sulfur dioxide also encourages producers to look for cleaner methods of generating electricity. Figure 16.4 [31.4] shows how producers have shifted away from coal, which is subject to the pollution tax, and towards low-sulfur coal and other cleaner fuels.

Let's review an Application that answers one of the key questions we posed at the start of the chapter:

2. What is the economic approach to global warming?

APPLICATION 2: THE EFFECTS OF A CARBON TAX

Scientists suggest that carbon dioxide, generated from burning carbon-based fuels, is accumulating in the atmosphere and, left unchecked, will lead to higher global temperatures. The cost of global warming is an external cost generated from the burning of carbon-based fuels. Keep in mind that if you drive you are a producer of carbon dioxide and a source of this external cost. This Application shows how a tax on carbon-based fuels would reduce the amount of carbon dioxide released into the atmosphere. In particular, taxes would be levied on gasoline, oil, and coal. Consumers should respond to higher fuel prices by using less carbon-based fuels by driving less and keeping their houses cooler in the winter. Producers should respond to higher fuel prices by finding alternatives to carbon-based fuels.

☞ The text suggests a tax rate of $0.28 per gallon on gasoline. How would you respond if the price of gas increased by $0.28 per gallon? Would you drive less? Think about getting a different car? Car pool or walk more? Would it matter if you believed the price change was permanent (like a tax) as opposed to temporary (from market changes)? A carbon tax of $0.28 will have only a significant impact on carbon dioxide emissions if people chose to drive less as a result of the higher prices.

16.3 [31.3] Traditional Regulation

Pollution regulation typically does not consist of taxes, but instead consists of regulation in which firms are told that they must reduce pollution by a given amount. The text shows why this regulation is not an efficient approach. In the example given in the text, a uniform regulation would lead to abatement costs of $7,000—$5,000 from firm H and $2,000 from firm L. You can see that society would prefer that firm L reduces pollution by two units at a cost of only $4,000.

A pollution tax would achieve this goal. When faced with a tax of $3,500 per unit, firm L would prefer to reduce pollution by two units at a cost of $2,000 per unit. Firm H would prefer to pay the tax rather than reduce pollution.

A command-and-control approach regulates not only the amount of pollution allowed, but also mandates the abatement technology to be used. This approach may discourage firms from seeking out lower-cost ways of reducing pollution. Command and control also discourages innovation in pollution control technology because the technologies to be used are already specified in the regulations.

In the market for the output good, the higher costs resulting from a uniform pollution reduction combined with the lack of incentive to develop new pollution reduction techniques would lead to a larger supply shift in Figure 16.4 [31.4]. The higher cost of regulation is passed along to consumers in the form of higher prices.

Let's review an Application that answers a key question we posed at the start of the chapter:

3. Are there different ways to reduce pollution or mitigate its effects?

> **APPLICATION 3: MERCURY IN TUNA**
> Mercury levels in tuna have risen. This Application illustrates how society can reduce its exposure to mercury, and suggests different costs. What you should notice is that the cost of capturing mercury is quite a bit higher, per kilogram of mercury avoided, than switching to another technology. This Application shows that there are often multiple paths, with different costs, to mitigating an externality.

16.4 [31.4] Marketable Pollution Permits

A more recent approach to pollution control is the **marketable pollution permit**. This is a system under which the government picks a target pollution level for a particular area, issues just enough pollution permits to meet the pollution target, and allows firms to buy and sell the permits. This is also known as a *cap-and-trade* system.

This system takes advantage of the principle of voluntary exchange:

The Principle of Voluntary Exchange
A voluntary exchange between two people makes both better off.

Think about firm H with an abatement cost of $5,000 per unit and firm L with an abatement cost of $2,000 per unit. Firm H will find it in its interest to purchase permits to pollute so long as the permit costs less than $5,000. If the permit costs more than $5,000, firm H would rather reduce pollution by that unit. Firm L will be interested in selling permits as long as they receive $2,000, the amount they would have to spend to reduce pollution by that unit. Firms H and L could certainly agree to trade permits for any price in between $2,000 and $5,000. With pollution permits, abatement will be done by low-cost firms thus reducing the cost of abating any given level of pollution.

 Remember

Marketable pollution permits use the principle of voluntary exchange and lower the cost of pollution abatement by encouraging low abatement cost firms to reduce pollution and sell their permits.

Figure 16.6 [31.6] in the text shows the market for pollutants in the Los Angeles area. Notice that the supply of permits is vertical at the chosen level. Pollution reduction over time is achieved in this instance by reducing the number of permits issued each year. The price of a permit is determined by the intersection of the supply curve and demand curve for the permits. The text points out that new abatement technology would lower the demand curve for permits as it would become less expensive to reduce pollution.

Let's review an Application that answers a key question we posed at the start of the chapter:

4.   What are the benefits of giving firms options for reducing greenhouse gasses?

APPLICATION 4: CHICAGO CLIMATE EXCHANGE
This Application shows that firms will take advantage of low-cost ways of reducing pollution. The Application indicates that the cost of converting electric generators from coal to natural gas would be $50 per ton of carbon abated. Instead of doing this, American Electric Power purchased 10,000 acres of land and planted walnut trees to offset carbon emissions. The cost was a mere $1.25 per ton of carbon abated.

16.5 [31.5] External Costs from Automobiles

Automobiles are a source of external costs. These costs come from three sources:
•   Pollution
•   Congestion
•   Collisions

Automobiles emit pollutants which contribute to smog. One estimate suggests that a $0.40 per gallon tax on gasoline would be needed to address the external costs of smog and other air pollution. Adding $0.28 per gallon for the carbon tax brings the total tax to $0.68. Figure 16.7 [31.7] shows the impact of a $0.68 increase in the gasoline tax in the market for gasoline. Imposing a tax would move the market from an outcome at point *a* to an outcome at point *c*. This would reduce the amount of gasoline purchased and burned and reduce the amount of pollution emitted by automobiles.

Pollution is not the only external cost. Additional cars on the road contribute to congestion which causes drivers to spend more time in traffic. Thus, another external cost is the opportunity cost of time spent in traffic. Singapore has begun charging drivers a "congestion tax" for driving during periods of high congestion.

Collisions are a final source of external costs. On average, one-third of the $300 billion cost of collisions is borne by the driver who did not cause the collision. Your book notes that in addition to taxes, this external cost could be imposed on collision, causing drivers in the form of higher insurance premiums for those who drove more miles per year.

Let's review an Application that answers a key question we posed at the start of the chapter.

    5.   What is the external cost of young drivers?

APPLICATION 5: YOUNG DRIVERS AND COLLISIONS
This Application illustrates that a vehicle mileage tax to offset the external costs of collisions would have to take into account the age of the person driving that mile. Young drivers, those under age 25, have an average external cost of $0.11 per mile driven. Middle-aged drivers, those between 25 and 70, have a much lower external cost of miles driven, about $0.034 per mile.

Activity

In this activity, you will find the private cost of reducing pollution from automobile emissions. In particular, you will look at the case of hybrid cars. (A hybrid is a car which runs on gasoline and some other fuel, typically electricity.) Toyota just introduced its hybrid Camry. The hybrid Camry has a base price of $7,455 more than the base price of the conventional gas-powered Camry. The hybrid's price is $3,105 more than the base price of a Camry XLE. The hybrid Camry has estimated gas efficiency of 43 mpg city and 38 mpg highway in contrast to the traditional Camry which gets 24 mpg city and 34 mpg highway.

Suppose you were considering buying a new Camry and were trying to decide whether to buy the hybrid Camry. Answer the following questions:

a. How many "city" miles do you drive in a year? _____ How many gallons of gasoline would you need to purchase to drive these miles in the standard Camry? _____ In the hybrid Camry? _____ (To find this, divide the miles by the mpg rating for each car.) How many gallons of gasoline would you save per year in city driving? _____

b. How many "highway" miles do you drive in a year? _____ How many gallons of gasoline would you need to purchase to drive these miles in the standard Camry? _____ In the hybrid Camry? _____ How many gallons of gasoline would you save per year in city driving? _____

c. What is the price of gasoline in your area? _____

d. How much money would you save on gasoline each year with the hybrid Camry? _____

e. Now, divide the price difference between the hybrid Camry and the regular Camry of your choice by the amount you would save on gas each year. This gives you a rough estimate of how many years it will take to save the difference in car prices. (This assumes for simplicity that interest rates are zero.) How many years would you have to drive the Camry to save enough gasoline to pay for the hybrid?

———————————

f. Why might this information discourage you from buying a hybrid car even though it would be better for the environment?

Answers

The answers to parts a through e will vary with the driving habits and location of the student. In part f you should see that a person driving a hybrid car pays a high price to avoid some pollution, and in fact, that person is unlikely to recover the additional cost of the hybrid vehicle under most driving conditions. If a person sees relatively few private benefits from reducing pollution, many people will be unwilling to pay these costs.

Here are sample calculations based on a driver who lives in a small town:

a. How many "city" miles do you drive in a year? 4,000 How many gallons of gasoline would you need to purchase to drive these miles in the standard Camry? 4,000/24 = 166.67 In the hybrid Camry? 4000/43 = 93 (To find this divide the miles by the mpg rating for each car.) How many gallons of gasoline would you save per year in city driving? 166.67 – 93 = 73.67

b. How many "highway" miles do you drive in a year? 2,000 How many gallons of gasoline would you need to purchase to drive these miles in the standard Camry? 2000/34=58.8 In the hybrid Camry? 2000/38=52.6 How many gallons of gasoline would you save per year in city driving? 6.2

c. What is the price of gasoline in your area? $2.20 per gallon

d. How much money would you save on gasoline each year with the hybrid Camry?
$2.20(73.67+6.2) = $175.71

e. Now, divide the price difference between the hybrid Camry and the regular Camry of your choice by the amount you would save on gas each year. This gives you a rough estimate of how many years it will take to save the difference in car prices. (This assumes for simplicity that interest rates are zero.) How many years would you have to drive the Camry to save enough gasoline to pay for the hybrid?
$3,105/175.71 = 17.67 years

f. Your answers to this question may vary, but as an example, you may be discouraged from buying a hybrid car when you realize that you will not save enough money on gasoline to pay the extra cost of the hybrid car.

As a result, you would be bearing a large cost to reduce pollution, while seeing very little direct benefit. If the cost of buying the hybrid exceeds the benefit that you would receive, you will not buy the car, even if it is better for the environment.

Key Terms

External cost of production: A cost incurred by someone other than the producer.

Marketable pollution permits: A system under which the government picks a target pollution level for a particular area, issues just enough pollution permits to meet the pollution target, and allows firms to buy and sell the permits; also known as a *cap-and-trade system*.

Pollution tax: A tax or charge equal to the external cost per unit of pollution.

Private cost of production: The production cost borne by a producer, which typically includes the costs of labor, capital, and materials.

Social cost of production: Private cost plus external cost.

Practice Quiz

(Answers are provided at the end of the Practice Quiz.)

1. Should society attempt to reduce pollution to zero?
    a. No, pollution is actually beneficial.
    b. No, because the marginal costs of pollution reduction would be likely to exceed the marginal benefits of pollution reduction at that level.
    c. Yes, regardless of cost, this is a good goal because all pollution is harmful.
    d. Only in those countries where pollution is very high does it make sense to attempt to eliminate all pollution.

2. Refer to the figure below. What is the optimum level of pollution abatement?

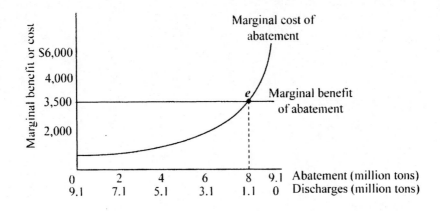

    a. Zero.
    b. Any level where the marginal benefit continues to be greater than the marginal cost, between zero and 8 million tons.
    c. 8 million tons.
    d. Preferably the maximum possible amount shown on the graph: 9.1 million tons of abatement, or zero discharges.

3. This question refers to the example in the text of reducing sulfur dioxide emissions. How do we determine the optimum level of pollution?

    In a figure that shows the marginal-benefit and marginal-cost curves for SO_2, abatement increases as we move to the right, while the amount of SO_2 discharged decreases. Under this scenario, an interpretation of the marginal benefit curve is as follows:
    a. The marginal-benefit curve shows that for each additional ton of SO_2 discharged into the atmosphere, the costs associated with premature deaths and health problems increase by about $3,500.
    b. The marginal-benefit curve shows that the more pollution we abate, the higher the marginal cost of abatement.
    c. The marginal-benefit curve shows that further abatement requires a switch from coal to natural gas, a more expensive fuel.
    d. The marginal-benefit curve is set at optimal level of pollution abatement.

4. *Social cost* refers to:
    a.   the firm's private costs.
    b.   external costs.
    c.   the sum of the firm's private cost and external cost.
    d.   the costs incurred by anyone outside the firm.

5. The idea of a *pollution tax* is to internalize the externality, which happens when:
    a.   the tax is greater than the external cost.
    b.   the tax equals the external cost.
    c.   the tax is less than the external cost.
    d.   the tax brings the external cost down to zero.

6. Refer to the figure below. What is the impact of a pollution tax on this graph?

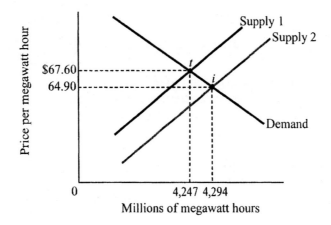

    a.   A higher price and higher equilibrium quantity.
    b.   A lower price and higher equilibrium quantity.
    c.   A higher price and lower equilibrium quantity.
    d.   A lower price and lower equilibrium quantity.

7. The main advantage of command-and-control policies is:
    a. the efficiency with which they reduce pollution.
    b. they generally have little effect on prices, especially energy prices.
    c. the incentive they provide to develop new technology that pollutes less.
    d. the predictability of pollution reduction.

8. Consider a power plant that produces five tons of waste for each unit of electricity generated. If the plant does not reduce the level of pollution, the cost of production is $48 per unit of electricity. The cost of production increases as the firm reduces the level of pollution. If the firm eliminates one ton of waste the cost of production is $50 per unit of electricity. With two units of reduction the cost is $55 per unit of electricity. The costs of electricity with three tons, four tons and five tons of reduction are $65, $80, and $100 respectively. If the government imposes a pollution tax of $10 per ton of waste, how many tons of waste should the plant eliminate?
    a. 1 ton.
    b. 2 tons.
    c. 3 tons.
    d. 4 tons.

9. A *marketable pollution permit* is:
    a. a permit that allows a firm to sell the right to pollute.
    b. a permit sold by one country that allows foreign firms to dump their waste in that country.
    c. a permit that allows the government to tax polluters.
    d. a permit firms buy that allows them to reduce the amount of pollution they generate.

10. This question relates to the example in your text on Dear Abby and environmental policy.

    There is usually more than one way to deal with a pollution problem. Which of the following is the fundamental economic question to ask?
    a. Which alternative fuel has the greatest impact on reducing pollution?
    b. Which cleanup method is superior to the others?
    c. How can traditional environmental policy be made more flexible?
    d. What is the most efficient and least costly way to reduce the problem?

11. Under a marketable pollution permits system:
    a. the government imposes a tax on each unit of pollution produced by a firm.
    b. the government directs a firm to produce a certain level of pollution using specific technology.
    c. the government subsidizes each unit of waste produced.
    d. the government assigns each firm rights to pollute, and these rights are transferable between firms.

12. A carbon tax is:
    a. an approach to reducing carbon emissions by imposing a tax equal to the marginal external cost of carbon.
    b. a way of increasing carbon emissions but reducing greenhouse emissions.
    c. a tax equal to the marginal social cost of carbon.
    d. actually a subsidy that nonpolluters can benefit from.

13. A carbon tax would reduce greenhouse emissions in several ways. Which of those ways is listed below?
   a.   The price of gasoline would increase.
   b.   People would drive less and buy more energy-efficient vehicles.
   c.   The tax would increase the price of electricity.
   d.   All of the above.

14. Which of the following would be an alternative to a tax or command-and-control policy to reduce pollution?
   a.   Allowing a firm to reduce pollution by supporting a project that reduces the pollution emissions of another firm.
   b.   Allowing a firm to reduce pollution by supporting a project that results in the absorption of pollutants.
   c.   Both of the above.
   d.   None of the above.

15. This question tests your understanding of Application 4 in this chapter: Chicago Climate Exchange. What are the benefits of giving firms options for reducing greenhouse gases?

   The Chicago Climate Exchange (CCX) allows firms to cut their emissions of greenhouse gases in different ways. When a firm joins CCX, it agrees to reduce its contribution to greenhouse gases by 4 percent within four years by: (1) cutting its own emissions, (2) paying for extra reductions by other firms, or:
   a.   paying for projects such as reforestation.
   b.   participating in auctions for carbon dioxide emissions.
   c.   convincing other firms to cut their emissions.
   d.   doing any combination of two of the three options above.

16. Refer to the figure below. How much is the gasoline tax in this graph and by how much does equilibrium price increase as a result of the tax?

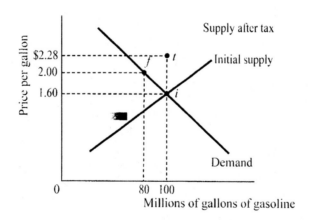

   a.   The tax is $0.68 per gallon, which causes an increase in equilibrium price by the full $0.68.
   b.   The tax is $0.68 per gallon, which causes an increase in equilibrium price by $0.40.
   c.   The tax is $0.28 per gallon, which causes an increase in equilibrium price by $0.68.
   d.   The tax is $0.40 per gallon, which causes an increase in equilibrium price by $0.68.

17. Refer to the figure below. How much of the tax is backward shifted?

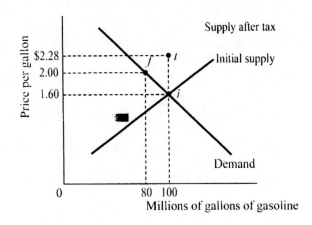

a. $0.28.
b. $0.40.
c. $0.68.
d. The entire amount.

18. Which of the following is the preferred method to reduce the external cost of traffic congestion according to an economist?
    a. With additional traffic, police dedicated specifically to enforcing anti-pollution laws.
    b. With a tax that varies with the level of traffic congestion.
    c. Establishing hours for driving, according to the last number on the license plate, odd or even.
    d. Issuing driving permits.

19. Describe the economist's preferred response to a pollution problem, and explain how the firm reacts to this response.

20. Explain how the marginal principle and the pollution tax work together to determine the optimal amount of pollution abatement.

21. Define marginal benefit and marginal cost as they apply to reducing output in a market that generates pollution. Use the marginal principle to explain how to reduce the amount of pollution generated in this market.

22. Describe and explain the traditional command-and-control regulatory policy, and explain its shortcomings.

23. Compare the outcome of a command-and-control policy to the outcome of a tax system.

24. Give three reasons why a traditional regulatory policy that mandates abatement technology is likely to be inefficient.

25. Explain what a marketable pollution permit is and how it works.

Answers to the Practice Quiz

1. b. As pollution abatement increases, the marginal costs of reducing one more unit increase (usually at an increasing rate) and the marginal benefits fall (because the environment has the capacity to absorb some small levels of pollution). Reducing pollution to zero is unlikely to be cost effective for most pollutants.

2. c. The optimum level of pollution abatement is where the marginal benefit of abatement equals its marginal cost, or at 8 million tons of abatement (or 1.1 million tons of discharges).

3. a. The marginal-benefit curve is a horizontal line because for each additional ton of SO_2 discharged into the atmosphere, the costs associated with premature deaths and health problems increases by the amount shown by that line.

4. c. The social cost of production is the sum of the firm's private cost and external cost incurred by others.

5. b. The idea of a pollution tax is to internalize the externality, which happens when the tax equals the external cost.

6. c. The pollution tax increases the cost of producing electricity, shifting the market supply curve to the left. The equilibrium moves from point i to point t. The tax increases the equilibrium price from $64.90 to $67.60 per megawatt hour and decreases the equilibrium quantity.

7. d. The government has traditionally preferred these measures because they are (relatively) easy for the government to implement and provide direct control.

8. c. The marginal benefit of reducing pollution is $10 per ton, which is the amount of tax avoided. Thus, the plant will reduce waste until its marginal cost is equal to its marginal benefit. This occurs when the plant eliminates 3 tons of waste and the production costs increase from $55 to $65.

9. a. A marketable pollution permit gives a firm the right to pollute. The firm can exercise its right or sell it in the open market for permits.

10. d. The economic question is: What is the most efficient and least costly way to reduce the problem? In some cases, it may be more efficient to prevent the pollution by switching to an alternative fuel or installing a catalytic add-on to the stove than to clean up the environment after it has been polluted by installing an air purifier. In other cases, cleanup will be more efficient than prevention.

11. d. Under a marketable permits system, the government gives each firm the right to pollute a certain amount, such as vouchers that let the holder emit 1 ton of waste. These vouchers can then be sold to other firms.

12. a. One approach to reducing carbon emissions is to impose a carbon tax equal to the marginal external cost of carbon. The tax would reduce greenhouse emissions in several ways.

13. d. The tax would reduce greenhouse emissions in several ways: The price of gasoline would increase, causing people to drive less and buy more energy-efficient vehicles. The tax would increase the price of electricity, decreasing the quantity of electricity demanded and the quantity of fossil fuels burned.

14. c. Firms can be allowed to meet pollution limits by reducing their own emission, supporting a project that either reduces the pollution emissions of another firm or results in the absorption of pollutants.

15. a. For the nation's largest electricity producer, for example, the cost of tree farming is $1.25 per ton of carbon absorbed, or "sequestered," which is small relative to the alternative—converting the company's generators from coal to natural gas at a cost of about $50 per ton of carbon abated.

16. b. The gasoline tax is $0.68 per gallon, which shifts the supply curve upward by the amount of the tax, and increases the equilibrium price by only $0.40.

17. a. The tax is $0.68. Of that $0.68, $0.40 is shifted forward on to consumers, and the rest ($0.28) is backward shifted on to input suppliers, who receive lower prices for crude oil.

18. b. The external cost from traffic congestion could be internalized with a tax that varies with the level of traffic congestion.

19. The economist's response to a pollution problem is to impose a pollution tax. A pollution tax is the tax or charge equal to the spillover cost per unit of waste. A pollution tax forces firms to pay for the waste they generate, which causes firms to produce less of the polluting good and also encourages firms to spend money to abate pollution. Pollution abatement is subject to diminishing returns. As firms continue to decrease the volume of waste they produce, it becomes progressively more expensive to decrease it further. The firms will question whether to continue to generate waste and pay taxes, or to spend some money to reduce waste. The marginal principle can be used to make these decisions.

20. The typical firm will decrease its waste in a manner consistent with the marginal principle. The firm's marginal benefit associated with reducing waste refers to the additional savings in terms of taxes reduced per unit of waste reduced. Marginal cost is the cost of cutting back additional waste. Additional efforts to decrease waste become progressively more expensive. As the volume of waste decreases, the cost of production increases while the tax cost decreases. The optimal amount of waste occurs when the marginal benefit equals the marginal cost of pollution abatement.

21. The marginal principle states that the level of an activity, such as producing output, should be set at the point at which marginal benefit equals marginal cost. The marginal benefit of reducing pollution is measured by the savings in pollution treatment costs associated with the decrease in output. The marginal cost is the loss of consumer and producer surplus associated with the disappearance of output produced and exchanged. To arrive at the optimal level of output, we decrease output one unit at a time and evaluate the impact of such reduction on marginal benefit and marginal cost. Output should decrease as long as the additional savings in pollution treatment costs are greater than the additional loss of surplus. Once the marginal benefit equals the marginal cost of output reduction, the reduction should stop.

22. The traditional command-and-control policy is an alternative to a pollution tax. It consists of controlling the amount of pollution generated by each firm in its production process. The problem with forcing the firm to use a particular pollution-control technology is that the mandated abatement technology is unlikely to be the most efficient. There are two reasons for inefficiency: 1) A single abatement technology is likely to be efficient for some firms but not for others; and 2) there is no incentive to cut the volume of waste below the maximum volume, or to develop better abatement technologies.

23. Because a command-and-control policy causes firms to use inefficient abatement technology, the policy will increase the firm's costs by a large amount. The supply shift resulting from the regulatory policy will be larger than the supply shift from the pollution tax. Compared to the pollution-tax policy, the command-and-control policy leads to a higher price and a smaller quantity.

24. 1) A single abatement technology is likely to be efficient for some firms but not for others. 2) There is no incentive to cut the volume of waste below the maximum volume allowed. 3) There is no incentive to develop better abatement technologies.

25. A marketable pollution permit is a permit that allows a firm to sell the right to pollute. The firm may exercise its right to pollute, or sell the permit in the open market. Government picks a level of pollution for a particular area; the government issues just enough permits to meet the pollution target; then, firms buy and sell the permits. Demand for the permits determines the price at which the permit will be traded. A firm is willing to sell its pollution permit if the increase in production cost from the sale of the permit is less than the amount it accepts for the permit. The purchase and sale of permits between firms allows the government to exploit the differences in abatement costs between firms, relying on the firms with low abatement costs to do most of the abatement. This is how a system of marketable pollution permits can achieve the same volume of pollution abatement at a lower cost than the traditional regulation policy.

17 [32]

The Labor Market, Income, and Poverty

Chapter Summary

This chapter examines how wages and employment levels are determined in competitive labor markets. Here are the main points of the chapter:

- The long-run demand curve for labor is negatively sloped because the output and input-substitution effects operate in the same direction: An increase in the wage decreases labor per unit of output and decreases the total output produced.

- An increase in the wage triggers income and substitution effects that operate in opposite directions, so an increase in the wage has an ambiguous effect on the quantity of labor supplied.

- The wage in a particular occupation will be relatively high if supply is small relative to demand. This will occur if (1) few people have the skills required for the occupation, (2) training costs are high, or (3) the job is dangerous or stressful.

- College graduates earn more than high-school graduates because a college education provides new skills and allows people to reveal their skills to employers.

- The trade-off with a minimum wage is that some workers earn higher income, but others lose their jobs.

- The wealthiest 20 percent of families in the Unites States earn about half of total income, while the wealthiest 10 percent earn 42 percent of total income. At the other end of the income distribution, the poorest 20 percent earn only 3.5 percent of total income.

- Poverty rates are relatively high among African Americans, Hispanics, high-school dropouts, and female-headed households.

Applying the Concepts

After reading this chapter, you should be able to answer these five key questions.
1. When the wage increases, will the typical person work more hours or fewer hours?
2. Does a living wage have the same effects as a minimum wage?
3. Who benefits from the immigration of low-skilled workers?
4. What explains differences in wages?
5. How does racial discrimination affect the labor market?

17.1 [32.1] The Demand for Labor

As in the case of many other economic decisions, the demand for labor will be governed by the marginal principle:

The Marginal Principle

Increase the level of an activity as long as its marginal benefit exceeds its marginal cost. Choose the level at which the marginal benefit equals the marginal cost.

🖺 Remember

Labor demand is a derived demand. That means that employers only hire labor in order to sell the product that labor produces.

The marginal benefit of labor is the money the firm earns by selling the output a worker produces. Table 17.1 [32.1] provides an illustration of this. The **marginal product of labor** is the change in output from one additional unit of labor. For worker 1, the MPL is 26 balls. Since each ball sells for $0.50, worker 1 adds $13 in revenue to the firm (26 balls sold for $0.50 each). This is worker 1's marginal-revenue product of labor. The **marginal-revenue product of labor** is the extra revenue generated from one additional unit of labor. In a perfectly competitive output market, MRP is equal to the price of output times the marginal product of labor.

☑ Key Equation

marginal-revenue product of labor = price of output x marginal product of labor

---

Worker 2 has a marginal product of 24 balls and a MRP = $12. Recall that the marginal product of labor falls as we add more units of labor due to the principle of diminishing returns.

Principle of Diminishing Returns

Suppose that output is produced with two or more inputs and we increase one input while holding the other inputs fixed. Beyond some point—called the *point of diminishing returns*—output will increase at a decreasing rate.

The MRP curve is the firm's short-run demand curve for labor. The **short-run demand curve for labor** is a curve showing the relationship between the wage and the quantity of labor demanded over the short run, when the firm cannot change its production facility. You can see that for any wage, or price of labor, the MRP curve tells us the number of workers a firm wants to hire. Since a demand curve relates the price of a good to the number of units of that good buyers want to buy, the MRP functions as the demand curve for labor.

Figure 17.1 [32.1] illustrates the MRP and the amount of labor demanded at that wage. When the wage rate in the market is $11, firms want to hire 3 workers. You can see this as point *a* in Figure 17.1 [32.1]. You can also see in Table 17.1 [32.1] that the third worker has a MRP of $11.

As the wage decreases to $8, the firm now finds it profitable to hire worker four, who has a MRP of $10, and will continue to hire up to point *b* on the MRP curve in Figure 17.1 [32.1].

Since MRP is the product of the price of the output good and the marginal product of labor, a change in either of these would change the demand for labor.

☞ Suppose the price of balls increased to $1 per ball while the wage remained at $8. Now, according to Table 17.1 [32.1], the firm would want to hire 7 workers. Since the firm wants to increase the number of workers while holding the wage constant, we have an increase in labor demand.

To find the market demand for labor, we simply sum the individual firm demand curves.

We don't have to worry about diminishing returns in the long run. The **long-run demand curve for labor** is a curve showing the relationship between the wage and the quantity of labor demanded over the long run, when the number of firms in the market can change and firms can modify their production facilities. The long-run demand curve for labor will still be downward sloping. There are two reasons for this:
- Output effect. This is the change in the quantity of labor demanded resulting from a change in the quantity of output produced.
- Input-substitution effect. This is the change in the quantity of labor demanded resulting from an increase in the price of labor relative to the price of other inputs.

📄 Remember

The long-run demand curve for labor is more elastic than the short-run demand curve.

17.2 [32.2] The Supply of Labor

Labor is supplied to the market by individuals who must determine how many hours they are willing to work at a particular wage rate.

〰 Study Tip

The wage rate can be thought of as the price of leisure. Why? You "buy" an hour of leisure time by not working for that hour and giving up the money that you would have made had you worked.

An increase in wages increases the price of leisure, leading to a substitution effect and an income effect. The **substitution effect for leisure demand** is the change in leisure time resulting from a change in the wage (the price of leisure) relative to the price of other goods. The **income effect for leisure demand** is the change in leisure time resulting from a change in real income caused by a change in the wage rate. The effects move in opposite directions with the substitution effect suggesting you should work more (take less leisure time) as the wage increases and leisure time becomes more expensive and the income effect suggesting you should work less (take more leisure time) as your purchasing power increases.

☞ Suppose you are a student worker in the economics department on your campus and further suppose that you have some control over the number of hours you work per week. Currently, you are working 12 hours per week for the minimum wage of $6.55 per hour and therefore earn $78.60 per week. As a result of student lobbying, your university agrees to increase student worker pay to $9.25 per hour. Will you:

- work less than 12 hours per week because of the higher wage? If so, the income effect for leisure demand has dominated the substitution effect.
- work 12 hours per week just as you did before? If so, the income and substitution effects have offset each other.
- work more than 12 hours per week because of the higher wage? If so, the substitution effect has dominated the income effect.

The **market supply curve for labor**, a curve showing the relationship between the wage and the quantity of labor supplied in the market, is the sum of the individual labor supply curves. In the nursing market, more hours of nursing labor will be supplied as the wage increases because:

- the average hours worked per week by existing nurses will stay relatively constant.
- more people will enter the nursing field attracted by the higher wages.
- existing nurses will migrate towards areas with higher nursing wages.

Let's review an Application that answers one of the key questions we posed at the start of the chapter:

1. When the wage increases, will the typical person work more hours or fewer hours?

APPLICATION 1: DIFFERENT RESPONSES TO A HIGHER WAGE
This Application shows three different responses to a higher wage. As the wage increases from $10 per hour to $12 per hour, nurses will have to determine whether to continue to work 36 hours per week or change their hours supplied. Studies have found that while some nurses may increase or decrease their hours supplied, the average nurse will continue to work 36 hours per week.

17.3 [32.3] Labor Market Equilibrium

Figure 17.3 [32.3] shows the equilibrium in the labor market at point *a* with a wage of $15 per hour and 16,000 hours of labor provided per day.

ᏗᎷ Study Tip

In any market, input or output, equilibrium will occur where the quantity supplied equals the quantity demanded.

We can analyze changes in labor demand and labor supply, as well as price floors (minimum wages) in the labor market just as we did in Chapter 4 when we studied demand and supply.

Remember from Chapter 4 that:

- as the demand for a good changes, price and quantity move in the same direction as demand.
- as the supply of a good changes, quantity moves in the same direction as supply, price moves in the opposite direction.
- price floors above the market price will lead to a surplus, or excess supply, in the market.

A minimum wage, illustrated in Figure 17.5 [32.5], is a price floor in the market for labor. As shown in the figure, the market will move from an equilibrium at point *a*, to a new price and quantity demanded at point *b*. At the price of $6.55 per hour, notice that people supply more hours of labor to the market than the number of hours of labor demanded by employers. The effects of the minimum wage are:
- higher wages for workers who keep their jobs.
- lost jobs for some workers as we decrease the quantity demanded for labor.
- higher prices for diners as the cost of producing meals increases.

A recent study suggested that a 10% increase in the minimum wage reduced the number of minimum wage level jobs by 1%.

Let's review two Applications that answer key questions we posed at the start of the chapter:

2. Does a living wage have the same effects as a minimum wage?

APPLICATION 2: CODES OF CONDUCT AND LIVING WAGES
Recently, there have been efforts by students to require the manufacturers of clothing with university logos to pay their overseas workers a "living wage," a wage high enough to support a family. Analytically this should have similar effects as a minimum wage. The Application does point out that if buyers are willing to pay more for goods made by workers earning a living wage, then there may be no employment effects as the cost of the living wage is borne by the consumers of the good.

3. Who benefits from the immigration of low-skilled workers?

APPLICATION 3: TRADE-OFFS FROM IMMIGRATION
Immigration increases the supply of labor as more workers are available to work at a given wage. An increase in market supply will increase the equilibrium quantity of the good, but will lower the price, or in this case, the wage. If immigrants are concentrated in low-skill jobs, we would expect low-skill native workers to see a decrease in their wages. As wage costs decrease, the supply of the goods produced by low-wage workers will increase and the price of those goods will fall. Lower prices benefit consumers of those goods.

17.4 [32.4] Explaining Differences in Wages and Income

Wages differ across occupations for five primary reasons:
- Few people with the required skills. When the supply of a good is relatively small, we expect the price of the good to be relatively high.
- High training costs. High wages are needed to compensate people for paying high training costs. For instance, a medical doctor will spend four years in medical school and then at least four more years in residency before starting to practice. The wages the doctor earns have to compensate for the expense of medical school and the low wages of residency.
- Undesirable working conditions. Night-shift workers typically earn more than day-shift workers doing the same job to compensate them for working at an undesirable time.
- Danger. A person doing a dangerous job requires a higher wage than someone doing a similar, but less risky job. (Think about working as an iron worker on the ground and working as an iron worker on tall buildings, you would need a higher wage to compensate you for the extra risk working on tall buildings.

- Artificial barriers to entry. Licensing boards restrict the supply of certain workers, thus forcing wages up.

Differences in wages are also observed between genders with women earning, on average, 80% as much as the typical male. Four reasons can also be offered:
- Differences in skills and productivity. Women, on average, have less education and work experience than men. A key reason for less experience is that many women interrupt their careers to raise families. The study referenced in the text suggests that differences in productivity is the most important factor in the wage gap between the genders.
- Differences in occupational preferences. Women are found more frequently in lower-wage occupations. To the extent that occupational choice reflects the preference of the worker, this would explain part of the wage gap.
- Occupational discrimination. If employers have a bias against hiring women in high skill/high pay occupations, we would observe a gender gap in wages. The study cited in the text attributes between 7% and 25% of the gender gap to discrimination.
- Wage discrimination. If employers pay women less than equally qualified men, we would see a gender gap in wages.

There is also a wage gap between members of different races. While some of the wage differences can be attributed to lower levels of skill and education, a study cited by the text suggests that discrimination lowers the wages of African American men by an average of 13%.

College graduates earn nearly twice as much, on average, as high school graduates. Part of this difference can be attributed to the **learning effect**, the increase in a person's wage resulting from the learning of skills required for certain occupations. It is also possible that a college degree provides information to potential employers about unobservable characteristics of a potential employee. This is known as the **signaling effect**, the information about a person's work skills conveyed by completing college.

Let's review two Applications that answer key questions we posed at the start of the chapter:

4. What explains differences in wages?

APPLICATION 4: THE BEAUTY PREMIUM
This Application reports on studies that show that people with above average looks earn more, and those with below average looks earn less holding other things constant. Biologists suggest that beauty can be a marker for positive underlying characteristics that employers value. Also, more attractive people seem to have more opportunities for professional experience and contacts which lead to higher wages.

5. How does racial discrimination affect the labor market?

APPLICATION 5: LAKISHA WASHINGTON VERSUS EMILY WALSH
This Application discusses two experiments showing the impact of racial discrimination in the labor market. In particular, this Application shows the advantages a Caucasian person has over an African American in securing an initial interview. Through cleverly designed experiments, researchers found that a Caucasian who has served 18 months in prison is just as likely to be interviewed as an African American without a police record. Additionally, applicants with names that can be identified as African American require 8 years of experience in order to have the same chance of securing an interview as an applicant with a Caucasian name and no experience.

17.5 [32.5] The Distribution of Income

 Remember

The median amount is the middle amount in a distribution. Half the observations lie above this amount and half lie below.

There are two income measures relevant for the discussion of income distribution:
- Market income. This is defined as all earning received from labor and capital markets.
- Disposable income. This is market income plus government transfers minus taxes paid.

There are three key factors that explain the large differences in market income earned by the top and bottom of the market income distribution:
- Differences in labor skills and effort. Higher skills and/or productivity are tied to higher wages.
- Luck and misfortune.
- Discrimination.

Table 17.3 [32.3] shows the income shares by quintile for selected years from 1970 to 2005. The data indicate that the income share of the top fifth rose over this time, while the income share of the rest of the population fell. Some of this is due to higher returns to education and skill brought about by:
- technological change. As technology has advanced, the demand for high-skilled workers has increased, while the demand for low skilled workers has fallen.
- increased international trade. This has allowed the United States to import goods produced by low-skilled workers, further reducing the demand for this type of labor.

Figure 17.7 [32.7] in the text graphs the percentage share of income for the top 10%, 5%, and 1% in the United States from 1920 to 1998. Income shares for all three groups fell during World War II and remained at or near those levels until the mid-1980s when those income shares began to increase back towards their pre-WWII levels.

17.6 [32.6] Poverty and Public Policy

 Remember

Poverty is defined as having household income below the amount needed to satisfy the "minimum needs" of the household.

Table 17.4 [32.4] shows the poverty rates for different groups in 2006. The overall poverty rate was 12.3%, but was much higher for blacks, Hispanics, and female-headed households.

Public policy towards poor families takes the form of means-tested programs. A **means-tested program** is a government spending program that provides assistance to those whose income falls below a certain level. Without these programs, the poverty rate in 2004 would have been 19.4%. If we include the value of non-cash transfers, such as food stamps, the poverty rate falls to 10.6%.

In 1996, the U.S. welfare system was overhauled with the passage of the Personal Responsibility and Work Opportunity Reconciliation Act of 1996. This Act restructured how welfare payments were made and placed limits on eligibility for these programs. In particular, recipients needed to participate in some type of work activity and could only receive cash assistance for 60 months.

Empirical evidence suggests that welfare recipients respond to work incentives and, in states with relatively large work incentives, welfare recipients work more hours and earn higher market income on average.

Activity

This activity will illustrate how an increase in output price or worker productivity increases the demand for labor, the number of workers hired at any particular wage. The activity compares new employment levels with those from Table 17.1 [32.1] and Figure 17.1 [32.1].

(1) Workers	(2) Balls	(3) Marginal Product of Labor	(4) Price of Balls	(5) Marginal Revenue Product of Labor (price of balls = $1)	(6) Balls	(7) Marginal Product from Column (6)	(8) Marginal Revenue Product of Labor (from column (7) and price of balls = $1)
1	26		$1		39		
2	50		$1		75		
3	72		$1		108		
4	92		$1		138		
5	108		$1		162		
6	120		$1		180		
7	128		$1		192		
8	130		$1		195		

a. Calculate the marginal product of labor and the marginal revenue product for columns 3 and 5.

b. Recall from Figure 17.1 [32.1] that at a wage rate of $11 per day 3 workers were hired when the price of output was $0.50 and 5 workers were hired at a wage of $8 per day. Find the number of workers hired at each wage when with the price of output increases to $1.

   Wage of $11 _____, wage of $8 _____.

c. Suppose that workers become more productive as reflected in column 6. Calculate the marginal product (column 7) and marginal revenue product at a price of $1 per ball (column 8).

d. Now, given the information in column 8, how many workers will be hired at a wage rate of $11? _____ At a wage rate of $8? _____.

Answers

a.

(1) Workers	(2) Balls	(3) Marginal Product of Labor	(4) Price of Balls	(5) Marginal Revenue Product of Labor (price of balls = $1)	(6) Balls	(7) Marginal Product from Column (6)	(8) Marginal Revenue Product of Labor (from column (7) and price of balls = $1)
1	26	26	$1	26	39	39	39
2	50	24	$1	24	75	36	36
3	72	22	$1	22	108	33	33
4	92	20	$1	20	138	30	30
5	108	16	$1	16	162	24	24
6	120	12	$1	12	180	18	18
7	128	8	$1	8	192	12	12
8	130	2	$1	2	195	3	3

b. Wage rate of $11, 6 workers. Wage rate of $8, 7 workers.
c. See columns 7 and 8 of the table.
d. Wage rate of $11, 7 workers. Wage rate of $8, 7 workers.

Key Terms

Income effect for leisure demand: The change in leisure time resulting from a change in real income caused by a change in the wage.

Input-substitution effect: The change in the quantity of labor demanded resulting from an increase in the price of labor relative to the price of other inputs.

Learning effect: The increase in a person's wage resulting from the learning of skills required for certain occupations.

Long-run demand curve for labor: A curve showing the relationship between the wage and the quantity of labor demanded over the long run, when the number of firms in the market can change and firms can modify their production facilities.

Marginal product of labor: The change in output from one additional unit of labor.

Marginal-revenue product of labor (MRP): The extra revenue generated from one additional unit of labor; MRP is equal to the price of output times the marginal product of labor.

Market supply curve for labor: A curve showing the relationship between the wage and the quantity of labor supplied.

Means-tested programs: A government spending program that provides assistance to those whose income falls below a certain level.

Output effect: The change in the quantity of labor demanded resulting from a change in the quantity of output produced.

Short-run demand curve for labor: A curve showing the relationship between the wage and the quantity of labor demanded over the short run, when the firm cannot change its production facility.

Signaling effect: The information about a person's work skills conveyed by completing college.

Substitution effect for leisure demand: The change in leisure time resulting from a change in the wage (the price of leisure) relative to the price of other goods.

Practice Quiz

(Answers are provided at the end of the Practice Quiz.)

1. Which of the following key principles of economics should be used to determine the quantity of labor the firm will hire?
    a. The principle of diminishing returns.
    b. The principle of opportunity cost.
    c. The marginal principle.
    d. The voluntary exchange principle.

2. Link one of the terms below to the following definition: "_____ is the change in a firm's output from having one additional worker."
    a. Marginal cost.
    b. Marginal revenue.
    c. Marginal product of labor.
    d. Marginal revenue product of labor.

3. Refer to the table below. What is the *marginal revenue product* of the 3rd worker?

Number of Workers	Balls per Hour	Price per Ball
1	26	$0.50
2	50	0.50
3	72	0.50
4	92	0.50
5	108	0.50
6	120	0.50
7	128	0.50
8	130	0.50

    a. $11.
    b. $12
    c. $22.
    d. $24.

4. As the number of workers increases,
    a. Marginal product of labor decreases and marginal revenue product of labor increases.
    b. Marginal product of labor increases and marginal revenue product of labor decreases.
    c. Both the marginal product of labor and marginal revenue product increase.
    d. Both the marginal product of labor and marginal revenue product decrease.

5. Refer to the figure below. When the hourly wage equals $8, how many workers should the firm hire?

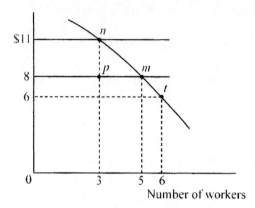

    a. 3 workers, because at that point the marginal benefit continues to be greater than the marginal cost of labor.
    b. 5 workers, where the wage equals the marginal revenue product of labor.
    c. 6 workers, which is a point on the downward-sloping curve below the horizontal line at $8.
    d. Anywhere between 3 to 6 workers, but not less or more than that.

6. Refer to the figure below. What could have caused the shift in the labor demand curve, from L_2 to L_1?

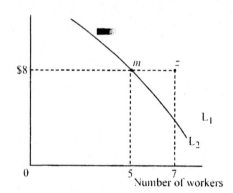

    a. A decrease in productivity.
    b. An increase in the wage.
    c. An increase in the price of the output.
    d. A decrease in the marginal product of labor.

7. The *long-run demand curve for labor* shows the relationship between the wage and the quantity of labor demanded:
    a. when the number of firms in the market can change.
    b. when firms in the market can modify their production facilities.
    c. when there are no diminishing returns.
    d. All of the above.

8. Which of the following concepts refers to a change in the quantity of labor demanded resulting from a change in the relative cost of labor?
    a. The output effect.
    b. The input-substitution effect.
    c. Neither the output effect nor the input-substitution effect.
    d. Both the output effect and the input-substitution effect.

9. Which of the following describes the effect of an increase in the wage on the demand for leisure?
    a. The substitution effect.
    b. The income effect.
    c. Both the substitution effect and the income effect.
    d. Neither effect.

10. According to the substitution effect, what is the impact of an increase in the wage?
    a. An increase in the opportunity cost of leisure.
    b. A decrease in purchasing power of an hour's worth of wage income.
    c. A decrease in the opportunity cost of leisure.
    d. An increase in the opportunity cost of work.

11. There is a positive relationship between the wage and the quantity of labor supplied in the market, *ceteris paribus*. Among the explanations for that relationship is that an increase in the wage affects:
    a. The hours worked per employee.
    b. Occupational choice.
    c. Migration.
    d. All of the above.

12. Refer to the figure below. In the strict terminology of supply and demand, we say that in order to get from point *e* to point *f* on this graph we need:

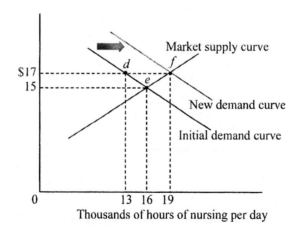

    a. An increase in demand and a corresponding increase in supply.
    b. An increase in quantity demanded and an increase in supply.
    c. An increase in demand and an increase in quantity supplied.
    d. A higher wage and a higher quantity of nurses hired, which in turn caused higher demand.

13. Refer to the figure below. Imposition of a minimum wage at $7.25 per hour in this graph:

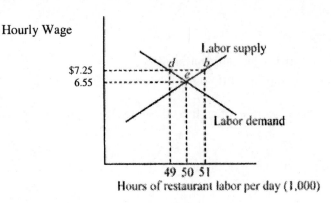

a. Decreases unemployment.
b. Increases unemployment.
c. Has no effect on employment.
d. Leads to equilibrium employment at $7.25.

14. This question tests your understanding of Application 2 in this chapter: Codes of conduct and living wages: Does a living wage have the same effects as a minimum wage?

One way to avoid job losses when the wage increases to the required "living wage" is if:
a. The increase in the wage increases the cost of producing T-shirts, so the price of T-shirts will increase.
b. Consumers respond by purchasing fewer T-shirts.
c. Firms produce fewer T-shirts.
d. Consumers are willing to pay a higher price for goods that are produced by living-wage workers.

15. Economists have estimated that the net effect of immigration on the U.S. economy is:
a. Positive. Immigration increases efficiency and the size of the overall economic pie.
b. Negative. Immigration ruins people's lives and reduces economic efficiency.
c. Mixed. The economy gains in some respects and loses in other ways, but the overall effect is neutral because the two cancel each other out.
d. Nonexistent. Immigration on the whole does not affect the economy.

16. Immigration creates winners and losers within the economy. Who are the winners?
a. Low-skill workers.
b. High-skill workers.
c. All workers.
d. None of the above. Immigration hurts all domestic workers.

17. The equilibrium wage in a given occupation will be high when:
a. supply is low relative to demand.
b. few people have the skills needed.
c. training costs are high.
d. the job is undesirable.
e. All of the above.

18. The signal of productivity that a college graduate provides by completing college is called:
    a.   the graduation gap.
    b.   the learning effect.
    c.   the achievement gap.
    d.   the signaling effect.

19. The percentages of total income earned by the highest and lowest fifths of the U.S. population are as follows:
    a.   the highest and lowest fifths earn less than the income groups in the middle.
    b.   the highest fifth earns 51% of the income and the lowest fifth earns 3.4% of the income.
    c.   the highest fifth and the lowest fifth earn almost equal shares, around 5% of the income.
    d.   the highest fifth earns 3.4% of the income and the lowest fifth earns 51% of the income.

20. Explain the concept of derived demand.

Answers to the Practice Quiz

1. c. The firm will pick the quantity of labor at which the marginal benefit of labor equals the marginal cost of labor.

2. c. The *marginal product of labor* is the change in a firm's output from having one additional worker.

3. a. The marginal product of the third worker is 22 units, and price is $0.50. Marginal revenue product equals marginal product times price, or 22 x $0.50 = $11.

4. d. Because of diminishing returns, the marginal product of labor (the change in output from one additional worker) decreases as the number of workers increases. Because the marginal product drops as the numbers of workers increases, the MRP curve is negatively sloped.

5. b. To determine how many workers to hire, the firm examines the relationship between the wage and the marginal revenue product of labor. The firm sets labor usage at the point where the marginal revenue product is equal to the wage.

6. c. An increase in the price of the output or in productivity of workers will cause the entire labor demand curve to shift to the right. At each wage, the firm will demand more workers.

7. d. The *long-run demand curve for labor* shows the relationship between the wage and the quantity of labor demanded over the long run when the number of firms in the market can change and firms in the market can modify their production facilities.

8. b. The input-substitution effect is the change in the quantity of labor demanded resulting from a change in the relative cost of labor.

9. c. An increase in the wage—the price of labor—has two effects on the demand for leisure: the substitution effect and the income effect.

10. a. As the wage increases, the opportunity cost of leisure increases, causing individuals to supply a greater quantity of labor. Therefore, the labor supply curve is upward sloping. But this occurs only if the substitution effect prevails over the income effect.

11. d. An increase in the wage affects the quantity of labor supplied in three ways: 1) Hours worked per employee, 2) occupational choice, and 3) migration.

12. c. As the demand curve shifts to the right, there is a move along the supply curve representing higher quantity supplied.

13. b. At $7.25, 51,000 workers are willing to work, but only 49,000 are hired.

14. d. In this case, the increase in cost and consequently the increase in the price of shirts would cause a smaller decrease in the quantity of T-shirts demanded, so fewer workers would lose their jobs.

15. a. Economists have estimated the net effect of immigration on the U.S. economy. George Borjas shows that immigration to the United States has a small positive effect, with the losses in wages of low-skilled workers more than offset by gains to consumers and firms.

16. b. Low-skill workers lose as a result of immigration because lower wages dominate the benefits of lower consumer prices, while high-skill workers benefit from lower prices.

17. e. According to the textbook, if supply is low relative to demand—because few people have the skills, training costs are high, or the job is undesirable—the equilibrium wage will be high.

18. d. The signaling effect states that there is an increase in a person's wage resulting from the signal of productivity provided by completing college.

19. b. Shares are as follows: lowest fifth: 3.4%; second fifth: 8.6%; third fifth: 14.3%, fourth fifth: 22.8%, and highest fifth: 51%.

20. Economists say that labor demand is a derived demand; that is, derived from the demand for the products produced by workers. Demand for resources is dependent on the demand for the outputs those resources can be used to produce. A firm demands inputs if, and only if, households demand the good or service produced by that firm.

18 [33]
Unions, Monopsony, and Imperfect Information

Chapter Summary

This chapter extends the discussion of the labor market beyond the world of the competitive labor market where each side takes the market wage as given. Here are the main points of the chapter:

- A union faces a trade-off between wages and total employment. An increase in the wage causes an output effect and an input-substitution effect that combine to decrease the quantity of labor demanded.
- The gap between the union wage and the nonunion wage will be relatively large when the price elasticity of demand for a product is relatively low. Demand is relatively inelastic in less competitive product markets.
- A firm facing a positively sloped labor supply curve must pay a higher wage to hire more workers, and the marginal labor cost exceeds the wage.
- The equilibrium employment in a monopsony is less than the equilibrium employment in a perfectly competitive market.
- In a labor market with asymmetric information about worker productivity, an increase in the wage may increase the average productivity of hired workers and increase profit.

Applying the Concepts

After reading this chapter, you should be able to answer these four key questions:

1. Is there a trade-off between union wages and the number of union jobs?
2. How does competition in the product market affect union wages?
3. Do firms face a positively sloped labor-supply curve?
4. When is it profitable to pay an above-market wage?

18.1 [33.1] Labor Unions

A **labor union** is a group of workers organized to increase job security, improve working conditions, and increase wages and fringe benefits. One primary type of labor union is a **craft union**, a labor organization that includes workers from a particular occupation, for example, plumbers, bakers, or electricians. The other primary type of labor union is an **industrial union**, a labor organization that includes all types of workers from a single industry, for example, steelworkers or autoworkers. The primary focus of unions is **collective bargaining**, negotiations between a union and a firm over wages, fringe benefits, job security, and working conditions. In collective bargaining, the union represents all covered workers in negotiations with the firm.

There are three key pieces of legislation related to unions:
- The National Labor Relations Act (Wagner Act) passed in 1935. This gave workers the right to join a union and required firms to negotiate with unions representing their workers. The National Labor Relations Board was created to oversee union organizing and activity.
- The Labor Management Relations Act (Taft-Hartley Act) passed in 1947. This law gave states the right to pass right-to-work laws. A **right-to-work law** is a law that prohibits union shops, where union membership is required as a condition of employment. The Act also allowed the government to stop strikes that "imperiled the national health or safety."
- The Labor Management Reporting and Disclosure Act (Landrum-Griffin Act) passed in 1959. This Act guaranteed free elections within unions, forced more financial disclosure from unions, and made theft of union funds a federal offense.

Estimates suggest that in the United States, union workers earn 10 to 20 percent more than similar non-union workers. Both the output effect and the input-substitution effect from the last chapter suggest that in exchange for higher wages, unions reduce employment in covered sectors.

The output effect, the decrease in output due to fewer units being sold, will be higher when:
- A large fraction of costs come from labor. The larger the fraction of labor costs, the greater the price increase for the final good.
- Demand is elastic. More elastic demand will have a greater quantity decrease in response to any price increase.

To prevent job loss from higher wages, unions typically negotiate work rules that increase the amount of labor needed to do a job. This is commonly called **featherbedding**, imposing work rules that increase the amount of labor required to produce a given quantity of output. By forcing labor costs higher, featherbedding may further decrease the output of the final good which is sold in the market.

On the positive side, unions may:
- Increase worker productivity by increasing communication between workers and management.
- Reduce turnover among employees.

Let's review two Applications that answer key questions we posed at the start of the chapter:

1. Is there a trade-off between union wages and the number of union jobs?

APPLICATION 1: TRUCKERS TRADE OFF WAGES AND JOBS
This Application illustrates the trade-off between wages and jobs for unionized truck drivers in response to the entry of nonunion trucking. Point *a* in Figure 18.2 [33.2] shows the initial wage, trucker point. As nonunion truckers became more common, the demand for union truckers fell. If wages remained constant at $20 per hour, union employment would have fallen from 526,000 truckers to 263,000 illustrated at point *b*. By allowing wages to fall to $14, union employment was able to move to 439,000 truckers, illustrated by point *c*.

2. How does competition in the product market affect union wages?

APPLICATION 2: COMPETITION REDUCES TRUCKER WAGES
In the full-truckload sector of the trucking market, entry is relatively easy as anyone with a truck and a license can enter the industry. In the less-than-truckload sector, it is more difficult to enter as more complex organization and support systems must be in place. Because of the ease of entry into the full-truckload sector, unionized truckers earn a smaller wage premium in this sector than in the less-than-truckload sector.

18.2 [33.2] Monopsony Power

A **monopsony** is a market in which there is a single buyer of an input.

ᗧᔍ Study Tip

A monopsony in the buyers' market is analogous to a monopoly in the seller market.

In a monopsony market, the buyer of the input faces the market supply curve for the input. As a result, the marginal labor cost of hiring another input is greater than the wage paid to the last worker. The **marginal labor cost** is the increase in a firm's total labor cost resulting from one more unit of labor. The reason is that the firm must increase the wages of all its workers in order to offer a higher wage to a new worker. (This is analogous to the price exceeding marginal revenue in a monopoly market.)

☑ Key Equation

marginal labor cost = wage paid to new worker + (change in wage x original quantity of labor)

A monopsonist will follow the marginal principle when choosing how many workers to hire and will hire to the point where the marginal-revenue product equals the marginal labor cost.

✈ The Marginal Principle
Increase the level of an activity as long as its marginal benefit exceeds its marginal cost. Choose the level at which the marginal benefit equals the marginal cost.

Figure 18.4 [33.4] of the text shows the monopsonist's decision. At point *a* the marginal-revenue product curve, the demand curve for labor, and the marginal labor cost curve intersect. At this point, 40 workers will be hired. The monopsonist will pay the wage required off the supply curve to hire 40 workers, in this case $4, illustrated at point *b*. The competitive labor market outcome will occur at point *c*, with a higher wage and greater employment than the monopsony result.

Table 18.1 [33.1] in your text illustrates the similarities between monopsony input markets and monopoly output markets.

When a market contains a monopoly seller of labor, such as a union, and a monopsony buyer of labor wage and employment levels will be determined by bargaining between the two parties. The actual wage will fall between the below-market wage of a monopsony market and the above-market wage of the union market.

A minimum wage can reduce monopsony power by allowing the firm to buy additional units of labor at a constant cost, at least up to the minimum wage. Figure 18.5 [33.5] in your text illustrates this. In this graph, until we reach point *d*, the marginal labor cost facing the firm is constant at the minimum wage of $7. At this wage the firm will hire 50 workers, found at point *e* in the Figure.

While true monopsony markets are rare in the real world, there are markets where hiring additional workers means increasing the wages of all workers in the market. In these cases, wages and employment will be lower than in a competitive labor market.

📄 Remember

If a firm must increase wages to all workers to attract additional labor, the marginal labor cost curve will lie above the supply curve for labor. In this case, wages and employment will be lower than in a competitive labor market.

Let's review an Application that answers one of the key questions we posed at the start of the chapter:

3. Do firms face a positively sloped labor-supply curve?

APPLICATION 3: PUBS AND THE LABOR-SUPPLY CURVE

This Application suggests that the labor-supply curve is in fact upward sloping and it uses clever intuition to do so. If the labor-supply curve was flat, then when workers left old jobs for new jobs, their wages would be the same. If this is the case, there is no reason to celebrate. The fact that workers celebrate new jobs and lament the loss of old jobs (if they are fired or laid off) suggests that the labor-supply curve is upward sloping.

ༀ Study Tip

Application 3 is a nice example of finding real-world situations to test economic theory. As you interact in the economy, try looking for similar tests of the theory that you have learned in this class.

18.3 [33.3] Imperfect Information and Efficiency Wages

The labor market is a mixed market, some workers are very productive, and other workers are not. It is difficult to know in advance whether you are hiring a high-productivity worker or a low-productivity worker.

☞ Think about sitting in a job interview. The interviewer asks you what you would consider your biggest weakness as an employee. Are you going to answer that you are a perfectionist who sometimes obsesses until a particular job is done, or are you going to answer that you are frequently lazy and unmotivated?

Every person interviewing for a job will say that they are a perfectionist. You know from co-workers you have had that this isn't the case.

In Table 18.2 [33.2], we see that we must pay at least $25 to hire a low-productivity worker and $50 to hire a high-productivity worker. Paying wages above $40 means we lose money on each low-productivity worker.

Table 18.3 [33.3] shows equilibrium wages with asymmetric information. Notice that at any wage below $50, we hire only low-productivity workers. At any wage above $50 we hire a mix of high- and low-productivity workers. The table illustrates that the wage will continue to rise until it reaches $60 at which point the expected marginal revenue product per worker will equal the marginal cost per worker.

Paying efficiency wages is the practice of paying a higher wage to increase the average productivity of the workforce. There are two other benefits from efficiency wages, both due to the fact that an employee will have difficulty finding another job paying above-market wages:
- Efficiency wages reduce shirking.
- Efficiency wages reduce turnover.

Let's review an Application that answers one of the key questions we posed at the start of the chapter:

4. When is it profitable to pay an above-market wage?

APPLICATION 4:
WHY DO LAW FIRMS PAY MORE FOR JANITORS AND SECRETARIES
Why would a janitor or secretary earn more in a law firm than if they worked elsewhere? This Application suggests that the reason is the cost of supervision. Because lawyers earn more, the cost of taking time to supervise janitors and secretaries is higher for a lawyer than it would be for someone in a lower paying occupation. By paying efficiency wages lawyers can spend less time supervision janitors and secretaries and more time working on billable cases.

Activity

Consider the labor market described in the following table. The wage rate is w, labor demand and labor supply are given as L^d and L^S and the marginal labor cost is MLC.

w	$L^d = MRP$	L^S	MLC
0	90	0	—
1	85	1	1
2	80	2	3
3	75	3	5
4	70	4	7
5	65	5	9
6	60	6	11
7	55	7	13
8	50	8	15
9	45	9	17
10	40	10	19
11	35	11	21
12	30	12	23
13	25	13	25
14	20	14	27
15	15	15	29
16	10	16	31
17	5	17	33
18	0	18	35

a. Fill in the marginal labor cost column.

b. In a competitive labor market, the market wage will be _____ and _____ workers will be employed.

c. Suppose a monopoly enforces a wage of $16 in the market. In this case, the number of workers employed will be _____.

d. If the labor market has only one buyer, there will be _____ workers employed and the wage rate will be _____.

Answers

a.

w	$L^d = MRP$	L^S	MLC
0	90	0	
1	85	1	1
2	80	2	3
3	75	3	5
4	70	4	7
5	65	5	9
6	60	6	11
7	55	7	13
8	50	8	15
9	45	9	17
10	40	10	19
11	35	11	21
12	30	12	23
13	25	13	25
14	20	14	27
15	15	15	29
16	10	16	31
17	5	17	33
18	0	18	35

b.   In a competitive labor market, the wage will be $15 and 15 workers will be employed.
c.   If a union raises the wage to $16, employment will fall to 10 workers.
d.   In a monopsony market, firms will hire 13 workers at a wage of $13.

Key Terms

Collective bargaining: Negotiations between a union and a firm over wages, fringe benefits, job security, and working conditions.

Craft union: A labor organization that includes workers from a particular occupation, for example, plumbers, bakers, or electricians.

Featherbedding: Work rules that increase the amount of labor required to produce a given quantity of output.

Industrial union: A labor organization that includes all types of workers from a single industry, for example, steelworkers or autoworkers.

Labor union: A group of workers organized to increase job security, improve working conditions, and increase wages and benefits.

Marginal labor cost: The increase in a firm's total labor cost resulting from one more unit of labor.

Monopsony: A market in which there is a single buyer of an input.

Paying efficiency wages: The practice of paying a higher wage to increase the average productivity of the workforce.

Right-to-work laws: Laws that prohibit union shops, where union membership is required as a condition of employment.

Practice Quiz

(Answers are provided at the end of the Practice Quiz.)

1. A perfectly competitive firm in the labor market will:
   a. have a marginal cost of labor that is equal to the market wage rate.
   b. face an upward sloping market supply curve for labor.
   c. face a downward sloping market supply curve for labor.
   d. set the marginal cost of labor equal to the marginal product of labor.

2. Select the best answer. A craft union is:
   a. an organized group of workers that can influence wages.
   b. an organized group of workers from a particular occupation like plumbers, bakers, or electricians.
   c. a union that includes workers from a single industry like steelworkers or autoworkers.
   d. a union that negotiates solely to obtain better working conditions.

3. Which of the following groups of workers had the highest unionization rates in the United States in 2007?
   a. All wage and salary workers as a whole.
   b. Public-sector workers.
   c. Private-sector workers.
   d. None of the above. All of the groups above had about the same unionization rates.

4. Which of the following pieces of legislation guaranteed workers the right to join unions and required each firm to bargain with a union formed by a majority of its workers?
   a. The Taft-Harley Act.
   b. The Wagner Act.
   c. The Landrum-Griffin Act.
   d. The Sherman Act.

5. Which of the following institutions was established to enforce the provisions of the Wagner Act?
   a. The National Labor Relations Board.
   b. The Toastmasters.
   c. The Air Traffic Controllers Association of America.
   d. The Jimmy Hoffa Workers of America.

6. What is the purpose of *right-to-work laws*?
   a. To ensure that unionized workers are given the right to work.
   b. To outlaw union membership as a precondition of employment.
   c. To ensure that workers can be employed without having to join a union.
   d. To prevent business firms from firing unionized workers.

7. Which of the following acts was a response to allegations of corruption and misconduct by union officials?
   a. The Wagner Act.
   b. The Sherman Act.
   c. The Landrum-Griffin Act.
   d. The Taft-Harley Act.

8. An increase in the wage decreases the quantity of labor demanded because of the output effect and the input-substitution effect. Which one is the input-substitution effect?
   a. As the wage increases, a worker will substitute income for leisure time.
   b. An increase in the wage increases a worker's real income in the sense that she can afford more of all goods, including leisure time.
   c. An increase in the wage increases the cost of production, and a firm will pass on the higher cost to consumers by increasing its product price.
   d. An increase in the wage increases the cost of labor relative to the cost of capital, and the firm will substitute capital for labor,

9. This question tests your understanding of Application 1 in this chapter: Truckers trade off wages and jobs: Is there a trade-off between union wages and the number of union jobs?

   Refer to the figure below. The figure shows the possible responses of union truckers to the entry of nonunion firms. In 1978, the union wage was $20 per hour and union employment was 526,000 truckers (point *a*). Which of the following best describes how union truckers reacted to the entry of nonunion firms?

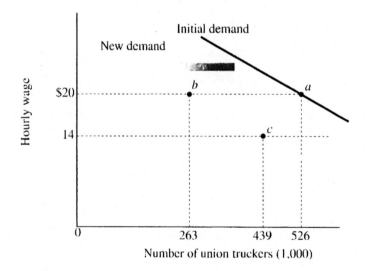

   a. The move from *a* to *b*.
   b. The move from *a* to *c*.
   c. The move from *a* to *b*, and then to *c*.
   d. The move from *a* to *c*, and then to *b*.

10. Fill in the blanks. Higher wages lead to a higher output price, less quantity demanded, and therefore less workers hired. This effect is particularly strong when the product's demand is _____ and labor costs are a _____ fraction of the costs.
    a. inelastic; large
    b. elastic; large
    c. inelastic; small
    d. elastic; small

11. *Featherbedding* is the practice of:
    a. guaranteeing a job for every worker who is a union member.
    b. giving preference to union members versus nonunion members for new jobs that become available.
    c. imposing work rules that increase the amount of labor required to produce a given quantity of output.
    d. giving workers all the tools that are necessary to produce a given quantity of output.

12. Which of the following statements about the effects of unions on worker productivity and turnover is correct?
    a. Unions may increase productivity and lower turnover.
    b. Unions may increase productivity, but also increase turnover.
    c. Unions may lower productivity and increase turnover.
    d. Unions have no impact on productivity and turnover.

13. To determine how many workers to hire, which key principle of economics should the profit-maximizing monopsonist use?
    a. The principle of opportunity cost.
    b. The marginal principle.
    c. The principle of diminishing returns.
    d. The principle of voluntary exchange.

14. Fill in the blanks: To hire more workers, the monopsonist must pay a _____ wage, so the marginal labor cost _____ the wage.
    a. higher...is greater than
    b. higher...is less than
    c. lower...is greater than
    d. lower...is less than

15. Just as a monopolist uses its market power to increase the price of output, a monopsonist uses its market power to:
    a. increase other input prices, but not the wage.
    b. decrease the wage.
    c. decrease the price of the output.
    d. increase the wage.

16. Refer to the figure below. What is the marginal labor cost of the 8th worker?

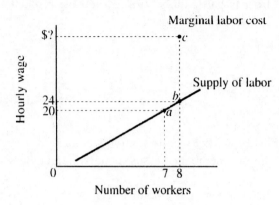

    a. $48.
    b. $56.
    c. $52.
    d. $38.

17. Refer to the figure below. If the firm decides to hire 40 workers, what wage will it pay to each worker?

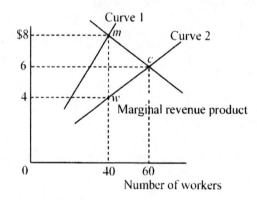

    a. $4.
    b. $6.
    c. $8.
    d. There is insufficient information to answer the question.

18. Refer to the figure below. Which of the supply curves does the monopsonist face in the presence of a minimum wage?

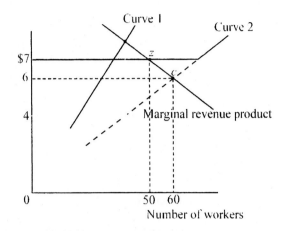

a. The solid line portion of Curve 2, but not the dashed segment.
b. Part of Curve 1 and part of the horizontal supply curve.
c. The solid line portion of Curve 2 and the entire horizontal line at $7.
d. The entire upward sloping Curve 2, including the dashed segment.

19. This question tests your understanding of Application 3 in this chapter: Pubs and the labor-supply curve: Do firms face a positively sloped labor-supply curve?

In which of the following situation is the labor supply curve is positively sloped?
a. When the labor market is perfectly competitive.
b. When the product market is perfectly competitive.
c. When the labor market is less competitive.
d. When workers earn a wage equal to the opportunity cost of their time.

20. What happens when there is asymmetric information in the labor market?
a. The firm hires only high-skill workers.
b. The firm must increase its wage in order to attract more high-skill workers.
c. The firm does not have to pay higher wages in order to attract higher-skilled workers.
d. The firm hires only low-skill workers.

21. Describe the problem of asymmetric information in the labor market.

22. What is an efficiency wage, and why do firms pay efficiency wages?

Answers to the Practice Quiz

1. a. One of the assumptions of perfect competition in the labor market is that a firm can hire an unlimited number of workers at the prevailing market wage, in other words, faces a horizontal supply curve of labor. This means that the marginal cost of labor is equal to the prevailing market wage.

2. b. A craft union includes workers from a particular occupation like plumbers, bakers, or electricians, while an industrial union includes all types of workers from a single industry like steelworkers or autoworkers.

3. b. Public-sector workers have a higher unionization rate than private sector workers or all workers as a whole. had a unionization rate of 37.5% in 2007.

4. b. The Wagner Act of 1935 guaranteed workers the right to join unions.

5. a. The National Labor Relations Board (NRLB) was established to enforce the provisions of the Wagner Act.

6. c. A piece of labor legislation gave government the power to the states to pass "right-to-work" laws. Right-to-work laws outlaw union membership as a precondition of employment.

7. c. The Landrum-Griffin Act was a response to allegations of corruption and misconduct by union officials.

8. d. The input-substitution effect states that an increase in the wage increases the cost of labor relative to the cost of capital, and the firm will substitute capital for labor, reducing the quantity of labor demanded.

9. b. Rather than accepting such a large reduction in union employment, truckers accepted a wage of $14 per hour, and total union employment in 1996 was 439,000. In other words, union truckers accepted lower wages in exchange for more jobs—or a smaller reduction in jobs.

10. b. If labor is responsible for a relatively large fraction of production costs, an increase in the wage will cause a larger increase in the product price than if it were a small fraction. If demand for the output is relatively elastic then a change in price causes a larger decrease in output than if demand were inelastic, and thus a larger decrease in the quantity of labor demanded.

11. c. Labor unions try to increase wages by imposing work rules that increase the amount of labor required to produce a given quantity of output—a practice called featherbedding.

12. a. According to the textbook, unions may increase worker productivity by facilitating communication between workers and managers. Also, unions lower turnover among workers.

13. b. This is the principle used in economics to determine the optimal level of an activity. The firm chooses the quantity of labor at which the marginal benefit of labor equals the marginal cost.

14. a. A monopsonist faces a positively sloped market supply of labor. To hire more workers, the monopsonist must pay a higher wage, so the marginal labor cost exceeds the wage.

15. b. A monopsonist (a single buyer) uses its market power to decrease the wage or other input prices.

16. c. The marginal labor cost equals the wage paid to new worker + (change in wage x quantity of original workers). In this case: 24 + (4 x 7) = $52.

17. a. The labor supply curve indicates that to hire 40 workers, the monopsonist must pay a wage of $4.

18. c. With a minimum wage, the supply curve is horizontal at the minimum wage up to the point where it intersects the original supply curve and then follows the original supply curve upward.

19. c. To hire more workers, the firm must pay a higher wage. Most workers will receive a wage that exceeds the opportunity cost of their time, so each worker gets a producer surplus.

20. b. The firm must increase its wage in order to attract more high-skill workers.

21. There is asymmetric information in the labor market because employers cannot distinguish between skillful and unskillful workers, or between hard workers and lazy workers. If the employer cannot distinguish between different types of workers, it will pay a single wage, realizing that it will probably hire workers of each type.

22. Paying efficiency wages is the practice of paying higher wages than average in order to increase the average productivity of the workforce. Firms pay efficiency wages to attract high-skill workers. The employer must pay a wage that exceeds the opportunity cost of high-skill workers. As the firm attracts more skilled workers, the average productivity of the workforce rises. By paying efficiency wages, the firm attempts to increase the average productivity of its workforce, and therefore its profit.

19 [18]
International Trade and Public Policy

Chapter Summary

This chapter discusses the benefits of specialization and trade and explores the trade-offs associated with protectionist policies. Here are the main points of the chapter:

- If one country has a comparative advantage vis-à-vis another country in producing a particular good (a lower opportunity cost), specialization and trade will benefit both countries.
- An import ban or an import quota increases prices, protecting domestic industries, but domestic consumers pay the price.
- Because the victims of protectionist policies often retaliate, the protection of a domestic industry can harm an exporting industry.
- A tariff, a tax on imports, generates revenue for the government, whereas an import quota—a limit on imports—generates revenue for foreigners or importers.
- In principle, the laws against dumping are designed to prevent predatory pricing. In practice, predatory pricing laws are often used to shield domestic industries from competition. Allegations of it are hard to prove.
- Under World Trade Organization (WTO) rules, each country may pursue its environmental goals only within its own borders.
- International trade has contributed to the widening gap between the wages of low-skilled and high-skilled labor. However, it also has reduced the relative prices facing the poor, offsetting some of the effects on inequality.

Applying the Concepts

After reading this chapter, you should be able to answer these four key questions:
1. Do tariffs (taxes on imported goods) hurt the poor disproportionately?
2. How much does it really cost to "save" a job that might be lost under free trade?
3. Does the concept of "unfair" competition make sense?
4. Why might international trade reduce measured inequality in the United States?

19.1 [18.1] Benefits from Specialization and Trade

Trade (voluntary exchange) between individuals and nations is based on the principle of opportunity cost.

 Principle of Opportunity Cost

The opportunity cost of an item is what you must sacrifice to get the item.

Table 19.1 [18.1] shows the opportunity costs of each good in Shirtland and Chipland. Chipland can produce either 120 shirts in one day or 120 chips in one day. This means that if it gives up production of 120 shirts, it gets 120 chips. The opportunity cost of a chip is then one shirt. Similarly, the opportunity cost of a shirt is one chip.

In Shirtland, giving up 108 shirts yields only 36 chips so the opportunity cost of a chip is 3 shirts. This is calculated as the 108 shirts sacrificed divided by the 36 chips gained. Similarly, the opportunity cost of a shirt is 1/3 of a chip. This is calculated as the 36 chips sacrificed divided by the 108 shirts gained.

Figure 19.1 [18.1] shows the production possibilities curves for Shirtland and Chipland. The **production possibilities curve** shows the possible combinations of products that an economy can produce, given that its productive resources are fully employed and efficiently used.

 Remember

> With no trade, an economy's production possibilities frontier also shows the possible consumption possibilities for the economy.

Chipland has the absolute advantage over Shirtland in the production of both chips and shirts. **Absolute advantage** is the ability of one person or nation to produce a product at a lower resource cost than another person or nation. Another way to think of this is that an economy has an absolute advantage in a good when it can produce more of that good in a given amount of time than can another economy.

Trade is based on comparative advantage. **Comparative advantage** is the ability of one person or nation to produce a good at a lower opportunity cost than another person or nation. Since the cost of a shirt is 1/3 of a chip in Shirtland, and one chip in Chipland, Shirtland should produce shirts since it has the comparative advantage, or lower opportunity cost. Chipland should produce chips since it gives up fewer shirts to produce a chip. Chipland has a comparative advantage in chip production because it has a lower opportunity cost for chips.

 Remember

> Even though Chipland can produce more shirts and more chips than Shirtland, it is still in Chipland's best interest to trade with Shirtland. This is because trade is based on comparative advantage—who can produce a good at the lowest opportunity cost.

Based on comparative advantage, Chipland will produce chips and buy shirts. Shirtland will produce shirts and buy chips. The terms of trade can be found from the opportunity costs for the two goods. The **terms of trade** is the rate at which units of one product can be exchanged for units of another product.

How many shirts will Shirtland give up to buy a chip? If Shirtland produced chips on its own, it would give up 3 shirts for each chip. This is Shirtland's opportunity cost, and the most it would be willing to pay for a chip. Chipland gives up one shirt each time it produces a chip and this is the least it would be willing to accept in trade for one chip. As a result, one chip will trade for somewhere between 1 and 3 shirts. Notice that these are simply the opportunity costs of the goods for each nation. Any trade between these two values will make both countries better off.

∂∽ Study Tip

Terms of trade are given by the opportunity costs of goods in the trading countries.

The **consumption possibilities curve** is a curve that shows the combinations of two goods that can be consumed when a nation specialized in a particular good and trades with another nation. We use the consumption possibilities curve to show the gains to Shirtland and Chipland from trading.

In Figure 19.2 [18.2] Panel A, we have the production possibilities curve for Chipland. Suppose that we start at point g, with Chipland producing 120 computer chips per day. If Chipland tried to produce shirts, it would have to give up one chip for each shirt. Suppose the terms of trade are 2 shirts per chip. Now when Chipland gives up a chip, instead of the one shirt it could receive if it produced shirts, it receives 2 shirts from Shirtland in return for selling a chip to Shirtland. At these terms of trade, Chipland is better off as it can now consume 119 chips and 2 shirts instead of the 119 chips and 1 shirt it could produce, and consume, without trade.

Panel B illustrates that Shirtland is better off as well. Starting from point a, if Shirtland wanted to produce a computer chip, it would have to give up three shirts without trade. By trading, Shirtland can send 2 shirts to Chipland and receive 1 chip in return. Thus, Shirtland is able to consume 106 shirts and 1 chip with trade instead of the 105 shirts and 1 chip it would have without trade.

∂∽ Study Tip

The consumption possibilities curve shows that trade allows countries to consume combinations of goods they could not produce on their own.

Trade rearranges employment in the two countries as well. As a result of trade, Chipland will choose to buy shirts instead of producing shirts. This means that workers in the shirt industry in Chipland will no longer be needed to make shirts. At the same time, Chipland will specialize in making chips and the chip industry will expand and this will increase the employment of chip makers.

19.2 [18.2] Protectionist Policies

Figure 19.3 [18.3] illustrates the effects of an import ban in Chipland. With trade, the shirt market is in equilibrium at point c with a price of $12 and a quantity of 80 shirts. All of these shirts are imported as no domestic supplier will sell shirts if the price is below $17. Without imports, the market supply shifts to the left (as the shirts from other countries are no longer offered for sale in Chipland) and the market reaches equilibrium at point a with a price of $25 and 60 shirts sold with all 60 shirts coming from domestic suppliers.

An **import quota** is a government-imposed limit on the quantity of a good that can be imported. Import quotas are illegal under international trading laws, however, exporting countries may agree to a voluntary export restraint. A **voluntary export restraint** is a scheme under which an exporting country voluntarily decreases its exports. A voluntary export restraint functions in the same way as an import quota. A **tariff** is a tax on imported goods. At times governments will issue **import licenses**, rights, issued by a government, to import goods.

ᠪ Study Tip

Any restriction on imports can be analyzed as a decrease in supply in the affected market.

Figure 19.4 [18.4] illustrates the impact of these trade restrictions. As long as some imports are allowed, the supply curve will shift to the left relative to the free-trade supply curve but will not shift as far left as the zero import case in Figure 19.3 [18.3]. Notice that the restriction on imports leads to an equilibrium at point *d* with a higher price and lower quantity than those under free trade. Point *e* shows the quantity supplied by domestic producers.

The price of shirts will increase to $20 regardless of whether a quota or tariff is used. The difference in the two approaches is who receives the $8 increase in price. With a tariff, this money is collected by the government and so in Figure 19.4 [18.4] the $8 increase in price for the 44 imported units would be collected as tax revenue by the home government. With a quota, importers and producers receive the extra $8 on those units.

Let's review an Application that answers one of the key questions we posed at the start of the chapter:

1. Do tariffs (taxes) on imported goods hurt the poor disproportionately?

> **APPLICATION 1: THE IMPACT OF TARIFFS ON THE POOR**
> Studies have found that the poor bear a larger burden from tariffs than do the rich. The first reason is that goods subject to a tariff tend to make up a larger part of the spending of the poor. The second reason is that most tariffs are applied to low priced, imported items, thus raising the price on goods that tend to be purchased more frequently by the poor.

19.3 [18.3] What Are the Rationales for Protectionist Policies?

There are three primary reasons for restrictive trade policies:
*   To shield workers from foreign competition.
*   To nurture infant industries until they mature.
*   To help domestic firms establish monopolies in world markets.

In many cases, industries affected by trade, such as textiles in the United States, are concentrated in relatively small parts of the United States. Politicians in those areas use trade policy to protect their constituents, even though it may cost other citizens.

Nurturing infant industries is justified in part by the concept of learning by doing. An **infant industry** is one that is at an early stage of development. **Learning by doing** refers to knowledge and skills workers gain during production that increase productivity and lower cost. As the industry matures, costs fall and the protection is less needed.

Airbus is an example of European governments using trade restrictions to assist a domestic firm to gain market share.

Let's review two Applications that answer key questions we posed at the start of the chapter:

2. How much does it really cost to "save" a job that might be lost under free trade?

APPLICATION 2: MEASURING THE COSTS OF PROTECTING JOBS
This Application illustrates the cost of saving U.S. jobs in certain industries. The Application states that each textile job saved from moving abroad costs the United States $199,241. The Application shows the five costliest jobs to save, with jobs in three industries costing the United States over $1 million per year to preserve.

3. Does the concept of "unfair" competition make sense?

APPLICATION 3: PROTECTION FOR CANDLE MAKERS
This Application reprints a satirical petition from the 1800s on behalf of French candle makers for protection from competition from the sun.

19.4 [18.4] A Brief History of International Tariff and Trade Agreements

This section describes a few major pieces of trade agreement.

The **General Agreement on Tariffs and Trade (GATT)** is an international agreement established in 1947 that has lowered trade barriers between the United States and other nations. The **World Trade Organization** was established in 1995 and oversees GATT and other international trade agreements, resolves trade disputes, and holds forums for further rounds of trade negotiations. The North American Free Trade Agreement (NAFTA) will eliminate all trade barriers between the United States, Canada, and Mexico. The European Union was formed to eliminate trade barriers between member states. The Asian Pacific Economic Cooperation was created to lower trade barriers between 18 member Asian nations. The U.S.-Central American Free Trade Agreement, if approved, will extend NAFTA-like provisions to five Central American countries.

19.5 [18.5] Recent Policy Debates and Trade Agreements

There are three recent policy debates discussed in this chapter:
1. Are foreign producers dumping their products?
2. Do trade laws inhibit environmental protection?
3. Does outsourcing and trade cause income inequality?

Dumping is a situation in which the price a firm charges in a foreign market is lower than either the price it charges in its home markets or the production cost. One reason we might see different prices between countries is price discrimination. **Price discrimination** is the process under which a firm divides consumers into two or more groups and charges a different price for each group buying the same product. A second reason is **predatory pricing**, a pricing scheme under which a firm decreases the price to drive rival firms out of business and increases the price when rival firms leave the market. It is very difficult to determine whether low prices in a market are caused by price discrimination, predatory pricing, or simply more competition in that market.

Environmental concerns arise in trade discussion particularly when the environmental standards in one country cannot be applied to producers in another country. The text demonstrated that the United States can impose certain regulations on foreign producers so long as all domestic producers are held to the same standard. For instance, the United States could limit the allowable levels of exhaust from automobiles as long as all producers that sell in the U.S. market are held to the same standard. A country, however, can't ban the imports of goods produced in other countries by methods of production that the home country outlaws. For example, both the United States, which tried to ban the import of net-caught tuna, and the European Union, which tried to ban the import of hormone-treated beef, have been found to be in violation of the WTO over those issues.

Outsourcing refers to firms producing components of their goods and services in other countries. Government can respond by enacting trade barriers to protect low-skilled jobs, or by easing the transition to an economy with fewer low-skilled jobs. To this point, outsourcing has affected low-skilled jobs. It is possible that jobs that require more skills could also be outsourced. There is still much to learn about the effects of outsourcing and international trade on wages and employment.

Let's look at an Application that answers one of the key questions posed at the start of the chapter.

4.   Why might international trade reduce measured inequality in the United States?

APPLICATION 4: TRADE, CONSUMPTION, AND INEQUALITY
This Application points out that while the income gap between rich and poor may be growing, thanks to trade the consumption gap may be getting smaller. Trade has lowered the price of many of the goods purchased by the poor or at least lowered the rate at which those prices rise. By lowering the relative prices of goods purchased by poor consumers trade has allowed poor families to enjoy higher living standards.

Activity

Consider Andy, who produces computer programs and hamburgers. In a given week (40 hours), Andy can produce 40 computer programs or 80 hamburgers along a linear production possibilities curve.

a.   Find the opportunity cost of computer programs and hamburgers for Andy.

b.   Can Andy consume 20 computer programs and 60 hamburgers?

c.   Suppose that Laura offers Andy three hamburgers for every computer program he writes for her. Will Andy make this trade?

d.   Suppose Andy specializes in programs and sells programs to Laura for hamburgers at the terms of trade from part c. Can he consume 20 computer programs and 60 hamburgers?

e.   Suppose Laura can only produce 45 hamburgers in a week. Does the fact that Andy has the absolute advantage in hamburger production change his desire to trade with Laura?

Answers

a. One computer program costs Andy 2 hamburgers. One hamburger costs Andy ½ of a computer program.
b. No, this point is outside his production possibilities curve. If Andy consumes 20 computer programs, he can consume at most 40 hamburgers.
c. Yes. It costs Andy 2 hamburgers to write a computer program, so he would gladly accept 3 hamburgers in trade for 1 computer program.
d. Yes. He will produce 40 programs and sell 20 of them. In return for the 20 programs, he will receive 60 hamburgers.
e. No, even though he has the absolute advantage in hamburgers, trade is based on comparative advantage and so this information is not relevant to the decision to trade.

Key Terms

Consumption possibilities curve: A curve showing the combinations of two goods that can be consumed when a nation specialized in a particular good and trades with another nation.

Dumping: A situation in which the price a firm charges in a foreign market is lower than either the price it charges in its home markets or the production cost.

General Agreement on Tariffs and Trade (GATT): An international agreement established in 1947 that has lowered trade barriers between the United States and other nations.

Import licenses: Rights, issued by a government, to import goods.

Import quota: A government-imposed limit on the quantity of a good that can be imported.

Infant industries: Industries that are at an early stage of development.

Learning by doing: Knowledge and skills workers gain during production that increase productivity and lower cost.

Outsourcing: Firms producing components of their goods and services in other countries.

Predatory pricing: A pricing scheme under which a firm decreases the price to drive rival firms out of business and increases the price when rival firms leave the market.

Price discrimination: The process under which a firm divides consumers into two or more groups and charges a different price for each group buying the same product.

Tariff: A tax on imported goods.

Terms of trade: The rate at which units of one product can be exchanged for units of another product.

Voluntary export restraint: A scheme under which an exporting country voluntarily decreases its exports.

World Trade Organization: An organization established in 1995 that oversees GATT and other international trade agreements, resolves trade disputes, and holds forums for further rounds of trade negotiations.

Practice Quiz

(Answers are provided at the end of the Practice Quiz.)

1. Specialization and trade are concepts based on a specific key principle of economics. Which one?
   a. The real-nominal principle.
   b. The marginal principle.
   c. The principle of opportunity cost.
   d. The principle of diminishing returns.

2. A *production possibilities curve* shows the possible combinations of:
   a. two sets of inputs, or productive resources available to an economy to produce output.
   b. two types of output that can be produced in an economy as full employment is maintained.
   c. quantities of output that are available at various price levels, during a given period, all else the same.
   d. the goods that can be produced by an economy at full employment over time as the economy grows.

3. Refer to the figure below. Assume that the economy always maintains full employment. What is the opportunity cost of increasing the production of shirts, from 54 to 60?

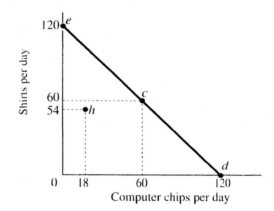

   a. Six shirts.
   b. Six chips.
   c. One chip.
   d. There is no way to determine the opportunity cost.

4. We say that a nation has a *comparative advantage* in producing a good if that nation:
   a. chooses autarky.
   b. has a lower opportunity cost for the production of that good.
   c. has a lower resource cost for the production of that good.
   d. All of the above.

5. Refer to the figure below. Which country in this graph has a comparative advantage in the production of shirts?

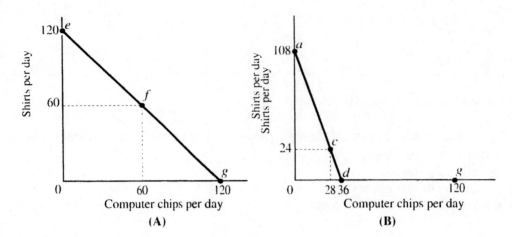

(A)   (B)

a. A
b. B
c. Neither country.
d. Both countries.

6. Only one statement below is entirely correct. Under specialization and trade, the consumption possibilities curve of a nation:
    a. lies above the nation's production possibilities curve because the nation has more options about how much to consume.
    b. lies above the nation's production possibilities curve because the nation has less options about how much to consume.
    c. lies below the nation's production possibilities curve because the nation has more options about how much to consume.
    d. lies below the nation's production possibilities curve because the nation has less options about how much to consume.

7. When a nation voluntarily decreases its exports in an attempt to avoid more restrictive policies, the nation is adopting:
    a. tariffs.
    b. quotas.
    c. voluntary export restraints.
    d. import licenses.

8. Refer to the figure below where one supply curve represents no trade and the other free trade. A country with policies that prevent trade will cause this market to settle in equilibrium at which point?

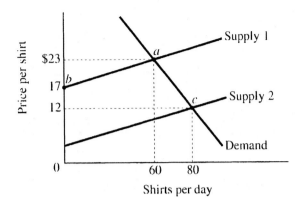

a. Point *b*.
b. Point *a*.
c. Point *c*.
d. This market may settle in equilibrium at any of the points shown after trade restrictions are imposed.

9. Which of the following is correct about voluntary export restraints (VERs)?
   a. VERs are illegal under global trade rules.
   b. Like a quota, a VER increases the price of the restricted good.
   c. A VER makes it more difficult for domestic firms to participate in the market.
   d. All of the above.

10. This question tests your understanding of Application 1 in this chapter: The impact of tariffs on the poor. Do tariffs (taxes) on imported goods hurt the poor disproportionately? Which of the following are reasons why tariffs fall disproportionately on the poor in the United States?
    a. Tariffs are usually placed on expensive goods, making those goods even less affordable for the poor.
    b. Tariffs are placed on goods that represent a higher fraction of the consumption of higher-income households than lower-income households.
    c. Within the category of goods for which tariffs are high, the highest tariffs fall on the cheapest products—precisely those that will be purchased by lower-income consumers.
    d. In general, to protect U.S. industries, tariffs are highest on capital-intensive goods; goods that use relatively more capital than labor.

11. Refer to the figure below. One supply curve represents the case of no trade, one supply curve represents the case of free trade and one supply curve represents the case of trade with a tariff. Which of the 3 represents the tariff case?

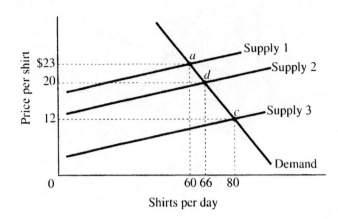

a. Supply 1.
b. Supply 2.
c. Supply 3.
d. None of the above.

12. Which of the following are possible reasons why countries restrict trade?
a. To shield workers from foreign competition.
b. To nurture "infant" industries until they mature.
c. To help domestic firms establish monopolies in world markets.
d. All of the above.

13. In addition to the nations involved in the WTO, which of the following is an association formed to lower trade barriers and promote international trade?
a. The North American Free Trade Agreement (NAFTA) between Canada, Mexico, and the United States.
b. The European Union (EU), which today includes close to 20 countries.
c. The leaders of 18 Asian nations have formed the Asian Pacific Economic Cooperation (APEC).
d. All of the above.

14. Based on the evidence concerning antidumping laws and predatory pricing, what is the position of economists about these issues?
a. Economists are skeptical about how frequently predatory pricing actually occurs versus price discrimination.
b. Economists believe that most nations use their antidumping laws to prevent unfair competition, not as protectionist policies in disguise.
c. Economists believe that antidumping laws are hardly ever used because they are an ineffective method of protecting domestic industries.
d. All of the above.

15. Nations that use trade restrictions to pursue environmental goals will:
    a. encounter resistance from the WTO.
    b. find support in the WTO because the WTO wants countries to pursue specific environmental goals.
    c. find that the WTO is neutral, neither supporting nor condemning a country's environmental goals.
    d. find support in the WTO but only as long as other WTO participants agree with the trade restrictions to be imposed.

16. Trade and specialization mean that individuals and nations:
    a. forget about borders.
    b. must surrender some of their independence and sovereignty.
    c. pay no attention to matters of independence and sovereignty, eventually becoming a single nation.
    d. can expand their independence and sovereignty.

17. Compare autarky equilibrium to equilibrium based on comparative advantage.

18. Protectionist policies are often defended on the grounds that they protect new or infant industries. Comment.

19. What are the WTO rules concerning trade that could harm the environment?

20. How is trade likely to affect the distribution of income?

Answers to the Practice Quiz

1. c. The opportunity cost of something is what you sacrifice to get it. Specialization and trade are based on the idea of sacrificing the production of some goods to concentrate on the production of others, based on comparative advantage.

2. b. The production possibilities frontier shows the possible combinations of two goods that can be produced by an economy, assuming that all resources are fully employed.

3. b. The opportunity cost is the slope of the production possibilities frontier. The information on the axes can be used to establish the value of the slope. The country can produce either 120 shirts when it produces no chips or 120 chips when it produces no shirts. Therefore, this country must give up one chip in order to increase the production of shirts by one. In this case, in order to increase the production of shirts by six, from 54 to 60, the production of chips must decrease by six.

4. b. The comparative advantage for a good means that a country can produce the good for the lower opportunity cost, in other words, give up less of an alternative good in order to make this.

5. b. The opportunity costs are as follows: The opportunity cost of shirts is: 1 chip for country A, and 1/3 chip for country B. Country B has a comparative advantage in the production of shirts because it sacrifices fewer chips to produce one shirt. Country B should therefore produce shirts.

6. a. Each consumption possibilities curve lies above the nation's production possibilities curves, meaning that each nation has more options about how much to consume under specialization and trade.

7. c. A voluntary export restraint (VER), where a nation voluntarily decreases its exports in an attempt to avoid more restrictive policies.

8. b. Restrictive trade policies would decrease the total supply, causing an increase in the price consumers have to pay for shirts and a decrease in the quantity available for them to buy.

9. b. Like a quota, a VER increases the price of the restricted good.

10. c. In general, to protect U.S. industries, tariffs are highest on labor-intensive goods; goods that use relatively more labor than capital. But these goods tend to be lower priced. That is why tariffs do fall disproportionately on the poor. Answer d says tariffs are highest on capital-intensive goods.

11. b. The tariff shifts the supply curve to the left from the free trade scenario of supply curve 3. The market moves upward along the demand curve to point d, which is between point c (free trade) and a (domestic supply only).

12. d. Three possible motivations to restrict trade are: to shield workers from foreign competition, to nurture "infant" industries until they mature, and to help domestic firms establish monopolies in world markets.

13. d. Nations have formed trade associations to lower trade barriers and promote international trade: The North American Free Trade Agreement (NAFTA) between Canada, Mexico, and the United States; The European Union (EU), which today includes close to 20 countries; and the leaders of 18 Asian nations have formed the Asian Pacific Economic Cooperation (APEC).

14. a. Many economists are skeptical about how frequently predatory pricing actually occurs versus price discrimination; they suspect that many nations use their antidumping laws as protectionist policies in disguise. Professor Thomas Prusa of Rutgers University has studied antidumping and found that it is a potent weapon for protecting domestic industries.

15. a. Nations that use trade restrictions to pursue environmental goals will encounter resistance because WTO rules mean that a nation can pursue its environmental goals only within its borders.

16. b. Trade and specialization mean that individuals and nations must surrender some of their independence and sovereignty.

17. Autarky equilibrium is a situation in which the economy chooses how to use its scarce resources to produce a certain amount of goods, in the absence of trade. It is similar to equilibrium based on comparative advantage in that both situations make full and efficient use of resources available. The difference lies in the combinations of output that are produced, and ultimately, in the amounts of goods that can be consumed. When a country chooses to specialize and trade based on comparative advantage, it shifts its production toward the goods for which it is more efficient relative to its trading partner. Once countries specialize and trade, the consumption possibilities frontier rises above the production possibilities frontier. By focusing on what each country does best, world output increases.

18. One possible answer is as follows: It would seem to make sense to protect domestic industries while they achieve the economies of scale and cost per unit of similar foreign competitors. But in reality, infant industries rarely become competitive with their foreign rivals. In the 1950s and 1960s, Latin American countries used tariffs and other policies to protect their young industries, but the industries never became as efficient as the foreign suppliers did. Additionally, once an industry is given tariff protection, it is difficult to take it away.

19. WTO rules concerning trade that could harm the environment state that a country can adopt any environmental standard it chooses, as long as it does not discriminate against foreign producers. For example, the U.S. can limit exhaust emissions of cars, as long as the rules apply equally to all cars—domestic and imports. The U.S. cannot ban imported goods that are produced in factories that generate pollution in other countries. The WTO recognizes that countries differ in the value they place on the environment.

20. Trade could lead to greater inequality of income and wages. If a country increases its exports of products requiring skilled labor, the demand for skilled labor and their wages will rise. And, if the country imports more goods requiring less-skilled labor, the wages of unskilled workers will fall.